iMovie® '09 and iDVD®
PORTABLE GENIUS

by Guy Hart-Davis

WILEY

Wiley Publishing, Inc.

iMovie® '09 & iDVD® Portable Genius

Published by
Wiley Publishing, Inc.
10475 Crosspoint Blvd.
Indianapolis, IN 46256
www.wiley.com

Copyright © 2009 by Wiley Publishing, Inc., Indianapolis, Indiana

Published simultaneously in Canada

ISBN: 978-0-470-47543-0

Manufactured in the United States of America

10   9   8   7   6   5   4   3   2   1

For general information on our other products and services or to obtain technical support, please contact our Customer Care Department within the U.S. at (877) 762-2974, outside the U.S. at (317) 572-3993 or fax (317) 572-4002.

Wiley also publishes its books in a variety of electronic formats. Some content that appears in print may not be available in electronic books.

Library of Congress CIP Data: 2009930064

WILEY

About the Author

Guy Hart-Davis is the author of more than 40 computing books, including *iLife '09 Portable Genius, Mac OS X Leopard QuickSteps,* and *How to Do Everything: iPod & iTunes 5th Edition.* He is also the coauthor of *iMac Portable Genius* and has been working with Macs for more than 20 years.

Credits

Executive Editor
Jody Lefevere

Project Editor
Chris Wolfgang

Technical Editor
Robert Barnes

Instructional Designer
Lonzell Watson

Copy Editor
Lauren Kennedy

Editorial Director
Robyn Siesky

Editorial Manager
Cricket Krengel

**Vice President and Group
Executive Publisher**
Richard Swadley

Vice President and Executive Publisher
Barry Pruett

Business Manager
Amy Knies

Senior Marketing Manager
Sandy Smith

Project Coordinator
Patrick Redmond

Graphics and Production Specialists
Jennifer Henry
Andrea Hornberger
Jennifer Mayberry

Quality Control Technician
David Faust

Proofreading
Penny Stuart

Indexing
Potomac Indexing

This book is dedicated to Rhonda and Teddy

Acknowledgments

My thanks go to the following people for making this book happen:

- Jody Lefevere for getting the book approved and signing me up to write it.
- Lonzell Watson for shaping the outline.
- Chris Wolfgang for running the editorial side of the project.
- Robert Barnes for reviewing the book for technical accuracy and making many helpful suggestions.
- Lauren Kennedy for copy-editing the book with a light touch.
- Jennifer Henry and Andrea Hornberger for laying out the book in the design.
- Penny Stuart for scrutinizing the pages for errors.
- Potomac Indexing for creating the index.

Contents

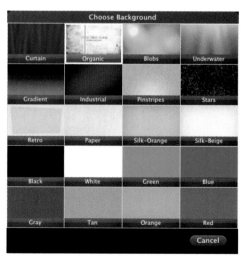

chapter 3

What Are My Video Import
Options?   30

chapter 4

Do You Have Tips for Fine-Tuning
Edits?   52

chapter 5

How Do I Make Video
Adjustments?   72

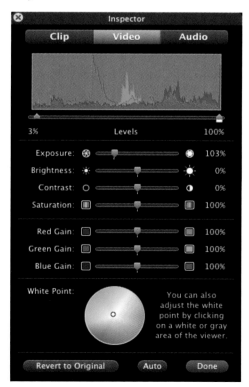

chapter 6

How Do I Create Cool Transitions,
Titles, and Effects?   92

chapter 7

What Should I Know about Audio
and Scoring My Movies?   122

chapter 8

What's the Best Way to
Manage My Video? 154

Some clips used in the project 'PF Project 1' are
not on the hard disk 'PostFlop'.

Copy the events (1.1 GB)

Copy the clips (88 MB)

Move the events (1.1 GB)

Cancel

chapter 10

How Can I Share
My Movies? 208

chapter 11

How Do I Create DVDs
Using iDVD? 224

chapter 12

Do You Have Any
Troubleshooting Tips? 264

Introduction

Digital camcorders and digital cameras have made it easy to capture video, and iMovie '09 makes it almost as easy — and fun — to turn your raw footage into a professional-looking, broadcast-quality movie.

iMovie '09 & iDVD Portable Genius shows you how to get up to speed with iMovie in the shortest possible time and get as much out of the application as you can. Here is a broad-strokes outline of what you can do with this book:

- **Find out about the new features.** iMovie '09 gives you great new features such as the Precision Editor for fine-tuning transitions; video stabilization for removing shake from clips; new effects such as cutaways, picture-in-picture effects, and green-screen superimposition; plus a wider selection of titles, transitions, and effects.

- **Pull together a high-quality movie within minutes.** Roaring up to speed with iMovie, you'll learn how to import video clips from a wide variety of DV camcorders and other sources, choose the footage you want, and then turn it into a movie complete with transitions, titles, and a soundtrack. When you need to put together a high-quality movie in short order, this is the way to go.

- **Bring in video from every source you have.** iMovie makes it easy to import video from most current DV camcorders, either using FireWire (for tape camcorders) or USB (for flash or hard-disk camcorders). But if Mac OS X identifies your camcorder as a digital camera, you may need to import movies using iPhoto rather than iMovie. Most likely, you will also need to import existing video files to use in your movies or bring your iMovie HD projects into iMovie '09.

- **Make precisely the edits you need.** Once you've placed video clips in the Project window, you can open the Precision Editor and adjust the transition from one clip to the next at the frame level. To keep total control, you can turn on the Fine Tuning controls so that you can select footage one frame at a time. Then trim your clips to the perfect length or split them up for use separately in different parts of a movie.

- **Adjust your video so that it looks great.** If a video clip suffers from camera shake, use iMovie's automatic stabilization to remove it and then tweak the adjustments manually if needed. Crop a clip down to show only the part you need, or rotate a clip you shot in the wrong orientation. Use the powerful tools in the Video pane to correct underexposure or overexposure, pump up the contrast and saturation, or give a color cast to a clip. Copy the painstaking adjustments you've made to one clip so that you can apply them to another clip in the blink of an eye.

- **Polish the video with transitions, titles, and visual effects.** To turn out a movie in record time, apply one of iMovie's themes, which give you a slickly finished movie with minimal effort. For greater control and originality, apply custom transitions to smooth or enhance the movement from clip to clip, add titles and credits — even insert an animated map if the movie needs it. For extra impact, display the Advanced tools and produce special effects such as cutaways or picture-in-picture scenes. You can also create slow-motion effects or play a clip backward.

- **Give your movie a powerful soundtrack.** With iMovie, iTunes, and GarageBand, your studio has all the tools you need to create a powerful, professionally edited soundtrack that fits your movie to a T. First, adjust the level of the audio recorded into your video clips and add fades where they're needed. Next, insert background audio and sound effects, and add voiceover narration where the movie needs it. When you need background music or a full soundtrack, harness the power of GarageBand to create the score you need and share it with iMovie.

- **Whip your video library into order.** Given half a chance, video files will merrily consume not only your Mac's hard drive but any external drives you connect. That means it's vital to understand the smart way in which iMovie handles your video footage; keep your Project Library in apple-pie order; and make the most of Events, Favorite and Rejected marking, and keywords to separate your sheep clips from your goat shearings. You can then use the Space Saver feature to reclaim precious drive space, or move a project to a different drive so that you can edit it using another Mac .

- **Include still photos in your movies.** If you have iMovie, you also have iPhoto, Apple's easy-to-use application that makes it easy to manage, improve and use your photos. iPhoto lets you pull in photos from your digital camera, crop them to size and fix problems, and then add them to your movie projects in iMovie. Once they're there, you can set a photo to play for as long as needed and add visual interest by panning and zooming over the photos with the Ken Burns effect. You can also capture still frames from your video clips and either use them in iMovie or export them back to iPhoto.

- **Share your movies with your family, your friends, or the world.** When your movie is ready for public consumption, use iMovie's built-in tools to share it with everyone who deserves the honor. Export the movie to iTunes so that you and your family can enjoy it on your computers, iPods or iPhones, or Apple TV; publish it straight to YouTube without fuss, or place it in your MobileMe gallery or on your iWeb site. To distribute the movie even more widely, export it to a QuickTime file that you can share with the whole world.

- **Create DVDs of your movies.** iDVD lets you burn your movies and other creations to DVD quickly and easily. Get up to speed on the iDVD workflow and user interface and set the application's preferences to make it work the way you want. You'll then be ready to bring your movies into iDVD, create an interface that complements the content, and then burn the result to DVD for distribution.

- **Troubleshoot problems.** Normally iMovie runs smoothly, and you can assemble, edit, and fine-tune your movies without trouble. But because iMovie must work with a wide range of video hardware, problems can crop up. You'll learn ways to make iMovie run as fast as possible; tricks to prevent the application from crashing or running unstably; and smart steps for solving problems when iMovie won't recognize your camcorder, import photos from iPhoto, or keep audio in sync.

iMovie '09?

To the swift and simple movie editing that iMovie '08 gave Mac users, iMovie '09 adds a slew of terrific new features — advanced drag and drop, a Precision Editor for transitions, a means of removing camera shake, and the list goes on. This chapter introduces you to the new features in iMovie and points you toward the chapters in which you'll find more coverage of them. It also covers the iMovie interface so you know what all the different elements do and what they're called.

Meeting the New Features in iMovie '09

iMovie '09's new features include advanced drag and drop; the Precision Editor; themes and maps; video stabilization; a wider selection of titles, transitions, and effects; and a new Library browser.

To open iMovie, click the iMovie icon on the Dock. I'll take you through what you need to know about the new features. After that, I'll discuss the main features of the iMovie window.

Note If the iMovie icon doesn't appear on the Dock, click the Desktop, choose Go ⇨ Applications, and then double-click the iMovie icon. Once iMovie is running, Ctrl+click or right-click the iMovie icon on the Dock and choose Keep in Dock to anchor it to the Dock.

Advanced drag and drop

iMovie '09 includes a new advanced drag-and-drop feature that enables you to edit your movies just as quickly and easily as in iMovie '08 but with extra power. As well as being able to add a clip to a project by simply clicking and dragging it to the Project window, you can also drop one clip on another clip and choose from a variety of advanced options (see figure 1.1).

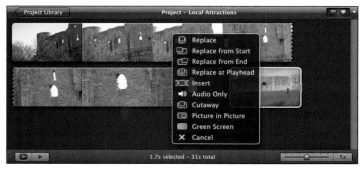

1.1 iMovie '09's advanced drag-and-drop tools enable you to create cutaways, picture-in-picture frames, and green-screen effects.

The four most useful advanced drag-and-drop features are:

- **Cutaways.** A *cutaway* is a scene where you paste a short clip over part of a longer one to give a different perspective. For example, in an interview, you can paste a shot of the interviewee starting to react to the question over a longer shot of the interviewer asking it. The cutaway replaces the part of the clip over which you paste it.

- **Picture in picture.** With picture in picture, you can inlay one clip in another clip, which can be useful for zooming in on a detail in the frame or for showing what's happening in two separate scenes at the same time. Figure 1.2 shows an example.

- **Green screen.** A green-screen effect enables you to "cut out" the subject of one video clip and overlay it on another video clip. You record the video clip you'll overlay using a green background that iMovie can eliminate automatically when you add the clip, making the background clip appear through all the areas that were green in the overlaid clip.

1.2 iMovie's picture-in-picture feature enables you to place one clip over another part of another clip. You can resize and reposition the overlaid clip as needed.

- **Audio only.** The audio-only effect enables you to use one video clip's audio as the audio for another clip. This is a great time-saver because you no longer have to create a separate audio-only version of the clip.

Note

Chapter 4 shows you how to use advanced drag and drop and the Precision Editor.

The Precision Editor

iMovie '09's new Precision Editor enables you to make exact edits to your video clips so that they play back precisely the way you want them to. The Precision Editor is a pane that appears in place of the Events pane (usually in the lower half of the iMovie window) and that gives you the power to zoom in on the transition between one video clip and the next.

Working in this magnified view, you can select the specific frames that you want to affect, rather than selecting roughly the right frame in the Project window. Figure 1.3 shows the Precision Editor with clips open for editing. The clip before the transition appears as the upper filmstrip; the highlighted area on the left shows the part of the clip that plays before the transition, while the darkened area on the right shows the part that doesn't play. The clip after the transition appears as the lower filmstrip; the darkened area on the left shows the part that doesn't play, while the highlighted area on the right shows the part of the clip that plays after the transition.

1.3 The Precision Editor gives you frame-by-frame control over transitions in your movie projects.

Themes and maps

When you need to whip together a movie in short order, you can use one of iMovie's themes. A *theme* is a set of animated titles and preset transitions that turns your raw footage into a watchable movie. Think of a theme as a shortcut for adding polish, coherence, and visual appeal to a movie.

You can switch from one theme to another as needed, even after you've added the text for the movie's titles. You can also customize a theme to make it look different. For example, you can change the transitions in the theme to a different type of transition, such as the widely useful Cross Dissolve.

You can apply a theme either when you create a new project or at any point afterward by using the General pane of the Project Properties dialog box (see figure 1.4). You can also remove the current theme by choosing None instead.

iMovie '09's new Maps and Backgrounds browser enables you to quickly add an animated map (for example, an old-world globe or an educational globe) or a colorful background to a movie project. The maps are great for documentaries, travelogs, and similar movies, while the backgrounds can help hold the audience's interest during a narrative or musical interlude.

1.4 You can switch a movie project from one theme to another at any point — or remove the theme.

Note Chapter 6 shows you how to work with themes and maps.

Stabilizing your video

One of the biggest problems with taking video is keeping the camcorder steady enough to prevent camera shake, especially when your subject is moving, you're moving, or both. Some camcorders include built-in image stabilization, but many don't, especially the pocket-size camcorders such as the Flip series from Pure Digital Technologies and its competitors.

Note Chapter 5 explains how to use iMovie's stabilization feature.

iMovie '09 enables you to automatically stabilize your video clips when you import them from the camcorder (or from files) or afterward — for example, when you realize that a clip is shaky enough to make the audience feel seasick. Figure 1.5 shows iMovie stabilizing a clip.

1.5 iMovie '09 can automatically stabilize video clips to reduce or remove camera shake and make them more watchable.

Genius iMovie's stabilization doesn't actually change the video clip — it just changes the way the clip plays. This means that you can increase or decrease the amount of stabilization as needed. You can even remove stabilization if you decide the cure is worse than the disease.

Titles, effects, and transitions

iMovie '09 provides more titles, effects, and transitions than iMovie '08. They enable you to do the following:

- **Titles.** iMovie's wider range of titles means you can add exactly the titles you need to a movie. You can easily place titles over clips or on their own, with colored or black backgrounds as needed.

Effects. iMovie '09 enables you to manipulate your footage in many more ways
than iMovie '08. Figure 1.6 shows the
Choose Video Effect dialog box, where
you can apply any effect from aged film
to a negative or X-ray.

Transitions. iMovie's transitions range
from the simple and subtle Cross
Dissolve to the dramatic revolving Cube
transition and the in-your-face Spin In
and Spin Out transitions.

1.6 iMovie enables you to apply 19 different
video effects with the click of a mouse — or
remove them by choosing None.

Genius

For most of us, iMovie '09's best effect is changing the speed of a clip. This means
you can create slow-motion effects or high-speed effects where you need them. You
can even make a clip play backward, which can be great for drama and comedy.

The new Library browser

To help you find the footage you need, iMovie
enables you to browse your video footage full
screen (see figure 1.7). You can even use Cover
Flow view to go through your video footage,
just as you use it in iTunes to flick through
your CDs by cover. See Chapter 3 for details.

1.7 Browsing your video footage full screen
makes it easier to find the parts you need.

Navigating the iMovie '09 Interface

This section shows you the main features of the iMovie '09 interface: the Project Library, the Project
window, the Viewer, the toolbar, the Event Library, and the Event browser. Figure 1.8 shows the iMovie

interface as a whole with the Project Library displayed and the Event Library in its standard position. The Project window doesn't appear because it shares the area occupied by the Project Library.

Toolbar   Project Library   Viewer

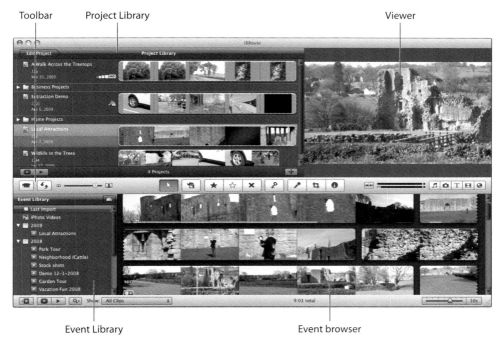

Event Library   Event browser

1.8 The iMovie window with a project selected in the Project Library

Project Library

The Project Library pane appears in the upper-left corner of the iMovie window by default. This pane lists all your movie projects, along with a few frames from each project to help you identify them, so you can easily move from one project to another.

When you're ready to work on a project, click it and then click Edit Project to hide the Project Library pane. You can also simply double-click the project to switch from the Project Library pane to the Project window.

From the Project Library (see figure 1.9), you can do the following:

- **Create a new project.** Click the New Project button or press ⌘+N.
- **See whether you've exported a project.** The screen icons to the right of a project's details show whether you've exported a project and whether you've shared it.

◉ **Play a project.** Click the project, and then click the Play Project from beginning button if you want to play the whole project in the Viewer. Click the Play Project full screen button if you want to play the project full screen.

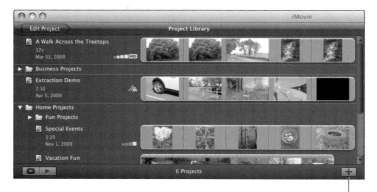

New Project

1.9 The Project Library is where you create new movie projects and organize your existing ones.

Project window

The Project window is where you assemble the footage for a movie project and add music, transitions, and titles to it. iMovie displays the current project in the Project window as a series of *filmstrips*, sequences of frames from the clips you're using.

You can take a wide variety of actions in the Project window by using the built-in controls (see figure 1.10), shortcut menus, and application menus, as you'll see in Chapter 2 onward. These are the basic moves:

◉ **Check the sharing.** The Shared to bar at the top of the Project window shows whether and where you've shared the project. If you've changed the project since you shared it, the Project window displays an out-of-date warning icon as well.

◉ **View the project.** Click the View button in the upper-right corner to view the project in a window. Click the Play Project from beginning button to play the project from the beginning. Click the Play Project full screen button if you want to view the project full screen.

◉ **Zoom in or out on the filmstrips.** Drag the Frames Per Thumbnail slider to the left to zoom out; drag it to the right to zoom in. Sometimes you'll need to see more frames on each filmstrip to reveal detail; other times you'll benefit from seeing more filmstrips in the Project window.

Sharing information

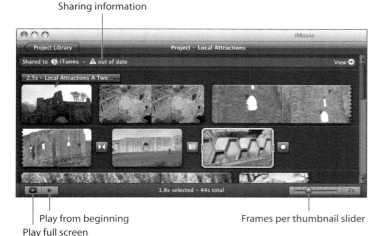

Play from beginning   Frames per thumbnail slider
Play full screen

1.10 A movie project open in the Project window.

To return from the Project window to the Project Library, click the Project Library button.

Viewer

The Viewer shows the current frame from the current video clip — the one you've selected by moving the mouse pointer over it or by clicking it. You can play the clip in the Viewer by pressing the spacebar, or play the whole movie project by clicking the Play Project from beginning button.

Most of the time, the Viewer doesn't display any controls. But when you need controls — for example, for cropping a video or for applying pan-and-zoom effects to a still photo — the Viewer displays them as an overlay.

Toolbar

Unlike most applications, in which the toolbar appears across the top of the window, the iMovie toolbar appears across the middle of the window. The toolbar contains most of the controls you use for manipulating content and for displaying other parts of the iMovie interface, such as the Music and Sound Effects browser or the Titles browser.

The buttons and controls are divided into several groups, as you can see in figure 1.11.

The first three controls at the left end of the toolbar let you import video, rearrange the iMovie window, and choose how big to display frames:

- **Open Camera Import Window button.** Click this button to open the Camera Import window so that you can pull in video from your camcorder.

- **Swap Events and Projects button.** Click this button to switch the Events area and Projects area of the iMovie window.

- **Thumbnails Size slider.** Drag this slider left to reduce the size of thumbnail pictures or right to enlarge them.

The next group of four buttons is for working with footage you've selected in a clip in the Event browser:

- **Add Selection to Project button.** Click this button to add the footage to your project.

- **Mark Selection as Favorite button.** Click this button to mark the footage as a favorite — footage you want to use.

- **Unmark Selection button.** Click this button to remove favorite or reject marking — for example, because you've decided you don't like the footage after all.

- **Reject Selection button.** Click this button to mark the footage as a reject.

The next group of three buttons enables you to manipulate a selected clip:

- **Voiceover button.** Click a clip in the Project window, and then click this button to start recording a voiceover for the clip.

- **Crop, Rotate, and Ken Burns button.** Click a clip in either the Project window or the Event browser, and then click this button to display cropping and rotation tools. If you click a still photo rather than a movie clip, you get the Ken Burns tools as well — tools for panning and zooming over the photo to emphasize the areas you choose and to add visual interest.

- **Inspector button.** Click a clip in either the Project window or the Event browser, and then click this button to display the Inspector window, which enables you to apply stabilization or adjust the video or audio settings.

Next, the Audio Skimming button enables you to turn audio skimming on and off. When audio skimming is on, you hear the audio as you skim through a clip. This can be useful for identifying the frames you want by sound; but high-speed audio tends to grate, so you can turn audio skimming off when you're picking video by sight rather than by sound.

The Volume meter shows the audio level of the left channel (above) and the right channel (below).

The five buttons at the right end of the toolbar enable you to open (from left to right) the Music and Sound Effects browser, the Photos browser, the Titles browser, the Transitions browser, and the Maps and Backgrounds browser.

Figure 1.11 shows the toolbar with its buttons labeled.

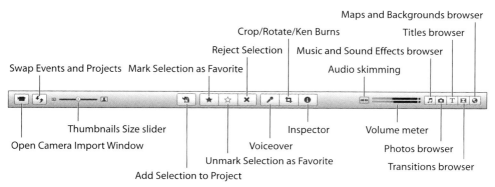

1.11 The toolbar appears across the middle of the iMovie window and gives you instant access to the most widely used controls.

Note   iMovie also contains advanced controls that appear on the toolbar when you select the Show Advanced Tools check box in the General pane of the iMovie Preferences window. You can learn more about these tools in Chapter 4 and subsequent chapters.

Event Library

This pane enables you browse the Events that contain all the movie footage you import into iMovie. If you don't need to keep the Event Library open once you've chosen the Event containing the footage you want, click the Show/Hide Event Library button to hide it and give yourself more space for the Event browser.

Genius   An *Event* is a tool for organizing your movie footage into categories. When you import video, iMovie creates Events automatically using the timecodes on the video, but you can also create your own Events as needed. You can move or copy a clip from one Event to another.

Event browser

The Event browser displays the clips of movie footage contained in the Event you've selected in the Event Library. These clips are called *filmstrips*. You use the Event browser to pick the footage you want to add to the Project Storyboard.

You can view a filmstrip quickly by moving your mouse pointer across it. This is called *skimming*. As you skim, iMovie plays the filmstrip in the Viewer using the speed at which the mouse pointer is moving. The image on the opening page of the chapter shows skimming a filmstrip. You can start playback at normal speed at any point by pressing Spacebar.

Note

To swap the positions of the Project Library or Project window (whichever is displayed) and the Event Library and Event browser, click the Swap Events and Projects button on the toolbar. Placing the Event Library and Event browser at the top of the iMovie window, next to the Viewer, can speed up the process of reviewing your clips and selecting footage

Movie Quickly?

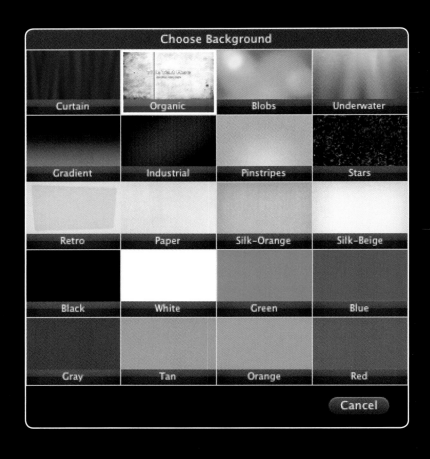

This chapter shows you how to use iMovie '09's powerful tools to put together a high-quality movie within minutes. First, you'll create a new iMovie project, choose between widescreen and standard formats, and apply one of iMovie's themes to it. Next, you'll import footage from your camcorder, quickly trim the footage to select the parts you want, and add them to a project. You'll then add a still image from iPhoto and adjust the transitions between the various clips. Finally, you'll add a title to the beginning of the movie, give the movie a soundtrack, and then play it back to see how it looks.

Creating a New Project

First, create a new project and choose settings for it. Here's how:

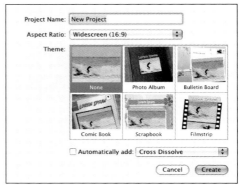

1. **Press ⌘+N to open the New Project dialog box (see figure 2.1).** You can also choose File ➪ New Project from the menu bar or click the New Project button (the + button) in the lower-right corner of the Project Library.

2. **In the Project Name box, type the name you want to give the project.**

2.1 Choose settings for the new project in the New Project dialog box.

Note

You can change the name and aspect ratio later if needed, so it's not vital to get the settings exactly right at this point.

3. **In the Aspect Ratio pop-up menu, choose the aspect ratio you want — the proportion of the frame's width to its height.** Your choices include:

   - **Widescreen (16:9).** Choose this aspect ratio (16 units wide by 9 units high) for playing back on a high-definition TV or a widescreen monitor. If you play the project back on a standard TV or monitor, the video appears letter-boxed, with black bands above and below it.

   - **Standard (4:3).** Choose this aspect ratio (four units wide by three units high) for playing back on a standard-shaped TV or monitor.

   - **iPhone (3:2).** Choose this aspect ratio (three units wide by two units high) for playing back on an iPhone or another device with a screen that's one-and-a-half times as wide as it is high.

4. **In the Theme section, make sure the None theme is selected.** You won't use a *theme* — a predefined set of scene transitions, titles, and other effects — for this movie.

5. **Select the Automatically add check box and choose Cross Dissolve in the pop-up menu.**

6. **Click Create.** iMovie creates the movie project for you, adds it to the Project Library, and then opens it in the Project window.

Genius

How iMovie '09 stores video and projects is complicated. The video clips are large, and iMovie lets you choose which drive to store them on; your Mac's hard drive is the best choice if it has space. The project file contains only details of which clips the movie uses and how (for example, play the first three seconds only), so it's small. iMovie automatically stores the project file in the ~/Movies/iMovie Projects folder (where ~ represents your home folder). See Chapter 8 for instructions on moving files to different drives.

Importing the Footage

Now import the footage you'll use in the movie. Follow these steps:

1. **Connect the camcorder to your Mac.** Most tape camcorders connect via FireWire; most tapeless camcorders connect via USB. For a USB connection, use a port on your Mac rather than on a USB hub connected to your Mac. Don't use the low-power USB port on a desktop Mac's keyboard — it doesn't provide enough power.

Note

The importing instructions in this section are for a tapeless DV camcorder — for example, one that records onto flash memory or a hard disk. If your camcorder records onto tape, the procedure is a bit different, but still straightforward. See Chapter 3 for instructions on importing video from tape.

2. **Switch the camcorder on and set it to Playback mode.** Some camcorders call this mode PC mode or VCR mode.

Genius

If your Mac doesn't recognize the camcorder and launch iMovie, you may need to plug the camcorder into a power outlet to convince the camcorder that it has more than enough power to transfer all your video.

3. **Your Mac should open or activate iMovie automatically when it notices the camcorder in Playback mode.** If not, try quitting iMovie (if it's running) and then reopening it manually.

4. **iMovie automatically generates thumbnail previews for the clips on the camcorder, and then displays the thumbnails in a panel at the bottom of the Import From window.** Figure 2.2 shows an example.

5. **Choose which clips you want to import:**

- If you want to import all the clips, simply click Import All, and go to the next step. Otherwise, click and drag the switch in the lower-left corner of the Import From window from Automatic to Manual. iMovie adds a check box to each clip (see figure 2.3).

- To play a clip, click its thumbnail, and then click the Play button on the toolbar across the middle of the window. You can then click the Previous button or the Next button on the toolbar to play another clip.

- Select the check box for each clip you want to import. If you want to import most of the clips, click Check All, and then clear the check boxes for those clips you don't want.

- Click Import Selected.

6. **When you click the Import All button or the Import Selected button, iMovie displays the dialog box shown in figure 2.4.**

7. **In the Save to pop-up menu, choose the hard disk on which you want to save the video.** Use your Mac's internal hard disk unless you've attached a fast external hard drive to give yourself extra space for working with video.

8. **Tell iMovie which Event to make the video part of:**

- To add the video to an existing event, select the Add to existing Event radio button, and then choose the Event in the pop-up menu.

2.2 iMovie shows you thumbnails of the clips on the camcorder.

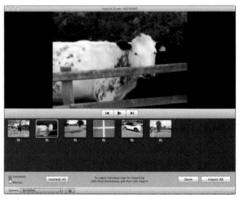

2.3 Move the switch to Manual to reveal check boxes for selecting the clips you want to import.

2.4 Choose which disk to save the video on, whether to create a new Event or add it to an existing Event, and whether to analyze it for stabilization.

To create a new Event, select the Create new Event radio button. Type the name for the new Event in the text box; iMovie suggests "New Event" and the date, but you'll find that more descriptive names are more helpful. Select the Split days into new Events check box if you want iMovie to create a separate event for each day on the imported video.

9. **If you want iMovie to apply stabilization to your clips, select the Analyze for stabilization after import check box.** Stabilization reduces or removes the camera shake that happens all too often on handheld video cameras.

Caution Applying stabilization makes importing the video take much longer. You may prefer to import your clips without analyzing them, pick the ones you want to use, and then apply stabilization only to those clips.

10. **Click OK.** iMovie starts importing the video, displaying a progress indicator so you can see how it's doing. iMovie displays an Import Complete dialog box to let you know when it has finished.

11. **Click OK to close the Import Complete dialog box.**

12. **Click Done to close the Import From window.**

Trimming and Assembling the Footage

Now that you've imported your movie footage into iMovie, review the footage and decide which pieces you want to use. iMovie enables you to add entire clips or parts of clips to the Project window from the Event browser.

If you've just this moment imported the footage, iMovie should be displaying it in the Event browser, as shown in figure 2.5. If it's not, click the Last Import item in the Event Library pane to make iMovie display the footage.

Each clip appears as a *filmstrip* — a sequence of frames at regular intervals throughout the clip (for example, one frame per second). To see the contents of a clip, move the mouse pointer over it. You can then move the red line of the Playhead across the clip by moving the mouse pointer or simply press Spacebar to play the clip in the Viewer.

Genius To change the size of the video thumbnails, drag the Thumbnails Size slider (on the toolbar) to the left or the right. To change the number of frames iMovie displays for a filmstrip, drag the Frames Per Thumbnail slider (in the lower-right corner of the iMovie window) to the left or right.

2.5 You'll find the footage you just imported in the Last Import Event in the Event Library.

When you've found a clip you want to use in your movie project, select the footage you want and add it to the movie project. Follow these steps:

1. **Click the point in the clip where you want to start using the footage.** iMovie selects a four-second chunk of the clip starting from where you clicked. iMovie displays a yellow border around the selected chunk.

2. **Click and drag the right selection handle to the point at which you want to stop using the footage (see figure 2.6).** The Viewer shows the current frame you're dragging over, so it's easy to see what you're doing.

3. **Click in the selection and drag it to the Project window.** iMovie displays a vertical green bar to show where the clip will land. The first clip goes at the beginning of the movie project, as you'd expect, but after that you can position each subsequent clip where you want it among the clips you've already added.

2.6 Click and drag the selection handle to select as much of a clip as you want to use.

Genius

If you want to select the whole of a filmstrip, Option+click it. Alternatively, Ctrl+click or right-click in the filmstrip and choose Select Entire Clip.

Because you chose to have iMovie add Cross Dissolve transitions, iMovie adds a transition at the beginning of the movie and between each pair of clips you add. The transition looks like two arrowheads pointing toward each other (see figure 2.7).

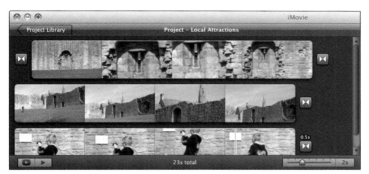

2.7 The arrowhead icons represent the transitions that iMovie adds to the movie project because of the project settings you chose.

To view the footage you've assembled so far, click the Play Project full screen button or the Play Project from beginning button in the lower-left corner of the Project window. You can also skim through the clips and transitions in the Project window by moving the mouse pointer across the clips and transition icons.

Use the same technique to add each of the other clips you want to use in the movie. The Event browser displays an orange bar across the bottom of the footage you've used for the project, so you can easily avoid adding the same footage twice.

Adding a Still Image from iPhoto

Now I'll show you how you can quickly add a still image from iPhoto to an iMovie project. This can be vital when you need to add information that you have only as a still image, but you can also use it to provide a change of pace in your movie.

Because going from movement to a still image can be jarring, iMovie automatically applies a Ken Burns Effect (panning over the photo and zooming in or out) to the still image to add movement and visual interest. You can adjust this effect as needed.

Here's how to bring a still image into iMovie from iPhoto and adjust the cropping and Ken Burns Effect:

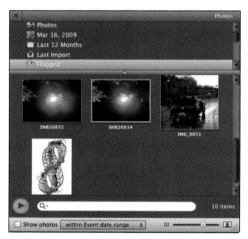

1. **Open the Photos browser pane (see figure 2.8).** Click the Photos Browser button on the toolbar or press ⌘+2.

2. **In the Albums lists at the top of the Photos browser pane, choose the album or other item that contains the photo you want.** For example:

   ● If the photo is in the last set of photos you imported, choose the Last Import item.

2.8 Use the Photos browser pane to quickly bring a still image from iPhoto into a project in iMovie.

   ● If you want to see the last year's worth of photos, choose the Last 12 Months item.

   ● If you prefer to browse by Event, click the Events item instead.

3. **Select the photo you want.** If you need to zoom in to see the photos larger, or zoom out to see more photos at once, click and drag the Thumbnails Size slider in the lower-right corner of the Photos browser pane.

4. **Click and drag the photo to the Project window.** iMovie displays a vertical green line to show where it will land.

5. **With the photo still selected, press Spacebar to play back the new clip consisting of the still image.** The photo appears in the Viewer, and you'll see the Ken Burns Effect that iMovie automatically applied.

6. **Press Spacebar again to stop playback.**

7. **In the Project window, move the mouse pointer over the photo's clip so that iMovie displays the Action button, which looks like a cog wheel.** Click the Action button and choose Cropping, Ken Burns & Rotation from the pop-up menu to display the cropping and Ken Burns tools.

8. **Customize the Ken Burns Effect like this:**

   ● Click the Ken Burns button if it's not already selected so that you see the Ken Burns controls (see figure 2.9).

Click and drag a corner or side of the green Start rectangle to select the photo size to display at the beginning of the pan and zoom. If necessary, click within the Start rectangle and drag it to select a different area of the picture. The green cross shows you where the middle of the Start rectangle is, and the yellow arrow shows you the direction and extent of the pan you'll get.

Click and drag a corner or side of the red End rectangle to select the photo size to display at the end of the pan and zoom. As with the Start rectangle, click within the End rectangle and drag it to select a different area of the picture. The red cross shows you where the middle of the End rectangle is.

Switch Start and End   Play clip

2.9 Customize iMovie's default Ken Burns Effect by resizing and repositioning the green Start rectangle and the red End rectangle. The yellow arrow shows you the direction and extent of the movement.

Click the Play Clip button to view the effect you've produced. Adjust the effect as needed. If you need to switch the Start rectangle and End rectangle, click the Switch Start and End button.

Click the Done button when you're satisfied with the effect.

9. **Choose how long you want to play the photo.** iMovie sets the duration to 4.0 seconds as a first step, but you can change it like this:

Move the mouse pointer over the photo's clip so that iMovie displays the Action button. Click the Action button and choose Clip Adjustments from the pop-up menu to display the Inspector window with the Clip tab selected (see figure 2.10).

Change the value in the Duration box to show the number of seconds you want.

Click the Done button.

2.10 You can quickly change the duration for which the still photo plays by using the Clip tab in the Inspector window.

Now play back your movie and make sure that the still image and its Ken Burns Effect works the way you want. If you're happy with the result, go on to the next section; if not, go back and adjust settings until you're happy with the movie so far.

Customizing Transitions

When you created this movie project, you chose to have iMovie automatically add a Cross Dissolve transition between each pair of clips. This provides an unobtrusive changeover: the first clip gradually dissolves into the second clip, and then the second clip appears without any traces of the first.

Note Cross Dissolve is the subtlest of the transitions, so it makes a good default. For other projects, you may want to try making a different default transition. Try out the transitions first, because some of the livelier ones (such as rectangles that spin in or out) are best kept for special occasions. See Chapter 6 for a detailed discussion of iMovie's transitions and when to use them.

If you decide that one trimmed clip in your movie will flow naturally into the next clip without the Cross Dissolve effect, remove the transition like this:

1. **In the Project window, click the transition you want to remove.**

2. **Press Delete.** iMovie displays the Automatic transitions are turned on dialog box (see figure 2.11), warning you that you need to turn off automatic transitions before you can change individual transitions.

2.11 When a movie project uses automatic transitions, you must turn them off before you can delete or change any of the transitions.

3. **Click the Turn Off Automatic Transitions button.** iMovie turns off automatic transitions and removes the transition you tried to delete.

Once you've done this, you can substitute another transition for one of your other existing transitions if you like. Here's what to do:

1. **In the Project window, double-click the transition you want to change.** iMovie displays the Inspector dialog box for transitions (see figure 2.12).

2. **Clear the Applies to all transitions check box.** You'd leave this check box selected if you wanted to change all the transitions.

3. **Click the Transition button.** iMovie displays the Choose Transition dialog box (see figure 2.13).

4. **Move the mouse pointer over a transition.** iMovie displays a preview of its effect in the Viewer window.

5. **Click the transition you want.** iMovie applies it and displays the Inspector dialog box again.

6. **Click the Done button to close the Inspector dialog box.**

Repeat the previous steps for each remaining transition you want to change.

Titling the Movie

By now, your movie should be looking pretty good. Next, give it an opening title:

1. **Click the Titles Browser button (the T button) near the right end of the toolbar to display the Titles browser (see figure 2.14).**

2. **Click the title style you want, drag it to the Project window, and drop it at the beginning of the project.** As with the clips, iMovie displays a vertical green bar when the mouse pointer is in the right place. iMovie then displays the Choose Background dialog box.

2.12 Use the Inspector dialog box for transitions to quickly apply a different transition between two clips.

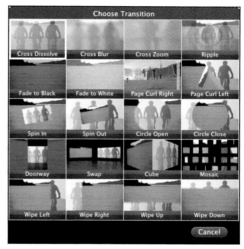

2.13 Pick a different transition in the Choose Transition dialog box.

2.14 The Titles browser provides a selection of title styles that you can customize as needed.

3. **Click the background color you want to give the title.** iMovie applies it to the title in the Viewer and closes the Choose Background dialog box.

4. **Click the placeholder text in the Viewer (see figure 2.15) and type your title text.**

5. **Click the Play button to see how the title looks.** Adjust it if necessary. For example, edit the text for fit or sense, or click the Show Fonts button in the Viewer and choose a different font.

2.15 Type your title text over the placeholder text, and then click Done.

6. **Click the Done button.** iMovie applies the title to the movie.

Adding Music

To finish off your movie project, add music to it like this:

1. **Click the Music and Sound Effects Browser button (the button with the musical notes) toward the right end of the toolbar to display the Music and Sound Effects browser (see figure 2.16).**

2. **Click the item that contains the music you want.** For example, click GarageBand to use one of your GarageBand compositions, or click iTunes to use a song from your iTunes library.

2.16 You can quickly add music to a movie project by dragging a song or other audio item from the Music and Sound Effects browser to the Project window.

3. **Click and drag the song or other audio item from the Music and Sound Effects browser to the Project window.** Drop the item outside any of the clip, transitions, and title boxes so that the background turns green. This means you're applying the audio to the whole project.

Now play back the movie from the beginning and see how it looks. For best effect, play the movie back full screen.

This chapter has introduced you to the essentials of creating a movie with iMovie. As you'll have noticed, the application offers far more options than I've covered here. The next eight chapters go into those options in detail, starting with the many ways you can import video content into iMovie.

What Are My Video Import Options?

Before you can make a movie, you need to get the raw materials — your video clips — into iMovie. You will usually need to decide between full high-definition video and a large frame size that uses less space. You also need to use different import methods for different camcorder types, for capturing from an iSight, and for importing existing video files. After you import the video, you'll probably want to review it in iMovie and choose the pieces you want to use.

Preparing to Import Video

Before you start hauling your video clips into iMovie, I'll go over the basics of importing. This will ensure that you know the essentials of what's happening right off the bat.

When you import video into iMovie, you need to make three main decisions: where to store the video clips, which Event to assign the clips to, and how to import high-definition video clips.

For most of iMovie's import methods, you get the same choices. Figure 3.1 shows the Import dialog box, which you use for importing existing movies from a disk or memory card and which contains the controls you use to make these choices.

3.1 The Import dialog box includes the controls you typically use for importing video into iMovie.

Choosing which disk to store the clips on

The Save to pop-up menu in iMovie's various import dialog boxes enables you to choose which disk to save the video clips on.

Video clips take up a lot of space — 40GB for an hour of high-definition video or 13GB for an hour of standard-definition video — so if you have a choice, you'll want to use the disk with the most free space. Normally, your Mac's internal hard disk is usually the best bet unless you've attached an external hard drive to give yourself extra space for working with video.

Genius

Your Mac's internal hard disk will give you faster performance than an external disk, even if you use a speedy FireWire 800 connection for the external disk. To make iMovie run as fast as possible, store your video files on your Mac's hard disk. If the disk is getting full, move files you no longer use to a backup (such as a DVD) and files you seldom use to the external disk.

Choosing which Event to assign the clips to

Your second decision is which Event you want to assign the video clips to. You can either use an existing Event, which is handy if the clips you're importing belong to a group of clips that you've already established, or create a new Event.

If you want to use one of your existing events, select the Add to existing Event option button and choose the Event in the pop-up menu.

Otherwise, select the Create new Event option button and type the name for the new Event in the text box.

Choosing how to import high-definition clips

Your third decision is how to import high-definition video clips. iMovie enables you to import high-definition video clips either at their full size (1920 x 1080 pixels) or at the size that iMovie calls Large, which uses 960 x 540 pixel resolution.

If you shoot high-definition video, this is a tough decision. For the highest quality, you'll probably want to import the clips at full size — but they take up a huge amount of space, and iMovie may run more slowly when you're manipulating them. Large takes up only a quarter of the space and looks pretty good, so it's well worth experimenting with this setting to see whether the quality is high enough for your needs.

You can choose the Import 1080i video as setting for each set of movie clips as you import them, but to save time, apply the setting you normally choose in the Video pane of the iMovie Preferences window. That way, you will need to change the setting only when you decide to import video clips in a different way than normal.

Here's how to choose your default setting:

1. **Open the iMovie Preferences window.** Choose iMovie ⇨ Preferences or press ⌘+, (comma).

2. **Click the Video button in the toolbar.** iMovie displays the Video pane (see figure 3.2).

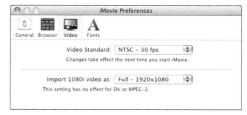

3.2 Choose your preferred Import 1080i video as setting in the Video pane of the Preferences window.

33

3. **Choose your preferred setting in the Import 1080i video as pop-up menu.** The choices are Full – 1920 x 1080 or Large – 960 x 540.

4. **Click the Close button (the red button) to close the iMovie Preferences window.**

With this essential information in mind, you're ready to throw at iMovie any of the kinds of video that it can handle.

Importing DV and HDV Footage from Tape

If your camcorder records on to tape, follow the steps in this section to import video clips.

1. **Connect the camcorder to your Mac via FireWire.** Most camcorders use a FireWire cable with a small, four-pin plug at the camcorder end and a regular, six-pin plug at the Mac's end. Others use a regular six-pin-to-six-pin cable.

Caution
Connecting a DV camcorder via FireWire can disconnect an external FireWire drive you're using. So before you connect your DV camcorder for the first time, close any files that you've opened from any external FireWire drive you're using, just in case the DV camcorder knocks the drive off your Mac's FireWire chain.

2. **Switch the DV camcorder to play mode or VCR mode.** When iMovie recognizes the DV camcorder, it automatically displays the Import From window (see figure 3.3). If you don't see the window, click the Open Camera Import Window button (you can also choose File ⇨ Import from Camera or press ⌘+I).

3.3 iMovie displays the Import From window when it recognizes that a DV camcorder is connected and switched on.

Importing all the footage from the tape

If you want to import all the video on the tape, follow these steps:

1. **Make sure the Mode slider in the lower-left corner of the Import From window is set to Automatic.**

2. **Click the Import button.** iMovie displays the sheet shown in figure 3.4.

3. **In the Save to pop-up menu, choose the hard disk on which you want to save the video.** Your Mac's internal hard disk is usually the best bet unless you've attached an external hard drive to give yourself extra space for working with video.

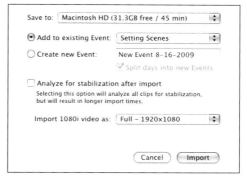

3.4 Choose which disk to save the video on and whether to create a new Event or add the video to an existing Event.

4. **Tell iMovie which Event to make the video part of.** Either select the Add to existing Event option button and choose the Event, or select the Create new Event option button and type a name for the Event.

5. **If you want iMovie to apply stabilization to your clips, select the Analyze for stabilization after import check box.** This feature adjusts your clips to compensate for camera shake.

Caution Applying stabilization can take quite a while, depending on how fast your Mac is and what else it's doing at the time. Usually, it's best to see which clips have the problem, and then stabilize only the ones you want to use.

6. **In the Import 1080i video as pop-up menu, choose whether to import high-definition video at the Full size or at the Large size.**

7. **Click OK.** iMovie rewinds the tape to the beginning, and then imports the video, displaying it in the Import From window as it does so.

8. **When iMovie displays the Camera Import Complete sheet (see figure 3.5), click OK.** You can now turn off your DV camcorder and start working with the video you've imported.

Camera Import Complete

About 5 minutes of video were imported and the tape was rewound.

OK

3.5 iMovie tells you when it has finished importing the video.

Importing selected clips manually

If you want to grab only some of the video from your camcorder, follow these steps:

1. **Move the mode switch in the lower-left corner of the Import From window to the Manual position.** iMovie displays the transport controls for the camcorder (see figure 3.6).

2. **Use the transport controls to reach the part of the tape you want to import.** For example, fast-forward to approximately the right part of the tape, play the video until where you want to start importing, and then stop it.

3.6 Move the mode switch to Manual to access iMovie's transport controls for your DV camcorder.

3. **Click the Import button.** iMovie displays the sheet for choosing where and how to save the video.

4. **In the Save to pop-up menu, choose the hard disk on which you want to save the video.**

5. **Choose whether to make the video part of an existing Event or to create a new Event for it, as discussed earlier in this chapter.**

6. **If you want iMovie to apply stabilization to your clips, select the Analyze for stabilization after import check box.** As before, applying stabilization will make the import take longer.

7. **In the Import 1080i video as pop-up menu, choose whether to import high-definition video at the Full size or at the Large size.**

8. **Click OK.** iMovie starts importing the video from the point you chose. Figure 3.7 shows an example of importing video clips manually.

9. **Click the Stop button when iMovie reaches the end of the video you want to import.** iMovie processes the clip you imported, and then displays the blue screen of the Import From window again.

10. **If you want to import more video from the DV camcorder, follow Steps 2 through 9 to select and import it.** When you've finished, click Done to close the Import From window.

3.7 Importing video clips manually from a tape camcorder.

Importing Footage from a Tapeless Camcorder

If your camcorder stores the video on a hard drive, memory card, or DVD, you should be able to import the video files like this:

1. **Connect the camcorder to your Mac via USB.** If possible, connect the tapeless camcorder to a USB jack on your Mac rather than on a USB hub connected to your Mac. Avoid using the low-power USB port on a desktop Mac's keyboard.

2. **Switch the camcorder on and put it into Playback mode.** Some camcorders call this mode PC mode or VCR mode.

3. **Your Mac should open or activate iMovie automatically when it notices the camcorder in Playback mode.** If not, try quitting iMovie (if it's running) and then reopening it manually.

4. **iMovie automatically generates thumbnail previews for the clips on the camcorder, and then displays the thumbnails in a panel at the bottom of the Import From screen.** Figure 3.8 shows an example.

3.8 When you connect a tapeless camcorder, iMovie shows you thumbnails of the clips it contains.

Note If your camcorder takes Advanced Video Coding High Definition (AVCHD) video, you need to have an Intel-based Mac to import the video. Even a powerful G5-based Mac can't handle AVCHD video.

5. **Choose which clips you want to import:**

   - If you want to import all the clips, simply click Import All and go to the next step. Otherwise, click and drag the switch in the lower-left corner of the Import From window from Automatic to Manual. iMovie adds a check box to each clip (see figure 3.9).

3.9 Move the switch to Manual to reveal check boxes for selecting the clips you want to import.

   - To play a clip, click its thumbnail, and then click the Play button. You can then click the Previous button or the Next button to play another clip.

   - Select the check box for each clip you want to import. If you want to import most of the clips, click Check All and then clear the check boxes for those clips you don't want.

   - Click Import Selected.

6. **In the Save to pop-up menu, choose the hard disk on which you want to save the video.**

7. **Choose whether to make the video part of an existing Event or to create a new Event for it, as discussed earlier in this chapter.**

8. **If you want iMovie to apply stabilization to your clips, as described in the previous section, select the Analyze for stabilization after import check box.**

9. **Click OK.** iMovie starts importing the video, displaying a progress indicator so you can see how it's doing. iMovie displays an Import Complete dialog box to let you know when it has finished.

10. **Click OK to close the Import Complete dialog box.**

11. **Click Done to close the Import From window.**

Importing Footage from a Digital Camera

If you've shot your video footage on a digital camera, import it using iPhoto rather than iMovie. You may also need to use this import method for some digital camcorders that Mac OS X identifies as digital cameras rather than as camcorders. Pocket-size digital camcorders are especially likely to appear as digital cameras.

Genius

If your camcorder or digital camera appears as a drive in your Mac's file system, it's better to import the files into iMovie as described later in this chapter. If it doesn't appear as a drive but it records videos onto a removable memory card, remove the card from the camcorder, insert it in a card reader connected to your Mac, and import the files from there.

Here's how to import video footage from a digital camera:

1. **Connect the digital camera to your Mac via USB and switch it on.**

2. **When Mac OS X notices the camera or memory card containing photos, it launches or activates iPhoto and prompts you to import the photos (see figure 3.10).**

3. **Type a descriptive name for the Event in the Event Name text box.**

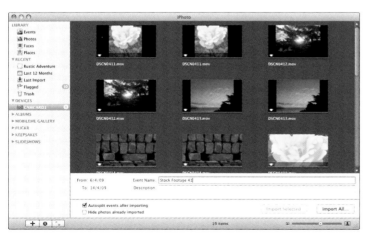

3.10 Mac OS X automatically opens iPhoto and displays thumbnails of the photos and videos on the camera or storage card you've connected.

4. **If you want, type a generic description for the photos or video clips in the Description text box.** You can give each photo or video clip its own description later.

5. **If you want iPhoto to split the photos and video clips into different Events by date and time, select the Autosplit events after importing check box.** iPhoto uses the Event length set in the Events pane in the Preferences window: One event per day, One event per week, Two-hour gaps, or Eight-hour gaps.

6. **If the camera or memory card contains photos or video clips you've imported before, select the Hide photos already imported check box to make iPhoto hide these items so you don't try to import them again.** Hiding the items you've already imported also enables iPhoto to show you the new items on the camera or memory card more quickly.

7. **Choose which photos or video clips you want to import.**

   - To import all the photos or video clips shown, click Import All.

   - To import only some of the photos or video clips, select them by dragging across a range or by clicking the first one and then holding down ⌘ while you click each of the others. Then click Import Selected.

8. **iPhoto imports the photos you chose, and then prompts you to delete the photos from the camera or memory card.**

9. **Click the Eject button next to the camera's listing in the Devices section of the Source list to eject the digital camera.** When the name of the digital camera no longer appears in the iPhoto Source list, you can turn the camera off and disconnect it.

Note Depending on the format in which the camcorder or digital camera stores its video clips, they may show up as dotted outlines in iPhoto rather than as visible previews. This doesn't mean the clips are damaged, just that iPhoto can't show previews. The clips will be fine when you get them to iMovie.

After importing the video clips into iPhoto, you can access them by selecting iPhoto Videos in the Event Library. From here, you can select footage, manipulate the video (for example, crop or rotate it), and drag it into a movie project. However, you cannot move a clip to another Event in iMovie.

Importing iMovie HD Projects

If you have movie projects you've created in iMovie HD (the iMovie version before iMovie '08, which has many advanced features), you can import them into iMovie '09 easily — at some cost. When you import an iMovie HD project, you get only the basics: iMovie replaces all transitions with Cross Dissolve transitions, removes all video effects, and omits the titles and music tracks.

iMovie automatically creates a new Event named after the imported project and places all the imported clips in it. It also creates a new movie project with the same name and adds to it the clips that were on the Storyboard in iMovie HD.

Here's how to import video from an iMovie HD project:

1. **Choose File ⇨ Import ⇨ iMovie HD Project.** iMovie displays the Import dialog box shown in figure 3.11.

2. **Navigate to the folder that contains the movie file, and then click the file.**

3. **In the Save to pop-up menu, choose whether to save the imported project to your Mac's hard disk or to another disk.**

4. **In the Import 1080i video as pop-up menu, choose whether to import high-definition video at Full size or whether to reduce it to the Large size.** If you're not importing high-definition video, you don't need to worry about this setting.

5. **Click Import.** You'll see a progress readout as iMovie imports the clips and generates the thumbnails.

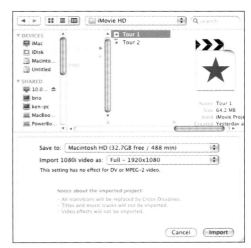

3.11 Bringing an iMovie HD project into iMovie '09 removes transitions, effects, titles, and music tracks.

After iMovie finishes importing the project, click the new Event in the Event Library and make sure that all the footage is there. Then click the new movie project that iMovie has created in the Project Library and verify that the movie has imported correctly.

Importing QuickTime and Other Movie Files

If you have movie files in QuickTime format or other movie formats (for example, AVI format) on your Mac's hard disk or on removable media, you can add them to the Event Library in iMovie so that you can use them in your movie projects.

To import a movie file, follow these steps:

1. **Choose File ⇨ Import ⇨ Movies.** iMovie displays the Import dialog box shown in figure 3.1, earlier in this chapter.

2. **Open the folder that contains the movie file, and then select the file or files.**

3. **In the Save to pop-up menu, choose the disk on which to store the imported file or files.**

4. **Choose whether to add the movie to an existing Event or create a new Event.**

5. **In the Import 1080i video as pop-up menu, choose whether to import high-definition video at Full size or at the smaller Large size.**

6. **In the lower-left corner of the dialog box, choose the Copy files option button or the Move files option button:**

   - Move the files if you want to manage your video footage through iMovie. Moving the files also avoids having them take up extra disk space on your Mac.

   - Copy the files if you want to be able to use the files from outside iMovie and you don't mind giving them extra space. If you're copying the files from an external drive, space may not be a concern anyway.

7. **Click Import.** iMovie copies or moves the files, imports the footage, and then displays the Event to which it has added the clips in the Event browser.

You can then review the imported clips as described later in this chapter.

Genius

You can also add a movie file to an Event in the Event Library by clicking the movie file in a Finder window and dragging it to the Event to which you want to add it.

Importing from an Analog Camcorder or Source

If you have an analog camcorder rather than a digital camcorder, or you need to import footage from another analog source (such as a VCR) to iMovie, you will need to convert the footage to digital video first.

The easiest way to do this is to use a DV camcorder that has an analog-to-digital pass-through system. Here's how this works:

1. **You connect the analog source to the DV camcorder's analog input, and then connect the DV camcorder's digital output to your Mac as usual.**

2. **You play the analog source into the DV camcorder's analog input.**

3. **The DV camcorder converts the analog input to digital video and passes it along to the Mac.**

4. **You import the video clips into iMovie on the Mac.**

The three steps from playback to importing in iMovie happen at the same time, so you end up recording in real time on your Mac from the analog source via the DV camcorder.

If you can't scare up a DV camcorder that can perform this neat trick, see if you can find a DV camcorder with analog inputs for recording from an analog source. In this case, you record from the analog source onto the camcorder's tape, then play back the recording and import it into iMovie as described earlier in this chapter. The disadvantage to importing video this way is that it takes twice as long, because both steps (recording to DV, and then recording from DV) take place in real time. But it works.

The third option is to beg, borrow, or buy an analog-to-digital converter box. This is a stand-alone unit that has analog inputs and a digital output. It works in much the same way as the DV camcorder with the analog-to-digital pass-through system described a moment ago: You play the analog source into the converter box; it outputs a digital video version and passes it along to the Mac; and you import the clips into iMovie. The conversion takes place in real time.

The main problem with analog-to-digital converter boxes is their cost: Most cost between $200 and $600, depending on the features you need.

Caution   iMovie doesn't recognize every analog-to-digital converter box, so be sure to read Mac-user reviews of any model you're thinking of buying. The Apple Store (http://store.apple.com) sells several models of analog-to-digital converters that should be fully compatible.

Importing from a DVD

You may need to import clips from a DVD because your camcorder records to DVD, because you have clips on a DVD that you're using to transfer or back up files, or because you want to use content from a commercial DVD. These three situations need different approaches, as explained in this section.

Importing from a DVD camcorder

If your camcorder records to DVD, the easiest way to import clips is to connect the camcorder to your Mac and import the clips using the technique explained earlier in this chapter for importing from a tapeless camcorder.

You can also remove the DVD from the camcorder, insert it in your Mac's optical drive, and then import files from there using the technique described for QuickTime and other video files earlier in this chapter.

Importing from a burned DVD

If you have burned video clips as files to a DVD, you can import them easily. Simply insert the DVD in your Mac's optical drive, and then use the technique described for QuickTime and other video files earlier in this chapter.

Importing from a commercial DVD

When you want to include content from a commercial DVD in a movie, you need to resolve two issues:

- **Getting the content off the DVD.** Most commercial DVDs are protected using the Content Scrambling System (CSS) to prevent unauthorized usage.

- **Getting permission to use someone else's copyrighted content.** See the end of the chapter for more details about copyright and where to request permission.

To get the content off the DVD, you need to use third-party software. Various commercial applications are available, but at this writing the best solution is a combination of two freeware applications:

- **VLC media player.** Download VLC media player from the VideoLAN Web site (www.video lan.org) and install it on your Mac. This gives you not only a versatile media player (which you may not need if you use iTunes and QuickTime) but also a DVD decrypter that HandBrake can use.

- **HandBrake.** Download HandBrake from the HandBrake Web site (http://handbrake.fr) and install it on your Mac. You can then run HandBrake and select the DVD you want to use. Choose the title that contains the chapters you want to extract, and then select the chapters you want. Choose the export format and resolution, and set HandBrake to extract the video to files you can use in iMovie.

Capturing Live Video from an iSight

Another option is to record video directly from an iSight video camera or a DV camcorder connected to your Mac. The iSight can be either built into your Mac or connected via FireWire.

To record live video, follow these steps:

1. **If you're using an external iSight or another external DV camera, connect it to your Mac via FireWire.** For a camera other than an iSight, turn its control knob to the Record position or Camera position (depending on the model).

2. **Open the Import From window by clicking the Open Camera Import Window button or choosing File ⇨ Import from Camera.** If you're using an external camera other than an iSight, the Import From window may open automatically when you switch the camera to the Record position or Camera position. Figure 3.12 shows iMovie ready to record from a built-in iSight.

3.12 The Camera Import window ready to import from a built-in iSight.

3. **If you have two or more cameras connected, choose the camera you want from the Camera pop-up menu.**

4. **If the Video Size pop-up menu appears, choose the resolution you want.** Some iSight cameras can provide different resolutions (for example, 640 x 480 or 1024 x 576), while others can manage only a single resolution.

5. **Aim the iSight or camera and any external microphone you're using.**

6. **Position your subject (for example, yourself) in the frame.**

7. **Click the Capture button (or the Import button) when you're ready to start recording.** iMovie displays the sheet shown in figure 3.13.

3.13 Choose where to store the footage, which Event to make it part of, and whether to split days into new Events.

8. **In the Save to pop-up menu, choose the hard drive on which you want to store the imported video.**

9. **Choose whether to add the files to an existing Event or whether to create a new Event using the usual techniques.** Select the Split days into new Events check box if you want iMovie to create a new event for each day you film. Unless the clock is ticking toward midnight or you're planning a marathon filming session, you don't normally need to worry about this check box when recording live.

10. **If you want iMovie to apply stabilization to your clips, select the Analyze for stabilization after import check box.** If the iSight is built into your Mac or mounted stably (for example, clipped to the screen or screwed onto a tripod), and the subject isn't dancing around, you shouldn't need to select this check box.

11. **Click OK.** iMovie starts recording through the camera.

12. **Click the Stop button when you want to stop capturing video.**

13. **Click the Done button when you're ready to close the Import From window.** iMovie adds your new footage to the Event you chose.

Browsing the Video You've Imported

After you import video, you'll probably want to browse through the imported clips, if only to make sure that all the footage has transferred successfully before you erase the tape or memory that contains it. You may also want to mark the footage you intend to use in your projects and the footage that's not worth using, leaving any footage between the two in a "maybe" status.

iMovie '09 enables you to browse your footage either in the Event browser or full screen. The Event browser gives you full control over what you're doing and lets you rate your clips, but browsing full screen gives you a better idea of the impact your footage will have when played at full size.

Browsing your footage in the Event browser

To view the clips in an Event, click the Event in the Event Library. iMovie displays the clips in the Event browser (see figure 3.14) as *filmstrips*, sequences of frames that show you the contents of the clips.

To change the size of the video thumbnails, drag the Thumbnails Size slider on the toolbar to the left or the right.

3.14 Viewing an Event's clips as filmstrips in the Event browser.

To change the number of frames iMovie displays for a filmstrip, drag the Filmstrip Length slider to the left or right. If you drag the slider all the way to the left, iMovie displays a single frame for each clip.

You can play clips in any of these ways:

- Double-click a clip to play it in the Viewer.
- To play a clip full screen, Ctrl+click or right-click it, and choose Play Full Screen.
- Click the Play selected Events from beginning button to play all the clips in the selected Event (or Events) in the Viewer.
- Click the Play selected Events full screen button to play all the clips in the selected Event (or Events) full screen. See the next section for details.

Skimming through a clip

To move through a clip at your own pace, position the mouse pointer over the filmstrip in the Event browser so that iMovie displays a red line representing the Playhead (see figure 3.15), and then move the mouse to the left or right to move through the frames. iMovie shows the current frame both in the Event browser and in the Viewer, so you can get a good view of what's happening. iMovie calls this technique *skimming*.

3.15 Drag the Playhead (the red line) to skim through a clip.

When you skim through a clip, iMovie plays the audio. If you don't want to hear the audio, click the Toggle Audio Skimming button on the toolbar (the button with the vertical red line) to turn off audio skimming. Click the button again when you want to turn it on again.

Switching the Event and Project areas

When you're reviewing your clips, you may want to switch the Event area and the Project area around so that the Event Library and Event browser appear at the top of the iMovie window along-side the viewer.

To switch the two areas, click the Swap Events and Projects button. iMovie swaps them over with a swirly animation. Click the button again when you want to switch the areas back.

Selecting the footage to keep

To save space on your Mac's hard drive, you'll usually want to trim down your clips by selecting only the footage you want to use. Use these techniques to select the footage:

- **To select a standard-length chunk of video, click the clip.** iMovie displays a yellow outline around it, starting from the point where you clicked. By default, iMovie selects four seconds (you can modify this in iMovie Preferences).

Note To change the number of seconds of video that iMovie selects when you click a clip, choose iMovie ⇨ Preferences, click the Browser tab, and then click and drag the Clicking in Events Browser selects slider to the number of seconds you want.

- **To select as much video as you want, click and drag through a clip.** iMovie displays a yellow outline around the part you've selected (see figure 3.16).

- **To change the length of the selection, drag the handle at either side to the left or right.** Alternatively, Shift+click another point in the clip to make the nearest handle snap to where you click.

- **To move the selection without changing its length, drag its top or bottom border to the left or right.**

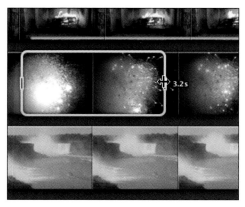

3.16 Click and drag to select as much of a clip as you want.

- **To select an entire filmstrip, Option+click it.** Alternatively, Ctrl+click or right-click and choose Select Entire Clip.

- **To select multiple filmstrips, click the first one, and then ⌘+click each of the others.** The first click gets you however many seconds iMovie is set to select, but as soon as you ⌘+click the second clip, iMovie selects the entire first clip as well.

Marking your clips as favorites or rejects

Once you've selected the footage you want, you can quickly mark it as a favorite. Similarly, you select footage you don't want to keep and mark it as a reject. Here's how:

- **Mark as a favorite.** Click the Mark Selection as Favorite button on the toolbar (see figure 3.17) or press F. iMovie puts a green bar across the top of the selected part of the clip.

3.17 Use these toolbar buttons to quickly mark favorites and rejects.

- **Mark as rejected.** Click the Reject Selection button or press R. iMovie puts a red bar across the top of the selected part of the clip.

- **Remove the marking.** Click the Unmark Selection button or press U. iMovie removes the green bar or red bar.

After marking favorites and rejects, you can narrow down the clips displayed by opening the Show menu and choosing Favorites Only, Favorites and Unmarked, or Rejected Only, as appropriate. When you want to see all the clips again, open the Show pop-up menu once more and choose All Clips from it.

Browsing your footage full screen

To browse your clips full screen, click the Event you want to browse (or click one Event and then ⌘+click to add others to the selection), and then press ⌘+G or click the Play selected Events full screen button in the lower-left corner of the iMovie window.

iMovie displays the Event's clips full screen with the thumbstrip and buttons at the bottom (see figure 3.18) and starts playing the clips. You can then take the following actions:

- **Pause playback.** Click the Play from beginning button.

- **Switch to viewing your projects.** Click the Show Projects or Events button to switch from Events to projects; click again to switch back.

- **Skim through clips.** Pause playback, click the clip you want on the thumbstrip, and then move the mouse pointer across the clip to move the red line of the Playhead.

- **Switch to Cover Flow view.** Click the Cover Flow view button to switch between the regular thumbstrip and one that has other Events or Projects displayed at angles at the ends. In Cover Flow view, you can quickly display another Event or project on the thumbstrip by clicking its thumbnail.

- **Exit full screen view.** When you've finished browsing full screen, click the Exit full screen button or press Esc to return to the iMovie window.

Play from beginning   Cover flow view

Show Projects or Events   Thumbstrip   Automatically hide thumbstrip
Exit full screen

3.18 Browse your Events full screen when you want to see the full impact of clips. You can switch between a regular thumbstrip and one that uses Cover Flow view, as shown here.

50

Do You Have Tips for Fine-Tuning Edits?

To create a tightly edited movie, first assemble the clips you want in the Project window in the right order. With that done, you can then use the Precision Editor to adjust the transition from one clip to another at the frame level. To work swiftly and exactly, you should enable the Fine Tuning controls and set iMovie's selection preferences to suit your needs. You can then select video footage a single frame at a time and trim your video clips to the perfect length for the movie. To make your footage easier to use in the ways you need, you can delete unwanted clips from frames. You can also split a clip up into two or three separate clips so that you can use them in different parts of your movie.

Creating a Movie from Clips

Once you've added video footage to the Event Library, you're all set to start creating your movie by assembling the clips you want in the right order. You got a taste of this in Chapter 2, but in this chapter I cover the details of what you can do and how you can save time and effort.

Your first step is to create a movie project and choose suitable settings for it. You may then want to adjust iMovie's preferences to match the way you prefer to work. You can then start dragging clips into the Project window.

Creating a new movie project

1. **Open the New Project dialog box (see figure 4.1).** Press ⌘+N or click the New Project button (the + button) in the lower-right corner of the Project Library.

2. **In the Project Name box, type the name you want to give the project.**

3. **In the Aspect Ratio pop-up menu, choose the aspect ratio you want.** Your choices are Widescreen (16:9), Standard (4:3), or iPhone (3:2).

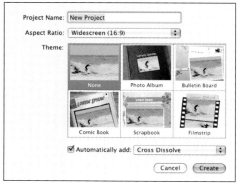

4.1 Choose basic settings for the new project in the New Project dialog box.

Note If you've already got a movie project ready for working on, use that project rather than creating a new one. It's still a good idea to check that the project's settings are suitable for your needs.

4. **In the Theme section, choose the theme you want to use, or choose None.**

- iMovie offers five themes: Photo Album, Bulletin Board, Comic Book, Scrapbook, and Filmstrip.

- Each theme is a predefined set of scene transitions, titles, and effects.

- The pictures in the New Project dialog box give you an idea of the differences among the themes. To see more detail on a preview, position the mouse pointer over its picture box, and then move the pointer around over the box to flick through the various pictures.

5. **Tell iMovie whether you want it to add scene transitions automatically.** How you do this depends on whether you selected a theme in Step 4:

   - **If you selected None:** Select the Automatically add check box and then use the pop-up menu to select the type of transition you want iMovie to apply throughout your project. Chapter 6 discusses the transitions in detail, but in general, the best transition for automatic use is Cross Dissolve. The example movies shown in this chapter have Cross Dissolve transitions automatically added.

   - **If you selected a theme:** In this case, iMovie selects the Automatically add transitions and titles check box for you. Deselect this check box if you don't want the automatic transitions and titles. (Normally, if you're using a theme, you will want to have automatic transitions and titles.)

6. **Click Create.** iMovie creates the movie project for you, adds it to the Project Library, and then opens it in the Project window.

Changing the properties for a movie project

Before you start adding video clips to your new project, check that its properties are set the way you want them. You can change project properties at any point, but getting them right at the start saves you time and effort in the long run.

Here's how to check and change the properties:

1. **Open the Project Properties dialog box.** If the project is open in the Project window, press ⌘+J or choose File ➪ Project Properties. Otherwise, Ctrl+click or right-click the project in the Project Library and choose Project Properties, or click it and use the keyboard shortcut or the menu command.

2. **Use the General pane (see figure 4.2) if you need to change the aspect ratio, choose a theme, or add automatic transitions.** See the discussion of these controls earlier in this chapter for details. If you've just created a movie project, you'll have chosen these settings already, so you probably won't need to change them again.

4.2 In the General pane of the Project Properties dialog box, you can change the aspect ratio, switch or remove the theme, and add transitions automatically.

3. **If you select the Automatically add check box to add automatic transitions and your project already contains clips, iMovie expands the dialog box as shown in figure 4.3.** Use the extra options to decide how to handle the ends of the project's current clips. They include:

- **Overlap ends and shorten clip.** iMovie moves each clip after the first to overlap its predecessor, and then applies the transitions. This is usually the best choice because you use only the footage in the clips. The one problem is when you've already set up your project with a carefully timed soundtrack: iMovie's shifting of the clips throws off the timing.

- **Extend ends and maintain duration (where possible).** iMovie extends the end of each clip to provide enough time for the transitions. To get this extra time, iMovie reveals extra frames you've hidden in the clip (more on this later in the chapter). If the clip doesn't contain any hidden frames at the end, iMovie can't extend the clip.

4. **In the Timing pane (see figure 4.4), choose transitions settings as follows:**

- **Transition Duration.** Click and drag the slider to set the length of the transition, from 0.5 seconds up to 4 seconds.

4.3 If you tell iMovie to add automatic transitions to a movie project, you need to decide whether to overlap the ends of the clips or extend the ends.

- **Theme Transition Duration.** Click and drag this slider to set the length of the theme transitions, from 0.5 seconds up to 4 seconds. This slider is disabled if you haven't selected a theme.

- **Applies.** These option buttons are available only if you deselect the Automatically add check box in the General pane. Select the Applies to all transitions option button if you want iMovie to use these settings for all transitions — those you've placed so far (if any) and those you add from now on. Otherwise, select the Applies when added to project option button to apply the duration only to clips you add from now on.

5. **Click and drag the Title Fade Duration slider to tell iMovie how long to fade the titles in and out.** You can set from 0 seconds to 2 seconds.

6. **Choose settings for still photos you add to the project:**

   • **Photo Duration.** Click and drag the slider to tell iMovie how long to play a photo for by default (from 1 second to 9 seconds).

   • **Applies To.** Select the Applies to all photos option button if you want to apply this duration to all photos you've already placed as well as to any you place from now on. Select the Applies when added to project option button if you want to apply the duration only to photos you place from now on.

   • **Initial Photo Placement.** In this pop-up menu, choose the standard placement for photos: Fit in Frame, Crop, or Ken Burns. You're just setting your default placement here; you can always change the placement for a photo after you place it.

7. **In the Initial Video Placement pop-up menu, choose the initial video placement: Fit in Frame, or Crop.**

8. **Click OK to close the Project Properties dialog box.** iMovie applies your preferences to the project.

4.4 Spend a minute setting default durations on the Timing pane of the Project Properties dialog box to reduce the number of changes you need to make later on in the project.

Adding video clips to the movie project

Follow these steps to add video clips to the movie project:

1. **In the Event Library, click the Event that contains the footage you want to use.**

2. **If you've marked the footage as favorites and rejects as discussed in Chapter 3, use the Show pop-up menu to make the Event browser display only the footage you want to see:**

   • **Favorites Only.** Choose this setting to hide all rejects and all unmarked footage.

   • **Favorites and Unmarked.** Choose this setting to show all the footage you haven't specifically rejected. This is a great setting if you've graded your clips into Yes (favorite),

Maybe (unmarked), and No (rejected) categories. You can also press ⌘+L to quickly choose this setting.

- **All Clips.** Choose this setting when you need to see every single clip. Normally the other settings are more useful.

- **Rejected Only.** Choose this setting when you realize that a vital clip is missing because you've rejected it by accident.

3. **Select a clip or part of a clip that you want to add:**

    - **Select a 4-second chunk.** Click the clip in the Event browser. iMovie displays a yellow outline around it, starting from the point where you clicked, as shown in figure 4.5.

4.5 Click to select a 4-second chunk of video beginning at the point you click.

Note By default, iMovie selects a 5-second chunk when you click a clip in the Event browser. You can change this behavior in the Browser pane of the iMovie Preferences window, as discussed later in this chapter.

- **Select a whole clip.** Option+click the clip. Alternatively, Ctrl+click or right-click the clip and choose Select Entire Clip.

- **Select as much video as you want.** Click and drag through a clip. iMovie displays a yellow outline around the part you've selected, together with a time readout (see figure 4.6).

- **To change the length of the selection, drag the handle at either side to the left or right.** Alternatively, Shift+click another point in the clip to make the nearest handle snap to where you click.

4.6 Click and drag to select as much of a clip as you want.

- **To move the selection without changing its length, drag its top or bottom border to the left or right.** The mouse pointer changes to a hand when it's in the right place for moving the selection rather than changing the length (see figure 4.7).

- **To select multiple clips, click the first, and then ⌘+click each of the others.** The first click gets you four seconds (or however many seconds iMovie is set to select), but as soon as you ⌘+click the second clip, iMovie selects the entire first clip as well. Figure 4.8 shows the Event browser with multiple clips selected.

4.8 You can also select multiple clips at once by ⌘+clicking.

4.7 You can drag a selection to the left or right to move it.

Genius

When you move a selection, drag the top or bottom part of the beginning or end border. That way, the Playhead is at the beginning or end of the selection, and you can see the details of the current frame in the viewer.

4. **Add your selection to the Project window:**

   - To add the selection to the end of the project, press E or click the Add Selection to Project button on the toolbar (see figure 4.9).

4.9 Click the Add Selection to Project button or press E to add the selected clip or clips to the Project window.

- To add the selection between two clips in the project, click inside your selection and drag it to where you want it. iMovie displays a green vertical bar when the mouse pointer is in the right place (see figure 4.10).

4.10 You can easily insert a selection between two clips in the Project window by using drag and drop.

- To insert the selection within a clip that's in the project, click inside your selection and drag it over the clip. Figure 4.11 shows an example. Move the Playhead so that your target frame appears in the viewer, and then release the mouse button. iMovie displays a pop-up menu with options (see figure 4.12). Click Insert on this menu.

4.12 Choose Insert from the pop-up menu to insert the selection within the clip.

4.11 Positioning a selection for inserting within an existing clip in the Project window.

5. **Play back the project and see how it looks:**

   - **Play the whole project in the Viewer.** Click the Play Project from beginning button near the lower-left corner of the Project window.

   - **Play the current selection.** Make a selection, and then press the / (forward slash) key. Press the / key again if you want to stop playback before the end of your selection.

Genius

To play just a couple of seconds of video, move the Playhead to where you want to start playback, and then press the [(left square bracket) key to play one second around that point or the] (right square bracket) key to play three seconds.

● **Play from a certain point in the viewer.** Move the Playhead to where you want to start playback, and then press the spacebar.

● **Play the whole project full screen.** Click the Play Project Full Screen button at the lower-left corner of the Project window.

● **Play part of the project full screen.** Move the Playhead to where you want to start playback, and then press ⌘+G.

Genius

If you find your movie looks weird when playing full screen, it may be because it's stretched out of its aspect ratio. Choose iMovie ⇨ Preferences, click the General tab, and use the Full-screen playback size pop-up menu to choose Actual Size or Half Size instead of Full Screen. Try playing back again, and Full Screen playback will have black borders rather than actually filling your screen, but the project will appear at its correct aspect ratio.

6. **Rearrange your clips as needed:**

● Select the clip you want to move, or select just part of it by clicking and dragging through it.

● Click inside the clip or selection and drag it to where you want to place it. As when placing a clip initially, you can drop the clip either between two clips that are already in the Project window or inside a clip.

Using the Precision Editor

One of the great new tools that iMovie '09 introduces is the Precision Editor. It enables you to easily adjust each transition so that it occurs at exactly the frames you want.

The Precision Editor works both with straight cuts from clip to clip — in other words, without any transition effect applied — and with transitions. With a straight cut, you can make sure the first clip ends and the second clip starts at exactly the right frames. And when you've applied a transition, you can use the Precision Editor to make sure that the transition doesn't obscure any footage you want the audience to see.

For example, if you're using a Fade to Black transition, iMovie increasingly darkens the last few frames of the first clip, and increasingly lightens the first few frames of the second clip. Similarly, if you're using a Cross Blur transition, iMovie slowly blurs the last few frames of the first clip, and slowly focuses the first few frames of the second clip. The Precision Editor enables you to make sure that the frames that are being darkened, lightened, or otherwise changed aren't ones that are vital for the audience to see. If they are, you can reposition the clips so that the essential frames remain visible despite the transition.

Here's how to open the Precision Editor:

1. **Move the mouse pointer over the clip that comes after the transition you want to adjust, or over the transition.** The Action button pops up.

Genius

If there's no transition between two clips, you can open the Precision Editor by double-clicking the gap between the clips. If there is a transition, you can open the Precision Editor by double-clicking the blank space above the transition icon and between the clips or — if you aim carefully — in the narrow gap between the transition icon and a clip.

2. **Click the Action button, and then choose Precision Editor (see figure 4.13).** iMovie displays the Precision Editor in the bottom half of the window, replacing the Event Library (if it was displayed) and the Event browser.

Figure 4.14 shows the Precision Editor open showing the transition between two clips. Here's what you need to know about the Precision Editor:

- The top filmstrip shows the frames from the first clip.

- The bottom filmstrip shows the frames from the second clip.

4.13 Opening the Precision Editor from the Action button on a clip

Play current edit
Show next edit
Show previous edit
Show/hide audio tracks
Show/hide extras

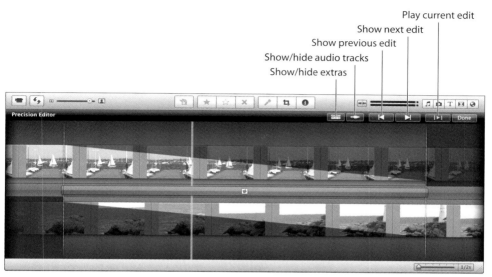

4.14 The Precision Editor enables you to adjust the transition between two clips so that it occurs at exactly the right frames.

- The blue bar in the middle represents the transition from the first clip to the second. If there's a straight cut from one clip to another, no blue bar appears.

- The brightened frames in both filmstrips represent clip footage that appears in the movie.

- The darkened frames in both filmstrips represent clip footage that doesn't appear in the movie.

- When you're using a transition, the diagonal separations of bright and dark within the transition zone in each filmstrip represent the progress of the transition. In the top film-strip, for example, the decreasing brightness indicates the increase of the transition effect (such as darkening or blurring).

- You can use the Playhead to play the filmstrips (move the mouse pointer across the film-strip) or the transition (move the mouse pointer across the transition bar).

Use any of the following techniques to adjust the transition:

- **Adjust the position of the transition relative to both clips.** Move the mouse pointer over the transition bar and then click and drag the bar left or right,

Note If you've used automatic transitions in your movie, you'll need to turn them off before you can change a transition using the Precision Editor. When you try to change a transition, iMovie displays the Automatic transitions are turned on dialog box to warn you of the problem. Click the Turn Off Automatic Transitions button if you want to go ahead and make the edit.

- **Include a particular frame in the transition.** Click the frame in the top filmstrip or the bottom filmstrip.
- **Change just the start point of the transition.** Click and drag the left edge of the transition bar.
- **Change just the end point of the transition.** Click and drag the right edge of the transition bar.

To view the transition in the viewer, click the Play Current Edit button in the upper-right corner of the Precision Editor. You can also play part of the transition by placing the Playhead with the mouse pointer and then pressing /. Press the [key to play one second of the transition or press the] key to play three seconds (if the transition is longer than that).

When you've finished editing the transition, you can move to another transition by clicking the Show Previous Edit button or the Show Next Edit button. This enables you to quickly work your way through all the transitions in a movie in turn.

When you've finished editing transitions, click Done in the upper-right corner of the Precision Editor to close the Precision Editor.

Note You can also use the Precision Editor to make the audio in two clips overlap. See Chapter 7 for details.

Enabling Fine Tuning and Setting Selection Preferences

As well as the regular selection tools that you've been using so far, iMovie also includes Fine Tuning controls that give you frame-by-frame control over what you're selecting.

Note

You can also make the Fine Tuning controls pop up by holding down ⌘+Option while working in the Project window.

iMovie doesn't display the Fine Tuning controls at first, so you need to reveal them before you can use them. While you're doing so, you may also want to choose selection preferences for the Event browser. Follow these steps:

1. **Choose iMovie ⇨ Preferences or press ⌘+, (comma).** The iMovie Preferences window opens.

2. **Click the Browser button to display the Browser pane (see figure 4.15).**

3. **Select the Show Fine Tuning controls check box.**

4. **If you want to change your selection settings, use the options in the lower half of the Browser pane:**

   - **Double-click to.** Choose the action you prefer to occur when you dou-ble-click an event: Edit or Play.

   - **Clicking in Events Browser dese-lects all.** Select this option button if you find it easier to select by clicking and dragging than by merely clicking.

4.15 Select the Show Fine Tuning controls check box in the Browser pane of the iMovie Preferences window to display the fine-tuning controls.

   - **Clicking in Events Browser selects entire clip.** Select this option button to make a click select an entire clip rather than just a chunk of it. Without this option button selected, you need to Option+click to select an entire clip.

   - **Clicking in Events Browser selects.** Select this option button, then click and drag the slider to choose how many seconds you want to select at the beginning of a clip you click in the Event browser. Select the Add automatic transition duration check box if you want iMovie to include the length of any transitions you've decided to apply automatically.

Genius

The default "Clicking in Events browser" setting is the Clicking in Events Browser selects option button, with the slider set to select a 4-second segment of the clip. Many people find this setting awkward because it is so different from the normal effect of clicking in most Mac OS X applications. If you are one of them, try selecting the Clicking in Events Browser deselects all option button instead.

5. **When you've finished choosing preferences, click the Close button (the red button) to close the Preferences window.**

Making Trim Adjustments

To make a clip play exactly the way you want it to, you can adjust its length in any of these ways:

- **Trim off selected footage.** Select the unwanted part of the clip and then delete it.
- **Keep only selected footage.** Select the part you want to keep and then trim off the rest.
- **Adjust the clip's playing length.** For this, you use the Trim Clip pane.
- **Make precise adjustments.** For these, you use the Fine Tuning buttons.

Note

Trim adjustments work only in the Project window, not in the Event browser.

Trimming off the beginning or end of a clip

When you need to trim off the beginning or end of a clip, follow these steps:

1. **Click the clip in the Project window to display a yellow selection rectangle around it.**
2. **Click and drag the left selection handle to the point at which you want to start deleting.** If you want to start deleting from the beginning of the clip, you don't need to move the selection handle.
3. **Click and drag the right selection handle to the point where you want to stop deleting.** If you want to stop deleting at the very end of the clip, you don't need to move the selection handle. Figure 4.16 shows an example of dragging the right selection handle.

4.16 Click and drag the yellow selection handle to select the part of the clip you want to delete. The white figures show the clip's length in seconds and tenths of seconds.

Genius

If you want to see a more precise measurement of clip length, make iMovie display the number of frames. Choose iMovie ➪ Preferences, click the General button, select the Display time as HH:MM:SS:Frames check box, and then close the iMovie Preferences window. You'll then see a readout such as 9:24 — 9 seconds and 24 frames. NTSC video has 30 frames per second; PAL video has 25 frames per second.

4. **Press Delete or choose Edit ➪ Delete Selection.**

Note

If you want to remove the selection and paste it into another part of the movie, Ctrl+click or right-click and choose Cut instead of deleting the selection. Move the mouse pointer to where you want to paste the selection, Ctrl+click or right-click, and then choose Paste.

Trimming a clip down to only the part you want

The other way to trim a clip is to select the part you want and then dispose of the rest. Here's how to do that:

1. **Click the clip to display a yellow selection rectangle around it.**

2. **Click and drag the left selection handle to the beginning of the part you want to keep.**

3. **Click and drag the right selection handle to the end of the part you want to keep.**

4. **Ctrl+click or right-click in the selection and choose Trim to Selection.** You can also choose Edit ➪ Trim to Selection from the menu bar. iMovie gets rid of the parts you didn't select, leaving those you selected.

Adjusting a clip with the Clip Trimmer

When you need to dig deeper into a clip than you can in the Project window, open the clip in the Clip Trimmer and trim it precisely there. Follow these steps:

1. **Move the mouse pointer over a clip, click the Action button that pops up, and then choose Clip Trimmer on the pop-up menu.** iMovie opens the Clip Trimmer (see figure 4.17).

Note

You can also open the Clip Trimmer by clicking a clip and then either choosing Window ➪ Clip Trimmer or pressing ⌘+R.

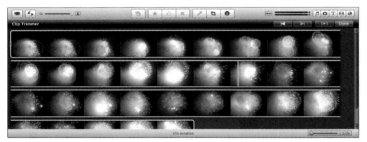

4.17 The Clip Trimmer appears in place of the Event browser and gives you a full-length view of the clip you're editing. The selection rectangle shows the part of the clip you're using.

2. **Change the part of the clip you're using.** For example:

   - Click and drag one of the selection handles to increase or reduce the amount of footage selected.

   - Click and drag the bottom edge or top edge of the selection rectangle to move it along the clip without changing its length.

   - Point at the end of the clip you want to move, and then press Option+left arrow or Option+right arrow to move it one frame at a time.

3. **To view the clip as you've currently cut it, click the Play Current Clip Segment button near the upper-right corner of the Clip Trimmer.**

4. **To move on to work with another clip, click the Show Previous Clip button or the Show Next Clip button.**

5. **When you've finished trimming clips, click Done to close the Clip Trimmer and display the Event browser again.**

Making a short adjustment with the Fine Tuning buttons

When you need to adjust the length of a clip by less than a second, use the Fine Tuning buttons.

Note Before you can use the Fine Tuning buttons, you'll need to select the Show Fine Tuning controls check box in the Browser pane of the iMovie Preferences window, as described earlier in this chapter.

Here's how to use the Fine Tuning controls:

1. **Move the mouse pointer over the clip in the Project window so that the Fine Tuning control buttons appear (see figure 4.18).**

2. **Click the Fine Tune Clip Start button or the Fine Tune Clip End button to display an orange handle for trimming the start or end of the clip.**

Fine tune clip start   Fine tune clip end

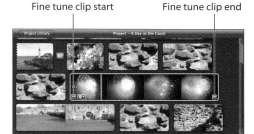

4.18 The Fine Tuning buttons and the Trim Clip button appear when you position the mouse pointer over a clip in the Project window.

Genius You can also display the orange handle for fine-tuning a clip by holding down ⌘+Option while you point to the clip's start or end. If you didn't select the Show Fine Tuning controls check box in iMovie's Preferences, you need to use this technique because the Fine Tuning buttons won't appear when you point to a clip.

3. **Click and drag the handle to the left or right, as appropriate.** Figure 4.19 shows an example of trimming the beginning of a clip. The readout shows the number of frames you moved the clip end and the current length of the clip.

4.19 Click and drag the orange handle to fine-tune the start or end of a clip.

Genius To quickly change the beginning or end of a clip by only a few frames, move the mouse pointer toward the end you want to affect. Press Option+left arrow to move the end to the left or Option+right arrow to move the end to the right.

Deleting Frames from Clips

To delete frames from a clip in a movie project, follow these steps:

1. **In the Project window, select the frames you want to delete.** Use the selection techniques discussed earlier in this chapter.

2. **Choose Edit ⇨ Delete or press the Backspace key.** iMovie deletes the extra frames so that they no longer appear in the Project window. When you delete frames from a clip in the project, you're not actually changing the underlying clip in your video library. What you're changing is the way that iMovie handles that clip for this project and this project only.

Note

For more detail on the smart way that iMovie handles your video clips, see Chapter 8.

Splitting Clips

Often, you need to split a clip into two so that you can use different parts of it easily in different sections of your movie.

Note

One reason for splitting a clip used to be so that you could insert another clip as a cutaway within it. But iMovie '09's new Cutaway feature means that you no longer have to split a clip manually so that you can insert another clip in it. See Chapter 6 for details.

From the Project window, you can split a clip into either two pieces (a beginning piece and an end piece) or three pieces (a beginning piece, a middle piece, and an end piece). Here's what to do:

1. **In the Project window, select the part of the clip that you want to split off from the rest.** You can split a clip into two parts by selecting either the beginning or the end, or split it into three parts by selecting a section in the middle (see figure 4.20).

4.20 To split a clip into three parts, select a section in the middle of the clip.

2. **Choose Edit ⇨ Split Clip.** iMovie splits the clip into the required number of parts. Figure 4.21 shows the clips after splitting.

4.21 The three clips resulting from the split

How Do I Make Video Adjustments?

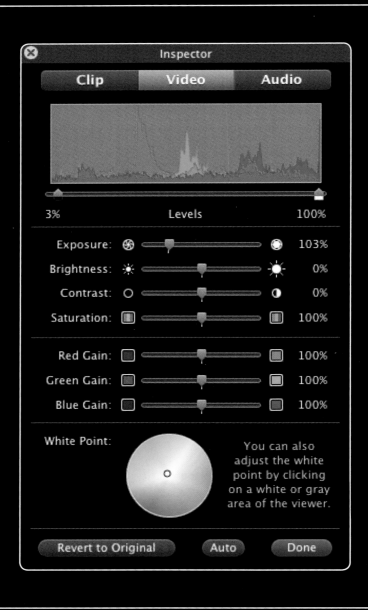

One of iMovie '09's most exciting new features is its capability to remove camera shake from clips by applying stabilization, enabling you to make even wobbly handheld footage look acceptable or good. You can also crop your video clips so that exactly the right piece appears in the frame or rotate a clip so that it plays in a different orientation from how it was filmed. When your clips suffer from exposure or color problems, you can use the Video pane in the Inspector dialog box to make the clips look great. Best of all, once you've applied fixes to one clip, you can quickly apply them to other clips by using cut and paste.

Using Automatic Video Stabilization

One of the biggest problems with portable camcorders is avoiding camera shake when you're capturing clips. Unless you have a very steady hand, carry pro tools, or use the right tricks, it's all too easy to move the camera enough to make the clips induce motion sickness.

iMovie '09's video stabilization feature helps you remove or reduce camera shake in your clips. You can have iMovie apply stabilization automatically, or you can apply it manually as needed. Whichever way you apply stabilization, you can adjust it to make the clips look right to you, or you can remove it completely if it doesn't help.

Understanding how stabilization works

Stabilization isn't a magic bullet for camera shake, but it can make a huge difference, especially with clips shot on a handheld camcorder rather than ones shot using a tripod.

What stabilization does is zoom in on the frame far enough to make room at each edge to crop off the part that has moved. For example, if the camera has wobbled to the left, cropping off the left-most part of the frame moves the frame back toward the right, helping to negate the movement; if the camera has moved down, cropping off the lower edge of the frame moves the frame back up. To maintain the aspect ratio of the video, iMovie has to crop each frame by the same amount.

The worse the camera shake in the clip, the more iMovie has to zoom in to fix the problem, and the more you lose from the outside of each frame.

Understanding how iMovie handles stabilization

iMovie handles stabilization in two parts:

1. **Analyzes a clip for stabilization.** iMovie examines the clips that make up the frame and determines how much shake there is by analyzing the differences between frames. By seeing whether the frame as a whole moves, rather than (say) just the subject moving, iMovie works out how bad the problem is and what degree of stabilization is needed to fix it (or whether it can't be fixed at all).

2. **Applies stabilization to a clip.** When you add a clip to a movie project in the Project window, iMovie by default automatically applies stabilization if you've already analyzed that clip for stabilization. Because iMovie has already analyzed the clip, there's no wait: iMovie simply sets the clip to be stabilized in the project, and processes the stabilization when you play back the clip or movie. If you haven't analyzed a clip for stabilization, iMovie doesn't apply stabilization when you add the clip to a movie project.

Note If you don't want iMovie to automatically apply stabilization to clips you've analyzed when you add them to the Project window, choose iMovie ➪ Preferences and click the Browser button. Deselect the Automatically stabilize clips that have been analyzed check box, and then close the iMovie Preferences window.

You can analyze a clip for stabilization when you import it from a camcorder (by selecting the Analyze for stabilization check box in the Import dialog box) or after you've added it to iMovie. Once the clip is in iMovie, you can analyze it for stabilization from either the Event browser or the Project window.

Analyzing a clip manually

Here's how to analyze a clip manually:

1. **If the clip is in the Event browser, Option+click the clip to select it.** If the clip is in the Project window, you don't need to select it.

2. **Ctrl+click or right-click the clip and choose Analyze for Stabilization from the shortcut menu.** You can also choose File ➪ Analyze for Stabilization if you prefer.

3. **As it is analyzing, iMovie displays the Analyzing for Stabilization dialog box (see figure 5.1).** Depending on the clip's length and resolution, and your Mac's speed and free resources, the analysis may take several minutes.

5.1 Wait while iMovie analyzes a clip for stabilization.

4. **When iMovie has finished analyzing the clip, it displays a red wavy line across the bottom of each section that requires stabilization.** Figure 5.2 shows an example.

5.2 A red wavy line indicates that a clip requires stabilization.

Applying stabilization to a clip manually

If you choose not to let iMovie automatically apply stabilization to previously analyzed clips you add to the Project window, you can apply stabilization manually. This is handy when you need to control which clips receive stabilization and which don't.

To apply stabilization to a clip manually, follow these steps:

1. **In the Project window, move the mouse pointer over the analyzed clip, click the Action button, and then choose Clip Adjustments from the pop-up menu.** iMovie displays the Clip pane of the Inspector dialog box for the clip (see figure 5.3).

2. **In the Stabilization area, select the Smooth clip motion check box.** iMovie displays the Maximum Zoom slider below the Smooth clip motion check box and sets it to the maximum amount of zoom iMovie has determined the clip will need for stability.

3. **Click Done to close the Inspector dialog box.**

5.3 Use the Clip pane of the Inspector dialog box to apply stabilization to a clip in the Project window.

Determining how much stabilization iMovie has applied

When you move the mouse pointer over a clip in the Project window that has stabilization applied, iMovie displays an icon in the clip's upper-left corner to indicate the stabilization and the degree applied. Here's what you need to know:

- **White hand on red background, black diagonal slash.** This symbol (see figure 5.4) means that iMovie couldn't stabilize the clip because the shake was so bad.

5.4 The black slash on this stabilization icon indicates that iMovie wasn't able to stabilize the clip.

- **White hand on red background.** This symbol (see figure 5.5) means that the clip needed extensive stabilization, so a lot of it has been cropped off.

- **White hand on orange background.** This symbol (see figure 5.6) means that stabilizing the clip required some zooming and cropping.

- **White hand on black background.** This symbol (see figure 5.7) means that the clip required little zooming or none at all.

5.5 This stabilization icon's red background means that the clip has extensive zooming and cropping applied.

5.6 This stabilization icon's orange background means that the clip has a moderate, but not extreme, amount of zooming and cropping applied.

5.7 The white hand on black background icon is good news — it means the clip needed little or no zooming.

Seeing how well the stabilization works

The next step is to see how well the stabilization works. Play the video clip and decide whether stabilization has improved matters, whether it needs further work, or whether you want to remove stabilization.

You may also find it helpful to skim through a stabilized clip, as this lets you compare different points in the clip more easily.

Why Stabilization Can Make Video Look Worse

Normally, stabilization improves video, turning unwatchable clips into watchable ones. But if your camcorder uses a *rolling shutter* — a shutter that exposes separate parts of the frame at different times rather than exposing the whole frame at once — stabilization can actually make a clip look worse.

This happens when the camcorder moves while the rolling shutter is exposing the frame. The frame itself appears distorted, because the different parts of the frame don't match up correctly. This is different from the usual problem of having each frame sharp and undistorted but with excessive movement from frame to frame.

If a clip contains such distortion from the camcorder moving during a rolling-shutter exposure, iMovie's attempt at stabilizing the video tends to make the camcorder's movement more evident rather than less.

If you run into this problem, remove stabilization from the clip and see if it looks better.

Adjusting the zoom level on stabilized video

iMovie automatically sets the zoom level that should produce the optimally stable video with as little cropping as possible, but often you'll need to adjust the zoom level to make the clip look the way you want it to. You can do this in the Project window but not in the Event browser.

To adjust the zoom level on stabilized video, follow these steps:

1. **In the Project window, move the mouse pointer over the stabilized clip, click the Action button, and then choose Clip Adjustments from the pop-up menu.** iMovie displays the Clip pane of the Inspector dialog box for the clip.

2. **Drag the Maximum Zoom slider to set the degree of zoom you want.** The farther in you zoom, the more stable the clip becomes, but the more of each frame you lose.

3. **Click Done to close the Inspector dialog box.** Play the clip and see if you're satisfied with the result; if not, repeat the steps and choose a different setting.

Removing stabilization from a clip

Sometimes you may find that stabilization doesn't help a clip enough to be worth cutting off the edges. When this happens, you can remove stabilization like this:

1. **Move the mouse pointer over the clip, click the Action button, and then choose Clip Adjustments from the pop-up menu.** iMovie displays the Clip pane of the Inspector dialog box.

2. **Clear the Smooth clip motion check box.**

3. **Click Done to close the Inspector dialog box.**

Cropping Your Clips

To get the best effect in your video, you may need to crop a clip so that only part of each frame appears on the screen. Cropping applies to an entire clip rather than just part of it, but you can split off the part you want to crop into a separate clip by using the technique described in Chapter 4.

Genius

You can crop a frame down to 50 percent of the original dimensions. Quality suffers when you crop an image because iMovie has to enlarge the remaining data to occupy the whole frame. But you can usually get good results if you crop standard-definition video only a modest amount. And if you have high-definition video, you can crop up to that 50-percent limit and still retain good quality.

Here's how to crop a clip:

1. **Click the clip in the Event browser or in the Project window.** iMovie displays the clip in the viewer.

2. **Click the Crop button on the toolbar (or press C).** You can also click the clip's Action button and choose Cropping & Rotation from the pop-up menu. iMovie displays the cropping and rotation buttons in the viewer. Figure 5.8 shows the cropping and rotation buttons with the Fit button selected.

5.8 The cropping and rotation tools in the viewer.

3. **Click the Crop button in the upper-left corner of the viewer.** iMovie displays green cropping handles and a frame in the viewer (see figure 5.9) and adds a red dot to the Playhead on the clip (see figure 5.10), indicating that the Playhead will remain stationary unless you click and drag it.

5.9 Click and drag the green cropping handles to select the part of the frame you want to keep. The green cross shows the middle of the cropping area.

5.10 The red dot on the Playhead indicates that the Playhead will remain stationary unless you click and drag it.

4. **Click and drag a corner handle to resize the cropping area proportionally.** iMovie stops you at the 50-percent limit of size and height if you drag that far.

5. **If necessary, reposition the cropping area by clicking and dragging anywhere in the rectangle.** The mouse pointer turns to a hand when it's in the cropping area.

6. **Check the effect of the cropping in either of these ways:**

    - Click and drag the red dot on the Playhead to skim through the crop.

    - Click the Play button in the viewer to play the clip.

7. **Click Done to apply your cropping.**

Rotating a Clip

Another iMovie effect you can apply to a clip is rotation. Again, this applies to the whole clip rather than part of it, so you may need to split a clip into smaller clips to separate the footage you want to rotate.

Genius

Rotation is a dramatic effect best used for special occasions, such as when you want to make a clip play upside down for laughs. But rotation can also be useful for rescuing clips recorded with the camcorder turned vertically for whatever reason — for example, to capture an unmissable shot, or because the video was recorded on a digital camera with which you often shoot stills in portrait orientation.

To rotate a clip, follow these steps:

1. **Click the clip in the Event browser or in the Project window.** iMovie displays the clip in the Viewer.

2. **Click the Crop button on the toolbar (or press C).** You can also click the Action button and choose Cropping & Rotation from the pop-up menu, but the other means are usually easier. iMovie displays the cropping and rotation buttons in the Viewer (see figure 5.11).

3. **Click the Rotate Counterclockwise button or the Rotate Clockwise button in the Viewer.** Each click gives you a 90-degree rotation in that direction.

4. **Crop the video to make it the right aspect ratio in its new orientation.** Figure 5.12 shows the same clip cropped to suit the project.

5. **Click Done to apply the rotation and any cropping.**

5.11 You can use rotation to fix video clips recorded in the wrong orientation or to create special effects.

5.12 Cropping the clip to fit the project loses much of the frame, but at least what remains is useable.

Making Color Adjustments

One of iMovie's slickest tricks is to adjust the color of your video clips. So if you find that a precious clip is overexposed or underexposed, or if the color balance makes everyone's otherwise healthy face look green, you may be able to save the day.

Note

Like cropping, color adjustments apply to an entire clip rather than part of it. So if only a part of a clip needs adjustment, you will need to split it off into a separate clip, as described in Chapter 4.

Opening the Video pane

To begin adjusting the color of your clip, open the Video pane of the Inspector dialog box and choose a suitable frame from the clip. Follow these steps:

1. **In the Project window or the Event browser, click the clip whose colors you want to adjust.** As expected, if you click the clip in the Event browser, the color adjustments apply to all projects that use the clip. If you click the clip in the Project window, the adjustments apply only to the current project.

2. **Open the Video pane of the Inspector dialog box (see figure 5.13).** The easiest way to do this is to press V, but you can also click the Action button on the clip and choose Video Adjustments from the pop-up menu, or double-click the clip and then click the Video button. iMovie also adds a Playhead with a red dot to the clip.

3. **Click and drag the Playhead dot to select a frame that gives you a good view of the colors you want to adjust.**

Black slider   Histogram   White slider

5.13 In the Video pane, you can correct the exposure, brightness, contrast, saturation, and color balance of your video clips.

Understanding the histogram

At the top of the Video pane of the Inspector dialog box is the *histogram*, a graphical diagram that shows how the colors in the selected video frame are distributed between pure black (at the left end, 0 percent) and pure white (at the right end, 100 percent).

The red, green, and blue show the individual red, green, and blue color channels in the image. For each of these color channels, the histogram represents the darker shades on the left and the lighter shades on the right.

That may sound daunting, but the histogram is at heart a bar graph that shows how much of each primary color the frame contains. The histogram may appear as overlapping ranges of red, green, and blue mountains, or as individual peaks showing where the colors are more concentrated.

As you change the settings in the Video pane, iMovie updates the histogram to show the current balance, so you can immediately see the effects of the changes you're making.

Genius

If you haven't worked with color adjustments before, the histogram and the adjustment sliders may seem off-putting at first. But if you click an unsatisfactory clip and start playing with the controls, you'll soon get the hang of it. You're not actually changing your video clip, just the way that it plays back, so any changes you make are fully reversible — just click the Revert to Original button if necessary.

Deciding what to adjust

The controls in the Video pane of the Inspector dialog box enable you to make huge changes to how your video looks, so you can rescue a clip that suffers from severe color or lighting problems or completely wreck a clip that looks fine. Therefore, it helps to have an idea of what you're trying to achieve.

To get an idea of the kind of color balance you like, skim through your video clips until you find a frame that has a color balance that looks right to you. Then press V (or click the clip's Action button and choose Video Adjustments from the pop-up menu that appears) to open the Video pane of the Inspector dialog box, and examine the histogram for that frame. Normally, you'll find that a frame with good color balance has data distributed all the way across the histogram, with several peaks where the color is most intense. Figure 5.14 shows the histogram for a frame with good color balance.

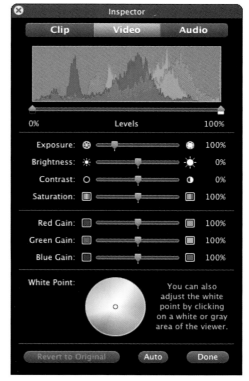

5.14 When a frame has a good color balance, the histogram shows data all the way across. The peaks show where the color is most intense.

I recommend proceeding in this order when you're fixing a video clip:

1. **Fix the white balance.**

2. **Correct any exposure problems.**

3. **Adjust the black and white tones.**

4. **Adjust the brightness and contrast.**

5. **Adjust the color saturation.**

6. **Adjust the red, green, and blue channels.**

Each step is optional — use it only if the clip needs it.

Adjusting the white balance

When working with video, you'll often find that the color balance isn't right. The lighting under which you shoot the video affects the *color temperature* you get in the frames. For example, if you shoot video under fluorescent light, you wind up with different colors than if you shoot the same subjects in sunlight.

Sometimes this is fine, but other times you'll want to fix it — for example, to make two clips shot under different lighting conditions have similar or identical colors.

Your first move toward fixing the color balance is to adjust the white balance. This means resetting the color that iMovie is treating as being white to the kind of white that you need it to be. For example, iMovie's white may look to you as though it's tinged with green. By showing iMovie what real white looks like to you, you can give it a reference point for how to change the other colors as well.

To adjust the white balance, display the Video pane of the Inspector dialog box, and then click in an area in the Viewer that should be plain white (even if it's currently some variation on white). As you can see in figure 5.15, the mouse pointer appears as an eye-dropper over the Viewer while the Inspector dialog box is open.

See what change this click produces. Ideally, it will fix the color problems in the video clip. More likely, you will need to click on several different points that should be white before you get the color balance you want.

5.15 To adjust the white balance, move the mouse pointer over the Viewer window and use the eye-dropper pointer to click on a point that should be plain white.

If you're not able to reach a suitable color balance by clicking in the Viewer window, click the color you want in the White Point color wheel in the Video pane of the Inspector dialog box. The colors here are packed pretty closely together, so you may have to click several times to hit the color you want.

Fixing exposure problems

What you'll typically want to do next is deal with any exposure problem in the video:

- **Underexposure.** A clip you shot in dark conditions — for example, outside at night or in a poorly lit room — may be underexposed. Not having received enough light, the darker areas look indistinguishable from the black areas. (If the clip is severely underexposed, most of each frame may appear black.) Figure 5.16 shows a sample frame looking underexposed.

- **Overexposure.** A clip you shot in bright conditions — for example, with strong sunlight glittering off waves and a beach — may be overexposed. Having received too much light, the brighter areas look white. (If the clip is hugely overexposed, most of each frame may appear white.) Figure 5.17 shows the same frame but overexposed.

To adjust the exposure of the clip, click and drag the Exposure slider. The scale goes from 0 percent to 100 percent, but generally you'll need to make only small changes to improve the clip's look considerably. Figure 5.18 shows the same frame looking much more lifelike.

5.16 In an underexposed frame, colors look darker than they should be, and darker areas may look black.

5.17 In an overexposed frame, colors look lighter than they should be, and lighter areas may look white.

5.18 Click and drag the Exposure slider until the colors look roughly how you want them.

Adjusting the black and white tones

After sorting out the exposure, look at the histogram again and see if you need to adjust the White slider or the Black slider. These sliders enable you to change the amount of white tones and black tones in the clip.

If the data reaches all the way from one side of the histogram to the other, and the peaks are fairly evenly distributed across the histogram rather than appearing all at one side or the other, you probably don't need to change the tones. But if there's a gap at either the left (black) end or the right (white) end of the histogram, or if all the peaks are on one side, try adjusting the sliders.

Click and drag the Black slider to the right if you want to add black tones to the clip; click and drag the White slider to the left to add white tones to the clip. You'll see the balance of the frame in the Viewer change as the histogram changes.

Caution When you drag the Black slider or White slider, you're removing some data from the video clip. (You're affecting only how the clip is played, not editing the underlying clip.) So avoid moving either slider so that any of the peaks in the histogram falls off the side unless you want to make extreme changes.

Adjusting the brightness and contrast

Next, you may need to adjust the brightness and contrast of the clip. *Brightness* enables you to make the clip look lighter or darker, and *contrast* enables you to increase the difference between the light tones and the dark tones.

Adjusting the brightness

If the clip is too dark as a whole after you've adjusted the exposure and the black and white tones, click and drag the Brightness slider to the right to lighten up the whole picture. The dark colors as well as the light colors become brighter, all by the same amount.

Similarly, if the clip is too light as a whole, click and drag the Brightness slider to the left.

Genius Think of brightness as shifting the histogram along to the right (increasing the brightness) or to the left (decreasing the brightness). The shape of the histogram remains the same, even though the colors become lighter or darker.

Adjusting the contrast

If the clip lacks enough difference between the light and dark tones (see figure 5.19), increase the contrast by clicking and dragging the Contrast slider to the right. Figure 5.20 shows the result.

5.19 A subject lacking in contrast.

5.20 The same subject with the contrast increased as far as it will go.

Similarly, if the contrast is too high and you want to produce a less extreme effect, click and drag the Contrast slider to the left.

Adjusting the color saturation

By this point, your video clip should be looking pretty good. But if you want to give the colors extra zip, or if you find the colors so garish you need to tone them down, you can adjust the saturation.

Click and drag the Saturation slider to the right to boost the colors, or drag it to the left to produce a calmer effect. Go easy on the saturation — normally, a small change will make all the difference you need. If your subject is already colorful, a major increase can quickly take the clip into the realm of the surreal (see figure 5.21).

5.21 A colorful Frisbee with the saturation increased to the max.

Genius

To make a color clip play in black and white, drag the Saturation slider all the way to the left. You may also want to increase the contrast to add impact to the black-and-white clip.

87

Adjusting the red, green, and blue

The final adjustment you can make to a video clip is to adjust its red gain, green gain, or blue gain. The Red Gain slider, Green Gain slider, and Blue Gain slider appear in the Video pane only if you've turned on the display of Advanced Tools like this:

1. **Choose iMovie ⇨ Preferences (or press ⌘+,) to open the iMovie Preferences window.**

2. **In the General pane, select the Show Advanced Tools check box.**

3. **Click the Close button (the red button) to close the iMovie Preferences window.**

Now click a clip, press V to open the Video pane of the Inspector dialog box, and the three color-gain sliders will be there (see figure 5.22). Click and drag a slider to the right to increase the amount of that color in the frame; click and drag it to the left to decrease the amount.

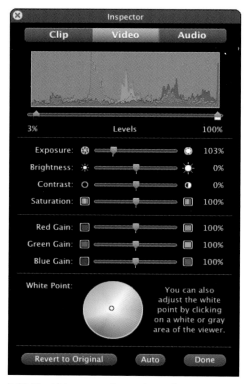

5.22 The Video pane shows the Red, Green, and Blue Gain sliders.

Genius

Apple hides the three color-gain sliders partly to keep the Video pane streamlined but mostly because you seldom need to use these sliders to fix color problems. Use the other controls to solve problems, and keep the color-gain sliders for when all else has failed to help or you need to create a special effect (such as applying an Incredible Hulk–style green tinge to a clip).

When you've finished adjusting the colors, click Done to close the Inspector dialog box.

Copying and Pasting Adjustments

Getting a video clip to look just right can take time and effort, particularly when you're making complex color adjustments as described in the previous section. iMovie has a great time-saver here: When you've adjusted a clip just the way you want it, you can apply the same adjustments to another clip by copying and pasting them.

Here's how to copy and paste adjustments:

1. **Ctrl+click or right-click the clip you fixed, and then choose Copy from the shortcut menu.** iMovie copies the details of all the adjustments you've made to the clip.

2. **Select the clip you want to adjust.** In the Project window, click the clip; in the Event browser, Option+click the clip. To adjust multiple clips, click the first, and then ⌘+click each of the others.

3. **Choose Edit ➪ Paste Adjustments, and then click the appropriate command on the Paste Adjustments submenu.** Alternatively, press the keyboard shortcut for the command. Table 5.1 explains the different adjustments you can paste and shows the keyboard shortcuts for them.

Restoring a Clip to How It Was Before

Because iMovie's editing is nondestructive, you can always restore a clip to the way it was before. To restore a clip, open the tool you used to edit it, and then remove the change you made. For example:

- **Remove cropping.** Click the clip, click the Crop button to display the cropping and rotation buttons, and then click the Fit button to fit the video back to the frame.

- **Remove color adjustments.** Click the clip, click the Inspector button, click the Video tab, click the Revert to Original button, and then click Done.

- **Remove rotation.** Click the clip, click the Crop button to display the cropping and rotation buttons, and then click the rotation button needed to put the clip the right way around again. Change the cropping as well if necessary.

Table 5.1 Paste Adjustments Commands and Keyboard Shortcuts

Paste adjustments	Keyboard shortcut	What it does
All	⌘+Shift+V	Pastes every adjustment you've made to the clip: video, audio, cropping, cutaways, video effect, stabilization, speed, and map style. Use this command with care, or be prepared to undo pasting if it makes changes you've forgotten you made to the source clip.
Video	⌘+Option+I	Pastes adjustments you've made in the Video pane of the Inspector dialog box, such as changes to white balance and saturation.
Audio	⌘+Option+A	Pastes audio adjustments made in the Audio pane of the Inspector dialog box, such as volume changes, ducking, and fading.
Crop	⌘+Option+R	Applies cropping and rotation adjustments.
Cutaway	⌘+Option+U	Applies the fading and opacity settings you've made to a cutaway clip.
Picture-in-Picture	⌘+Option+U	Applies the border, position, dissolve, and drop-shadow settings you've made to a picture-in-picture clip.
Green Screen	⌘+Option+U	Applies the background color subtraction and background cropping adjustments you've made to a green-screen clip.
Video Effect	⌘+Option+L	Applies the video effect, such as Dream or X-Ray.
Stabilization	⌘+Option+Z	Applies the same stabilization settings — whether stabilization is on and, if so, the degree of zoom.
Speed	⌘+Option+S	Applies the speed adjustments you've made (for example, slow motion).
Map Style	⌘+Option+M	Applies the style of the map in the source clip to the map in the destination clip.

How Do I Create Cool Transitions, Titles, and Effects?

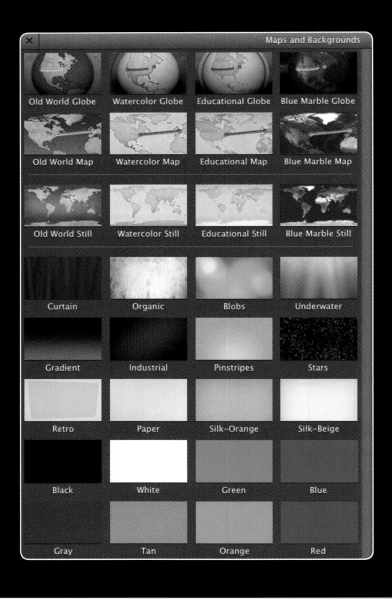

To add pizzazz, you can apply one of iMovie's slick themes to either a new movie or one you've already created. Your movie will probably also need transitions to smooth the movement from one clip to the next, and it will almost certainly require titles to provide its name and credits; it may also need a map to show where it takes place. Display iMovie's Advanced Tools so that you can create effects such as cutaways, picture in picture, or superimpose an actor or presenter on another clip by using a green screen.

Applying Themes

A *theme* is a predefined set of transitions, titles, and effects that you can use to give a movie a finished feel. You can apply a theme when you start creating a movie or at any point after that.

To apply a theme when you create a movie, click the theme you want in the Theme area of the New Project dialog box.

To apply a theme to a movie you've already created, press ⌘+J or choose File ⇨ Project Properties to display the Project Properties dialog box, and then click the theme in the Theme area of the General pane.

In either case, you can select the Automatically add transitions and titles check box if you want to have iMovie add them. Transitions and titles are an important part of themes, so when you do apply a theme, you'll probably want to select this check box.

When you're applying a theme to a movie that already contains clips, there's one complication: You need to decide how to deal with the ends of clips. iMovie displays an extra section at the bottom of the Project Properties dialog box (see figure 6.1) with two option buttons:

- **Overlap ends and shorten clip.** iMovie moves each clip after the first to overlap its predecessor, and then applies the transitions. This is usually the best choice because you use only the footage in the clips. The one problem is when you've already set up your project with a carefully timed soundtrack: iMovie's shifting of the clips wrecks the timing.

6.1 If you tell iMovie to add automatic transitions to a movie project, you must decide whether to overlap the ends of the clips or extend them.

- **Extend ends and maintain duration (where possible).** iMovie extends the end of each clip to provide enough time for the transitions. To get this extra time, iMovie reveals extra frames you've hidden in the clip — usually a problem because these are frames you've chosen not to use. If the clip doesn't contain any hidden frames at the end, iMovie can't extend the clip anyway.

When you've chosen the theme and settings, click Create to close the New Project dialog box or click OK to close the Project Properties dialog box.

Adding Transitions

When one clip of your movie ends, the next clip begins. The changeover between the two is called the *transition*. If you don't apply one of iMovie's transition effects, you get what's called a *straight cut* — iMovie jumps straight from the last frame of the first clip to the first frame of the second clip.

If those last and first frames are similar in content, a straight cut can work well. If the contents are substantially different, a straight cut can produce a jarring effect. Sometimes, you may want to give the audience that jar, but often, you will want to treat your viewers more gently. To reduce the abruptness of the change between two clips, you can apply one of iMovie's transition effects to the transition between those clips.

Genius You can also use iMovie's transition effects to emphasize the movement from one clip to another or to encourage the viewer to interpret the relationship of the clips in a certain way.

Opening the Transitions browser

To start working with transitions, open the Transitions browser by clicking the Transitions browser button on the toolbar, choosing Window ⇨ Transitions, or pressing ⌘+4. Figure 6.2 shows the Transitions browser.

Adding transitions automatically

The easiest way to add transitions to a movie project is to have iMovie add them automatically for you. You can do this either when you create the movie project or at any time afterward.

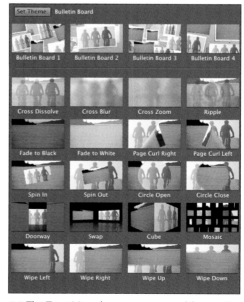

6.2 The Transitions browser pane enables you to apply any of iMovie's 20 transitions to your clips in moments. Point to a transition to preview its effect within the browser pane.

To create a new project, click the New Project button in the Project Library or press ⌘+N to open the New Project dialog box.

To add transitions to an existing project, open the Project Properties dialog box. From the Project window, press ⌘+J or choose File ➪ Project Properties. From the Project Library, Ctrl+click or right-click the project and choose Project Properties from the context menu, or click the project and press ⌘+J or choose File ➪ Project Properties.

In either the New Project dialog box or the General pane of the Project Properties dialog box (see figure 6.3), set iMovie to add transitions automatically like this:

- **When you use a theme.** Select the Automatically add transitions and titles check box (refer to figure 6.1).
- **When you don't use a theme.** If you select None in the Themes box, select the Automatically add check box, and then choose the transition type from the pop-up menu.

6.3 Select the Automatically add check box in the General pane of the Project Properties dialog box to make iMovie add transitions to a movie project.

Click Create to close the New Project dialog box or OK to close the Project Properties dialog box, and iMovie starts adding the transitions for you.

Adding transitions manually

To have the most control over your movies, you'll typically want to add transitions manually between clips. Here's how to do that swiftly and smoothly:

1. **Open the Transitions browser.** Click the Transitions Browser button on the toolbar or press ⌘+4.

2. **In the Transitions browser, click the transition type, drag it to the Storyboard, and then drop it between the clips you want to affect.** iMovie displays a vertical green bar to show where the transition will land (see figure 6.4) so you can tell when you've dragged to the right place.

When you drop the transition, iMovie displays an icon representing the transition. Each transition type has a different icon, but some of the icons are hard to decipher at first. For example, the icon shown in figure 6.5 represents the Ripple transition.

6.4 Click and drag the transition you want to the gap between two clips.

6.5 iMovie adds an icon that represents the transition. The icon shows the transition's type.

Play back the transition — or skim it by moving the mouse pointer over it — to check that it looks the way you want it to. If necessary, change the settings for the transition, or change to another transition.

Genius

If possible, stick with just one transition type to give your movie a consistent look, or use Cross Dissolve transitions and one other type of transition. Using many different types of transitions tends to grate on the audience.

To delete a transition, Ctrl+click or right-click it, and then choose Delete Selection. To replace a transition with another transition, click and drag the replacement transition on top of the existing transition.

Note

If you didn't apply a theme for your project, but you did select the Automatically add check box for transitions in the Properties sheet for the movie project, iMovie automatically adds transitions of the type you choose. If you want to prevent iMovie from doing this, Ctrl+click or right-click the movie project in the Project Library, choose Project Properties, clear the Automatically add check box, and then click OK.

Changing to a different transition

When you need to change from one transition from another transition, you don't even need to remove the original transition from between the two clips. Click and drag another transition from the Transitions browser onto the existing transition, and iMovie replaces the existing transition with the new transition.

Play back the new transition and see if it needs any changes. For example, you may need to adjust the frames at which the transition starts and ends, or adjust the transition's duration, as discussed next.

Changing transition duration

When you add a transition between two clips, iMovie automatically sets its duration to the time set on the Timings pane of the Project Properties dialog box. In most movie projects, different transitions (and different clips) need different lengths, so you'll probably want to treat the default duration only as a starting point.

You can change the duration of a transition like this:

1. **Double-click the transition in the Project window to open the Inspector dialog box for transitions (see figure 6.6).**

2. **In the Duration box, type the length you want to use for the transition:**

   - If you've selected the Display time as HH:MM:SS:Frames check box in the General pane of the iMovie Preferences window, type the time in seconds and frames — for example, 1:15 represents one second and 15 frames, or one and a half seconds in the NTSC video format.

   - Otherwise, type the time in seconds — for example, 1.5 for one and a half seconds.

6.6 The Inspector dialog box enables you to quickly change the length of a single transition or all the transitions in your movie project.

Caution

Don't select the Applies to all transitions check box in the Inspector dialog box for transitions. Having iMovie automatically change the length of transitions can wreak havoc with the timing of a movie project. If any clip is too short for the length you set, the transition will be shorter. If you then change the length of a clip, or the playback timing for a still, iMovie changes the length of its transitions without consulting you.

3. **If you want iMovie to apply this duration to all the transitions, select the Applies to all transitions check box.** Normally, you will not want to do this.

4. **Click Done.** iMovie closes the Inspector dialog box and applies the change.

Caution iMovie limits any transition to occupying only up to half of a clip (so that you can also put another transition at the other end of the clip). This can be a problem with short clips, as you cannot set an exact transition length longer than half the clip; if you try to set the transition longer, iMovie automatically shortens the transition.

Changing the default duration

As you've just seen, you can change the default duration of a movie project's transitions directly from the Inspector dialog box for transitions. You can also change the default duration by adjusting the Transition Duration slider in the Timing pane of the Project Properties dialog box (see figure 6.7), which you open by pressing ⌘+J or choosing File ➪ Project Properties. You can set the default duration to any length between 0.5 seconds (roughly the length of a sneeze) and four seconds (a short fit of coughing). If you're using HH:MM:SS:Frames timing, the minimum length is 0:15 (15 frames) for NTSC video.

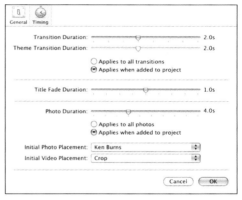

6.7 In the Timing pane of the Project Properties dialog box, you can change the default duration for transitions but choose to apply the default duration only from now on.

The advantage to making the duration change in the Timing pane is that you can choose how to apply the change:

- **Applies to all transitions.** Select this option button to set all the transitions in the movie project to the time the Transition Duration slider is showing. All the existing transitions get this duration, as do all transitions you add from now on.

Caution Select the Applies to all transitions option button only if you're prepared to have iMovie automatically change the length of every transition you've added to your movie project. Normally, this is a recipe for disaster.

⊘ **Applies when added to project.** Select this confusingly-named option button to apply the duration only to transitions you add from now on. Any transitions already in the movie project don't change. This is usually what you want.

Removing transitions

To remove a single transition, simply click it in the Project window and then press Backspace or choose Edit➪ Delete Selection. You can also Ctrl+click or right-click the transition and choose Delete Selection from the shortcut menu.

You can also remove all transitions that iMovie has automatically added from a movie project; if the movie project uses a theme, removing the automatic transitions removes the automatic titles too. Here's what to do:

1. **Press ⌘+J or choose File➪ Project Properties to display the Project Properties dialog box.**

2. **In the General pane, deselect the Automatically add check box (when you have chosen None in the Theme box) or the Automatically add transitions and titles check box (when you have chosen a theme).** iMovie reveals an extra section at the bottom of the Project Properties dialog box (see figure 6.8) where you can decide how to deal with the automatic transitions and titles (for themes only).

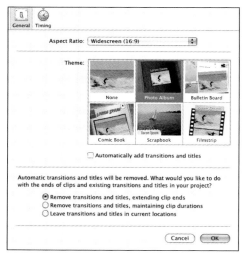

3. **Select the appropriate option button:**

    ⦿ **Remove transitions and titles, extending clip ends.** Select this option button if you want iMovie to

6.8 When removing all automatically added transitions and titles, use the three option buttons to decide how to handle the clip ends.

extend the clip ends to compensate for the removed transitions and titles, keeping the movie the same length. The advantage of this is that your soundtrack will still fit. But if you've cropped the clips to show what you want, this is not a good choice.

⊙ **Remove transitions and titles, maintaining clip durations.** Select this option button if you want to keep the clips the same length. Your clips will look the way you
intend them, but the movie will become shorter, and your soundtrack will be thrown
out of kilter. Usually, this is the best choice, especially if you haven't yet worked
extensively on the movie's soundtrack.

⊙ **Leave transitions and titles in current locations.** Select this option button if you
just want to stop iMovie from adding any more transitions. Your current transitions
and titles remain in place.

4. **Click OK.** iMovie closes the Project Properties dialog box and removes the transitions
and titles.

Adding Animated Titles

Usually, a movie will need one or more title screens at the beginning to present its name, the
director's name, and maybe set the scene for the audience. At the end, it will probably need credits — perhaps many of them. In between, you may need to add further text screens to give the
audience vital information.

To start working with titles, open the Titles
browser by clicking the Titles Browser button
on the toolbar, pressing ⌘+3, or choosing
Window ⇨ Titles. Figure 6.9 shows the Titles
browser.

Understanding the types of titles

iMovie provides more than 30 different styles
of titles (plus four extra theme-related styles if
you've applied a theme to the movie). Many
of the titles are animated, which can be highly
effective if used in moderation. To see a preview of a title's animation effect, hover the
mouse pointer over the title thumbnail in the
Titles browser.

6.9 The Titles browser gives you instant access to
all iMovie's various titles.

You can either superimpose a title on a video clip or use it on its own. In most cases, you'll use the animated titles on their own.

You can use the static title styles on their own or superimposed over a clip. For example, you can use the Lower Third title style to identify what's on-screen or provide a name for an upcoming video segment without obscuring much of the frame. Figure 6.10 shows an example of a Lower Third title.

6.10 You can superimpose titles on existing video clips. With the Lower Third style, most of the frame remains visible.

Adding a title

To add a title, simply click it in the Titles browser and drag it to where you want to place it on the Storyboard.

Applying a title on its own

Here's how to place the title on its own:

1. **Click and drag the title to the Project window so that iMovie displays a vertical green bar between clips where you want to place it.**

2. **Drop the title in the Project window.** iMovie displays the Choose Background dialog box (see figure 6.11).

3. **Click the background color or pattern you want to use for the title.** iMovie extends the movie by adding enough frames to cover the duration of the title (four seconds, by default) and displays a title box over the new frames.

4. **Type the title text, as described later in this chapter.**

5. **Change the duration of the title, as described later in this chapter.**

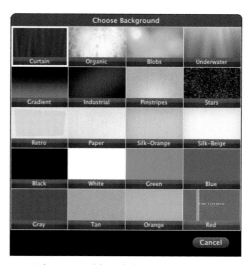

6.11 When you add a title between clips, click the background you want in the Choose Background dialog box.

Superimposing a title on a clip

To superimpose the title on a clip, click and drag it to the clip on which you want to place it. You can drag it to the middle of the clip to use the title for the entire clip, to the beginning to use it for the first part of the clip, or to the end to use it for the last part.

As you drag the title, iMovie displays shading on the clip and a time readout so you can see what's covered (see figure 6.12). The title appears above the clip in a little balloon, and you can drag the sides of the balloon to extend or shorten the time the title appears. You can fine-tune these settings later as needed.

Applying theme titles

As you saw earlier, if you apply a theme to your project, you can have iMovie add some titles and transitions automatically. Applying a theme adds these two titles to your project automatically:

6.12 When you drag a title onto a clip, the shaded area and time readout show you where and how long the title will play.

- **An opening title.** This title is the name of your project superimposed on the first few seconds of the movie.

- **A closing title.** This title displays "Directed By" followed by your user account name, which is superimposed over the last few seconds of the movie.

iMovie also adds four theme-related title styles to the top of the Titles browser, so you can also add your own theme titles.

Editing titles

After adding the title to the movie, edit the title's text by clicking its box in the Project window and then working in the Viewer. Click to select a line of the placeholder text, and then type the text you want.

Most of the title styles include a subtitle. Select that line too and type a subtitle if you want one; if not, just press Delete to delete the subtitle.

Here's how to change the font used:

1. **Select the part of the title you want to affect.**

2. **Click Show Fonts to display the Choose Font dialog box (see figure 6.13).**

3. **In the left column, click the font you want.**

4. **In the middle column, click the color you want.**

5. **In the right column, click the size you want.** These are relative sizes, from 1 (smallest) to 9 (largest), not point sizes.

6. **In the Style area, click a button to apply boldface, italic, or outline.**

7. **In the Alignment area, choose left, center, right, justified, or right alignment.**

8. **Click Done when you're satisfied with the font formatting.**

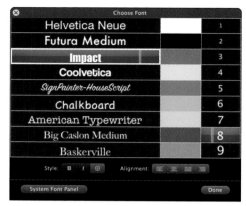

6.13 The Choose Font dialog box gives you quick access to popular fonts, colors, sizes, and styles. You can also change the alignment.

If you want greater control over the fonts, click System Font Panel in the Choose Font dialog box to open the Font panel (see figure 6.14). You can then choose font options using the same techniques as in many Mac OS X applications. When you've finished using the Font panel, either click Done to stop editing the title or click iMovie Font Panel to return to the Choose Font dialog box.

Changing title duration and fade

Here's how to change how long a title appears on-screen, and how quickly it fades in and out:

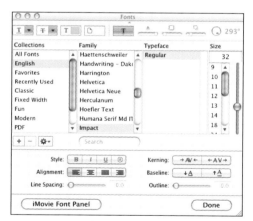

6.14 To access a full range of font formatting options, open the Font Panel.

1. **In the Project window, double-click the title's box.** iMovie displays the Inspector dialog box for the title (see figure 6.15).

2. **In the Duration box, set the time you want to display the title:**

If you've selected the Display time as HH:MM:SS:Frames check box in the General pane of the iMovie Preferences window, type the time in seconds and frames — for example, 4:20 represents four seconds and twenty frames.

Otherwise, type the time in seconds — for example, 4.5 for four and a half seconds.

3. **In the Fade In/Out area, choose one of the following options:**

Select the Project setting option button to use the time set in the Timing pane of the Project Properties dialog box.

Select the Manual option button to create a custom fade, and then drag the slider to set the length of the fade in and out.

4. **Click Done to close the Inspector dialog box.**

If you find that you need to change the duration of every title fade, change the project setting like this:

1. **Press ⌘+J or choose File ⇨ Project Properties to open the Project Properties dialog box.**

2. **Click the Timing button to display the Timing pane.**

3. **Click and drag the Title Fade Duration slider to set the fade time you want.** The minimum time is 0 seconds; the maximum time is 2 seconds. The slider offers these limits and preset intervals between them.

4. **Click OK to close the Project Properties dialog box.**

Changing the background text block color

To change the background text block color used for a title, follow these steps:

1. **Double-click the color block's box in the Project window to open the Inspector dialog box.**

2. **Click the Background button (which shows the name of the current background) to display the Choose Background dialog box.**

6.15 Choose the duration and fading for a title in the Inspector dialog box.

3. **Click the color block you want.** iMovie applies the color block and displays the Inspector dialog box.

4. **Click Done to close the Inspector dialog box.**

Genius

If none of iMovie's background text blocks is suitable for your movie, you can create your own background text block using a graphics application such as Photoshop Elements, Photoshop, or GIMP. Add the graphics file to iPhoto, and then bring it into iMovie from there. See Chapter 9 for details on importing graphics from iPhoto.

Using special characters

Most of your titles will probably need only characters you can type from the keyboard. But if you need special characters — anything from mathematical symbols to currency symbols, from Greek letters to Braille characters — you can insert them like this:

1. **Open the title for editing as usual.** Position the insertion point where you want the special character to appear.

2. **Choose Edit ⇨ Special Characters to open the Characters palette (see figure 6.16).**

3. **In the View pop-up menu at the top, choose the types of characters you want to browse through.** Choose All Characters if you want to see the full range of what's available, including scripts from all over the world. Choose Roman if you want to see characters conventionally used in English-language writing.

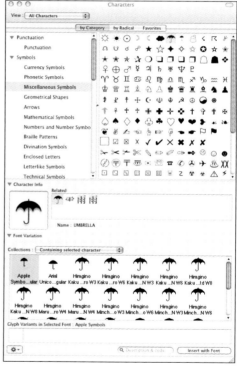

6.16 Use the Characters palette to insert an unbelievable range of characters in your titles when you need them.

4. **In the box on the left, select the category of characters you want — for example, Miscellaneous Symbols.**

5. **In the box on the right, click the character you want.**

6. **To see more information on the character, including related characters you may want to use instead, look at the Character Info area.** If this area is collapsed, click the disclosure triangle to display it.

7. **If you want to view variations on the character, look at the Font Variation area.** If this area is collapsed, click the disclosure triangle to display it. You can then click the variation you want.

8. **Click Insert to insert the character.**

9. **If you've finished using the Characters palette, click its Close button (the red button in the upper-left corner) to close it.**

Adding Animated Maps

iMovie '09's new animated maps give you a great way to locate where in the world your movie is taking place or to spice up a travelog or documentary. You can add a map in moments, and then tweak it to show exactly the places you want.

iMovie has four map styles: Old World, Watercolor, Educational, and Blue Marble. Each is available in three styles:

- **Spinning globe.** For example, Old World Globe.
- **Animated flat map.** For example, Watercolor Map.
- **Still flat map.** For example, Educational Still. iMovie automatically applies the Ken Burns effect — panning and zooming — to the map to give it eye appeal. You can adjust this effect as discussed in Chapter 9.

Here's how to add a map to a movie project:

1. **Click the Maps and Backgrounds browser button on the toolbar or press ⌘+5 to open the Maps and Backgrounds browser pane (see figure 6.17).**

2. **Click the map type you want, and then drag it to the Project window.** When iMovie displays a vertical green bar between the right two clips, drop the map there. iMovie automatically displays the Inspector dialog box for maps (see figure 6.18).

3. **In the Duration box, type the duration you want to give the map.** As usual, enter the duration in seconds and tenths of seconds (for example, 3.4s) unless you're using HH:MM:SS:Frames measurements, in which case use seconds and frames (for example, 3:15 for three seconds and 15 frames).

4. **If you want to apply a video effect, click the Video Effect button, and then click the effect in the Choose Video Effect dialog box.** See the end of this chapter for details on the video effects.

5. **Choose the start location like this:**

   - Click the Start Location button. iMovie displays the Choose Location dialog box (see figure 6.19).

   - Type the city, place name, airport code (for example, JFX or LAX), or — if you happen to know them — the coordinates for the location.

   - Pick the location from the list that iMovie displays in the main part of the dialog box.

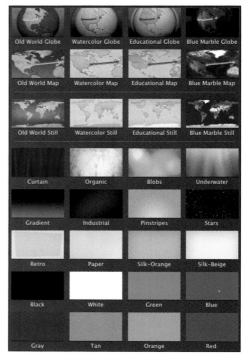

6.17 Use the Maps and Backgrounds browser pane to quickly add an animated map to a movie project.

6.18 Set up the map's details in the Inspector dialog box.

In the Name to display on map box, change the name if needed. For example, you may prefer to use a friendly name rather than the airport code and city name.

Click OK to close the Choose Location dialog box.

6.19 Choose the start location or end location by city, place name, or airport code. You can also use decimal coordinates if you know them.

6. **If you're using a map with an end location, select the End Location check box.** Click the End Location button, and then choose the location as described in the previous step.

Note If you decide your map would look better the other way around, click the Swap starting and ending locations button to the right of the locations buttons. It's the button with the symbol like a rotated S.

7. **Click Done to close the Inspector dialog box.** iMovie applies the start and end locations to the map.

8. **Ctrl+click or right-click the map in the Project window and choose Play from the shortcut menu to play the map in the viewer.**

Making iMovie Display the Advanced Tools

Before you can create a cutaway, a picture-in-picture effect, or a green screen effect (all discussed in the remainder of this chapter), you must make iMovie display the Advanced Tools, which it hides by default. Follow these steps:

1. **Choose iMovie ➭ Preferences or press ⌘+, (comma).** The iMovie Preferences window opens.

2. **If the General pane (see figure 6.20) isn't displayed, click the General button to display it.**

3. **Select the Show Advanced Tools check box.** iMovie displays the Advanced Tools.

6.20 In the General pane of the iMovie Preferences window, turn on the display of Advanced Tools.

4. **Click the Close button (the red button) or press ⌘+W to close the iMovie Preferences window.**

When you've displayed the Advanced Tools, you will see several additional controls in the iMovie window (figure 6.21 shows these controls), and iMovie will behave in different ways when you drop one video clip on another clip. Here are brief details on the additional controls, which you'll use in later chapters of this book:

- **Comment Marker button.** Drag this button to a frame to create a comment marker, a named location in your project. You use comment markers to move about your movie project swiftly while you're creating it.

- **Chapter Marker button.** Drag this button to a frame to create a chapter marker, a point the viewer can quickly move to in the finished movie or on a DVD you create of it. For example, clicking the Next button on a DVD player moves to the next chapter marker.

- **View or Select Markers pop-up menu.** Open this menu and choose the comment marker or chapter marker to which you want to move.

Chapter Marker

Comment Marker | View/Select Markers

Show/Hide Keyword Filtering Pane   View Keywords for Selection

6.21 The iMovie window with the Advanced Tools displayed.

- ◎ **Arrow button.** Click this button to turn off quick-selection mode. In quick-selection mode, you can select footage by clicking and dragging across it.

- ◎ **View Keywords for Selection button.** Click this button to display or hide the Keywords dialog box, which you use to apply keywords to video clips. For example, you can mark a clip as being Landscape or City.

- ◎ **Show or Hide Keyword Filtering pane button.** Click this button to display the Keyword Filtering pane, an area in which you can select the keywords for which you want to see matching video — for example, all the footage you've tagged with Landscape or City.

Creating Cutaways

A *cutaway* is a scene where you paste a short clip over part of a longer one to give a different perspective. For example, in an interview, you can paste a shot of the interviewee starting to react to the question over a longer shot of the interviewer asking it. The cutaway replaces the part of the clip over which you paste it.

111

The great advantage of a cutaway over simply inserting one clip in another clip is that the length of the original clip doesn't change: Instead of inserting, say, a two-second clip inside another clip and needing to adjust the audio to compensate, you can simply keep the audio playing in real time. This can save you not only considerable editing effort but also problems with audio synchronization.

Creating a basic cutaway

Here's how to create a basic cutaway:

1. **Make sure that the Advanced Tools are displayed, as discussed earlier in this chapter.** Choose iMovie ➪ Preferences, select the Show Advanced Tools check box in the General pane, and then close the iMovie Preferences window.

2. **Add the main clip to the Project window and set it up to play as you want it.** This is the clip in which you will insert the cutaway clip.

3. **In the Event browser, select the footage for the cutaway.**

4. **Drag the cutaway footage to the main clip in the Project window.** Position the Playhead over the frame at which you want to start the cutaway. Figure 6.22 shows an example.

6.22 To create a cutaway clip, drag a selection over the part of the existing clip where you want to start the cutaway.

5. **Release the mouse button.** iMovie displays a pop-up menu of options, including advanced options (see figure 6.23).

6. **Choose Cutaway from the pop-up menu.** iMovie inserts the clip at a smaller size above the clip on which you dropped it, starting at the point you chose (see figure 6.24). The cutaway clip has a gray border.

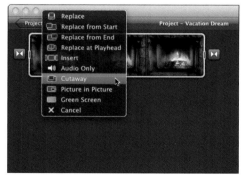

7. **Play back the cutaway and check that it appears the way you want.** You can also skim through the cutaway by moving the Playhead with the mouse pointer.

6.23 The pop-up menu includes advanced options when the Show Advanced Tools check box is selected.

8. **If necessary, adjust the cutaway:**

   * **Move the cutaway.** Click the cutaway clip, and then drag it to the left or right.

   * **Shorten or lengthen the cutaway.** Click the cutaway clip, and then drag either the left border or the right border to the position needed.

   * **Make precise adjustments.** Move the mouse pointer over the cutaway clip, click the Action button, and then

6.24 iMovie displays the cutaway clip above the main clip and puts a gray border around it.

   click Clip Trimmer to open the cutaway clip in the Clip Trimmer.

Adjusting the audio in a cutaway clip

When you add a cutaway clip, iMovie plays the audio in both the main clip and the cutaway clip during the cutaway section. Occasionally this creates exactly the effect you need, but in most cases, you'll need to adjust the audio levels. To do so, use the techniques explained in the next chapter.

Fading a cutaway in and out

Sometimes a cutaway works best with a straight cut between the main clip and the cutaway clip, but often you'll want to fade the cutaway in and out to create a softer transition between the two. Here's how to do that:

1. **Move the mouse pointer over the cutaway clip, click the Action button, and then click Clip Adjustments.** iMovie displays the Clip pane of the Inspector dialog box (see figure 6.25).

2. **In the Cutaway Fade section, select the Manual option button, and then drag the slider to set the length of the fade.**

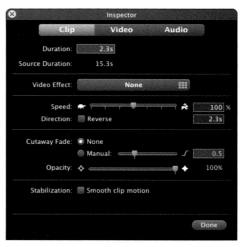

6.25 Use the Cutaway Fade controls in the Clip pane of the Inspector dialog box to fade a cutaway clip in and out.

3. **Play back or skim the cutaway to check the effect.** Adjust it if necessary.

4. **Click Done to close the Inspector dialog box.**

Making the original video show through the cutaway

Another effect you may sometimes want to create is showing the original video clip through the cutaway by making the cutaway translucent. To do so, open the Clip pane of the Inspector dialog box (click the Action button, and then click Clip Adjustments), and then drag the Opacity slider. At 0% opacity (the left end of the slider) the clip doesn't show at all, while at 100% opacity, it is fully revealed. Figure 6.26 shows the effect of changing the opacity.

Creating Picture-in-Picture Effects

iMovie '09's new picture-in-picture effect enables you to inlay one clip in another clip. This is great for various effects, such as showing what's happening in two different scenes at the same time or for zooming in on a detail in the subject while still showing the main clip.

Here's how to create a picture-in-picture effect:

6.26 By reducing the opacity of the cutaway clip, you can make the original clip show through it to different degrees.

1. **Make sure that the Advanced Tools are displayed, as discussed earlier in this chapter.** Choose iMovie ➪ Preferences, select the Show Advanced Tools check box in the General pane, and then close the iMovie Preferences window.

2. **Add the main clip to the Project window and make any adjustments needed.** For example, trim the clip or crop it. This is the clip in which you will insert the picture-in-picture clip.

3. **In the Event browser, select the footage for the picture-in-picture clip.** Either select a whole clip or just the frames you want to use from a clip.

4. **Drag the selection to the main clip in the Project window.** Position the Playhead over the frame at which you want to start the picture-in-picture effect.

5. **Release the mouse button.** iMovie displays a pop-up menu of options, including advanced options.

6. **Choose Picture in Picture from the pop-up menu.** iMovie inserts the clip at a smaller size above the clip on which you dropped it, starting at the point you chose, with a yellow selection border around it and a red dot on the Playhead (see figure 6.27). iMovie displays the combined pictures in the viewer (see figure 6.28).

6.27 iMovie displays the picture-in-picture clip at a smaller size above the host clip and stops the Playhead.

6.28 The viewer shows the position and size at which the inset clip appears on the other clip.

7. **Resize and reposition the picture-in-picture clip.** To resize it, click and drag one of the corner handles. To reposition it, click in the picture and drag it to where you want (see figure 6.29).

8. **Click the Play button in the viewer to play back the two clips and make sure your settings work.** If not, tweak them until they do.

9. **Click Done to hide the editing tools.** iMovie displays a blue border around the picture-in-picture clip, so you can tell at a glance what kind of advanced clip it is.

6.29 Resize the picture-in-picture clip and position where you want it to appear over the other clip.

Superimposing a Subject with a Green Screen

One of iMovie '09's most impressive tricks is creating a *green screen* effect. This is where you record a video clip in front of a green backdrop that you can then tell iMovie to eliminate, leaving just the subject of the video. You can then impose this subject on another video clip.

For example, you can make a video of yourself presenting information and then place yourself (but not your background) over other footage — great for documentaries. Or you can superimpose live actors on a computer-generated backdrop.

Genius

Green screen is like Photo Booth's effects that put you in front of the Eiffel Tower, tropical fish, or another background by analyzing your background and then digitally removing it. Green is used for the background because cameras' image sensors are more sensitive to green than other colors. Similar techniques use blue screens — widely used for putting weather forecasters in front of the maps they're presenting — or magenta screens.

Shooting a green screen video

The first step — and the tricky part — is to shoot video of your subject in front of a green background. Follow these steps:

1. **Script and plan the scene.** For example, if the subject will be presenting information on a topic, write the script. Decide where the subject will appear in the frame; depending on what you're creating with the green screen, you may want to have the subject at the side of the screen rather than in the center.

2. **Set up a solid green backdrop.** If you're buying paint or cloth for the background, look for "chroma key green" — that's the color the pros use.

3. **Set up your lights to light the subject from various angles.** Try to make sure that the lights won't cast shadows on the subject or make the subject cast shadows on the backdrop.

4. **Make sure your subject isn't wearing green, because otherwise iMovie may eliminate part of the subject.** Green eyes are okay, but that's as much green as you can have.

5. **Record your video.** At the end of each take, pause the camera, have the subject leave the scene, and then take a few frames of only the background. This helps iMovie to work out what's the subject and what's the background.

After you shoot your green screen video, import it into iMovie as usual. Play it back, make sure it looks satisfactory in itself, and split it up into clips as needed. If the clips need cropping, crop them to the right dimensions.

Creating the green screen effect

When your green screen clip is ready for use, superimpose it like this:

1. **Make sure that the Advanced Tools are displayed, as discussed earlier in this chapter.** Choose iMovie ➪ Preferences, select the Show Advanced Tools check box in the General pane, and then close the iMovie Preferences window.

2. **Add the main clip to the Project window and set it up to play as you want it.** This is the clip in which you will insert the green screen clip.

3. **In the Event browser, select the footage for the green screen clip.** If you need the whole clip, select it; otherwise, select just the footage you want.

4. **Drag the selected footage to the main clip in the Project window.** Position the Playhead over the frame at which you want to start the cutaway.

5. **Release the mouse button.** iMovie displays a pop-up menu of options, including advanced options.

6. **Choose Green Screen from the pop-up menu.** iMovie inserts the green screen clip at a smaller size above the host clip and displays a yellow selection border around it (see figure 6.30). iMovie also displays the green screen clip over the background clip in the viewer and shows its cropping tools (see figure 6.31).

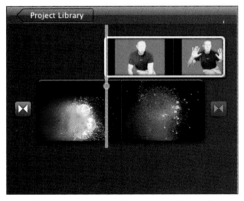

6.30 The green screen clip appears above the host clip and at a smaller size.

6.31 In the viewer, you see the green screen clip superimposed on the background clip, together with cropping tools.

7. **Click the Cropped button in the viewer.** iMovie displays an outline with four control points around the area it is allotting to the green screen's subject (see figure 6.32).

8. **Drag the control points to frame your subject (see figure 6.33).**

6.32 Often you can get better results by using the cropping tools to tell iMovie where the subject is in the green screen clip.

6.33 Drag the control points to improve the cropping on the green screen clip.

9. **Click the Play button in the viewer to play back the superimposed clip and the background clip.** Make sure you haven't cropped too aggressively. For example, if the subject of the green screen clip moves, you may need to crop less tightly to avoid costing the subject body parts.

10. **When the cropping is right, click Done.** iMovie displays a green border around the clip to indicate that it's a green screen (see figure 6.34).

11. **Double-click the green screen clip to display the Clip pane of the Inspector dialog box (see figure 6.35).**

12. **Select the Subtract last frame check box to tell iMovie to remove the extra color-reference frame that you recorded at the end of the clip without the subject.**

Caution If you didn't record a color-reference frame without the subject at the end of the clip, don't select the Subtract last frame check box — if you do, iMovie may subtract part of the subject instead.

13. **Click Done to close the Inspector dialog box.**

6.34 A green border indicates that the clip is a green screen.

6.35 The Clip pane of the Inspector dialog box for a green screen clip includes the Subtract last frame check box.

Note

Once you've created a green screen clip, iMovie considers it part of the clip to which you've attached it. If you move the host clip to a different part of the project, the green screen clip goes along for the ride, which is handy. If you delete the host clip from the Project window, you delete the green screen clip as well.

Adjusting the audio for the green screen clip

iMovie plays the audio for both the green screen clip and the host clip at the same time. To get the right balance of sound, you'll usually need to adjust the audio levels in the clips. See Chapter 7 for details.

Applying Cool Video Effects

iMovie includes a battery of neat effects that you can apply to your video clips to make them look different, special, or plain odd. For example, you can flip the video horizontally (switching left and right), make it look black and white or dreamlike, or make it look like a film negative with all the colors reversed.

Here's how to apply an effect.

1. **Select the clip you want to affect.**

2. **Open the Clip pane of the Inspector dialog box.** The easiest way to do this is to press the letter I or double-click the selected clip. You can also click the Action button and choose Clip Adjustments from the pop-up menu.

3. **Click the Video Effect button in the middle of the Clip pane to display the Choose Video Effect dialog box (see figure 6.36).**

4. **Move the mouse pointer over an effect to make iMovie apply the effect in the viewer so that you can see how it looks.** iMovie displays a Playhead that you can drag to preview the effect along the clip rather than on a still frame.

6.36 Use the Choose Video Effect dialog box to preview 19 different video effects on a clip.

5. **Click the effect you want.** iMovie closes the Choose Video Effect dialog box, and the Inspector dialog box reappears.

6. **Click Done to close the Inspector dialog box.**

Creating Slow-Motion and High-Speed Effects

You can create slow-motion and high-speed effects by changing the speed at which a clip plays back. This is a great new effect that can make a huge difference in your movies. You can even make a clip play backward for dramatic effect.

To change a video clip's playback speed or direction, follow these steps:

1. **Select the clip you want to affect.**

2. **Open the Clip pane of the Inspector dialog box (see figure 6.37).** For example, press the letter I or double-click the selected clip.

3. **Drag the Speed slider along the Tortoise–Hare axis.** You can set anywhere from 12.5% slow-motion to 800% rapid-fire mayhem. The box under the percentage readout shows how long the clip plays for at the adjusted speed, either in minutes, seconds, and tenths of seconds or in minutes, seconds, and frames (if you've selected the Display time as HH:MM:SS:Frames check box in the General pane of the iMovie Preferences window).

6.37 In the Clip pane of the Inspector dialog box, you can slow a clip down, speed it up, or reverse it.

4. **Press Spacebar to preview in the viewer how the clip plays at this speed.**

5. **If you want to reverse playback, select the Reverse check box.** Again, press Spacebar to preview the effect.

6. **Click Done when you're satisfied with the result.** iMovie closes the Inspector dialog box.

Caution

You can type a custom value in the percentage box (for example, 173%) to make a clip play at exactly the speed (or for exactly the time) you need. Generally, it's better to use the increments on the slider. In early versions of iMovie '09, custom playback speeds sometimes caused audio synchronization problems.

What Should I Know about Audio and Scoring My Movies?

		Music and Sound Effects
×		

Foley

Name	Artist	Time
Alarm Clock Bell.caf	Apple Inc.	0:09
Antique Clock Strike.caf	Apple Inc.	0:49
Barn Door Close.caf	Apple Inc.	0:04
Barn Door Open.caf	Apple Inc.	0:03
Bell Tower.caf	Apple Inc.	0:09
Bubbles.caf	Apple Inc.	0:10
Camera Shutter.caf	Apple Inc.	0:01
Cash Register.caf	Apple Inc.	0:01
Clock Wind Up.caf	Apple Inc.	0:32
Coin Drop on Concrete.caf	Apple Inc.	0:02
Coin Drop on Wood.caf	Apple Inc.	0:02
Combination Lock Opening.caf	Apple Inc.	0:05
Door Air Lock Closing.caf	Apple Inc.	0:05
Door Metal Squeak.caf	Apple Inc.	0:03
Door Vault Closing.caf	Apple Inc.	0:04
Door Wood Squeak.caf	Apple Inc.	0:02
Footsteps.caf	Apple Inc.	0:12
Grandfather Clock Strike.caf	Apple Inc.	1:07
Packing Boxes.caf	Apple Inc.	0:04
Radio Tuning 01.caf	Apple Inc.	0:04
Rescue Helicopter.caf	Apple Inc.	0:31
School Bell Ringing.caf	Apple Inc.	0:03
Scuba Breathing.caf	Apple Inc.	0:54
Squeeze Toy.caf	Apple Inc.	0:01
Traffic Helicopter.caf	Apple Inc.	0:31
Walkie Talkie Garble.caf	Apple Inc.	0:09
Walkie Talkie Static.caf	Apple Inc.	0:01

Q

27 items

A great movie needs a soundtrack to match, and iLife gives you heavy-hitting tools for creating exactly the audio you need. Normally, you'll start by adjusting audio levels in video clips and arranging any fading in or out they need. You can then add background music, sound effects, and narration, and adjust the levels to make the right parts audible. When you need more powerful audio tools than iMovie itself offers , you can enlist GarageBand to create a custom soundtrack for your movie.

Adjusting Audio Levels in Clips

iMovie enables you to adjust the audio level at which the audio in a video clip or in an audio clip plays back. You can also create fade-in and fade-out effects as necessary, and you can quickly copy audio adjustments from one clip to another clip.

Adjusting audio volume and fading

When you add music, sound effects, or a voiceover to movie footage that already contains audio, you usually need to adjust one or more of the audio clips to make sure the parts you want to hear are audible. You can also adjust the audio that's part of the video clip, which is useful when you need to boost it, reduce it, or suppress it altogether.

To adjust a clip's volume, fading, and normalization, follow these steps:

1. **Click the audio clip you want to adjust.** For example, click a Voiceover Recording clip or the music clip. To work with the audio in the video track, click the video clip.

2. **Click the Inspector button on the toolbar or press I to display the Inspector dialog box with the Audio pane displayed (see figure 7.1).**

3. **Drag the Volume slider to increase or decrease the volume.** You can mute the track altogether by dragging the slider all the way to the left.

4. **Apply ducking if the track needs it.** *Ducking* means reducing the volume of the other tracks while this track plays, and then restoring their volume. To set ducking:

7.1 Use the Audio tab in the Inspector dialog box to change the volume on an audio clip.

- **Drag the Reduce volume of other tracks slider to the left or right.** iMovie automatically selects the Ducking check box for you. (You can select it first manually if you prefer.)

- **Listen to the effect to see if your track is audible over its competition.** Increase or decrease the ducking as needed.

5. **If you want to create a gradual fade-in instead of using iMovie's automatic rapid fade-in, select the Manual radio button in the Fade In area.** Drag the slider to the right to set the number of seconds and frames the fade-in occupies. The maximum setting is 2 seconds.

6. **If you want to create a gradual fade-out instead of using iMovie's automatic rapid fade-out, select the Manual radio button in the Fade Out area.** Drag the slider to the right to set the number of seconds and frames the fade-out occupies. As with the fade-in, the maximum setting is 2 seconds.

7. **If your audio was recorded at different volumes, try clicking the Normalize Clip Volume button to even it out.** If you don't like the result, click the Remove Normalization button.

8. **To work with another clip, click it, and then repeat Steps 3 to 7.**

9. **When you finish working with audio, click Done to close the Inspector dialog box.**

Copying and pasting audio adjustments

When you've finished making audio adjustments to one clip, you can quickly apply them to one or more other clips that need the same treatment. This saves you from repeating exactly the same edits for a mind-numbing number of different clips.

Here's how to apply the audio adjustments to another clip:

1. **Ctrl+click or right-click the clip you fixed, and then choose Copy from the shortcut menu.** iMovie copies the details of all the adjustments you've made to the clip, including the audio adjustments.

2. **Select the clip you want to adjust.**

    - In the Project window, click the clip; in the Event browser, Option+click the clip.

    - To adjust multiple clips, click the first, and then ⌘+click each of the others.

3. **Choose Edit ⇨ Paste Adjustments ⇨ Audio or press ⌘+Option+A.**

Adding Background Music

Background music is music that plays right through the movie (but you can choose where to start and stop playback). Background music can be either a single song file or an iTunes playlist containing songs you've selected. Other audio — the audio recorded in your video clips, or sound effects or narration you attach to particular clips — plays through or over the background music.

Adding a song or audio clip as a background

Here's how to add a song or audio clip as a background for a movie:

1. **Open the Music and Sound Effects browser (see figure 7.2).** The easiest ways to do this are to click the Music and Sound Effects browser button on the toolbar or press ⌘+1.

2. **In the Music and Sound Effects browser, choose the item that contains the music or sound effect you want:**

   - **iMovie Sound Effects.** Choose this item to see iMovie's wide range of sound effects — everything from ambient sounds to a train passing.

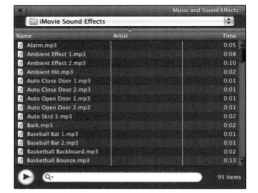

7.2 Use the Music and Sound Effects browser to add a song or audio clip as background audio for a movie.

   - **iLife Sound Effects.** Choose this item to see the hundreds of sound effects available to the iLife applications. Choose one of the folders — Ambience, Animals, Booms, Foley (see the nearby Genius), Jingles, Machines, People, Sci-Fi, Sports, Stingers, Textures, Transportation, and Work–Home — to see only the effects that folder contains.

Genius

Foley effects are extra, everyday sound effects usually added after a movie has been shot. (The name comes from Jack Foley, a pioneering Hollywood sound engineer.) iLife's Foley effects include cash registers ringing, clocks striking, footsteps, and so on.

   - **GarageBand.** Choose GarageBand to see the songs you've composed in GarageBand.

   - **iTunes.** Choose iTunes to see all the songs in iTunes.

   - **A playlist or playlist folder.** Choose a particular playlist or playlist folder in iTunes to see only the songs in that playlist or the playlists in the folder.

3. **Find the song or sound effect you want.** If you're looking at a long list, click in the Search box and start typing a word to find matching items.

4. **To preview a song or sound effect, double-click it.** You can also click an item and then click the Play button in the lower-left corner of the Music and Sound Effects browser. Press Spacebar or click the Play button to stop playback, or simply double-click another item to preview that item.

5. **Click the song or sound effect, drag it to the Project window, and drop it in the background well — that is, in open space not occupied by a clip, title, or other object.** When the item is over the background well, iMovie displays a green border around all the clips visible in the Project window and applies green shading to everything within the border (see figure 7.3).

7.3 The green border and shading indicates that iMovie will apply the sound effect or song as background music to the whole movie.

After you drop the background music, iMovie displays a green border and background around only those clips for which the background music will play. For example, if your movie is ten minutes long, and you add a background song that's five minutes long, only the clips in the first five minutes will have the background music. If the background music is longer than the movie, iMovie displays an icon showing two notes and an ellipsis (…) over the last clip (see figure 7.4).

When you add a piece of background music, iMovie sets it to start right at the beginning of the movie. Often, this is what you want; but if you want to make the music start after the beginning of the movie, you can easily do so.

7.4 The Notes icon indicates that the background music continues past the end of the movie.

127

Genius When iMovie places a piece of background music at the very beginning of a movie, it considers the music to be *floating* and gives it a green background. If you add another piece of background music, iMovie sets it to start after the first. Here, "float-ing" doesn't mean that the music moves around, but that iMovie, not you, has cho-sen the music's placement. The opposite of floating is *pinned*, which means you've placed the music where you want it. Pinned items have a purple background, so you can easily see which items you've placed.

Trimming a clip with the Clip Trimmer

Use the Clip Trimmer to trim off any parts of the audio clip that you don't want to play. Here's how to use the Clip Trimmer:

1. **Click the Action button for the background audio clip and choose Clip Trimmer from the pop-up menu.** iMovie opens the audio clip in the Clip Trimmer (see figure 7.5).

7.5 The Clip Trimmer shows a graphical representation of the waveform in the audio clip. You can trim the audio clip by dragging the yellow handle at the left end or at the right end.

2. **If you need to zoom in on the clip so that you can see its waveform in more detail, click and drag the Frames Per Thumbnail slider to the left.** If you need to shorten the clip so that you can fit more of it into the Clip Trimmer, click and drag the Frames Per Thumbnail slider to the right.

3. **If you need to trim the start of the clip, click and drag the yellow selection handle at the beginning to the right.** iMovie skims through the waveform as you drag so that you can hear which part you've reached.

4. **If you need to trim the end of the clip, click and drag the yellow selection handle at the end to the left.**

5. **Click the Play Current Clip Segment button (the button with the Play symbol between two vertical lines) to hear how the clip sounds.** Make any further trimming needed.

Marking key moments with beat markers

When editing your clip in the Clip Trimmer, you may also want to mark key moments in the clip so that you can synchronize your video clips with them. For example, you can align a cymbal crash with a change of scene or a drum roll with the entry of your movie's villain.

Adding a beat marker

To mark a moment, place a beat marker in the clip. You can place beat markers in any of four ways:

- **Click the Beat Marker button and drag to where you want the beat marker to appear on the waveform (see figure 7.6).**

7.6 Click and drag a beat marker to mark a key moment on a clip's waveform. Each beat marker appears as a light-gray vertical line.

- **Position the Playhead where you want to place the beat marker, and then press M.**

- **Set the clip playing, and then press M to mark each beat.** If your timing is good, this is a great way of marking the beats quickly and effectively.

- **Position the Playhead when you want to place the beat marker, Ctrl+click or right-click, and then choose Add Beat Marker from the shortcut menu.**

Note

If the audio clip plays alongside a video clip at the point where you add the beat marker, iMovie automatically splits the video clip into separate clips at the beat marker. You can then easily swap in a different video clip for that beat by dragging another clip on top of that clip, and then choosing Replace from the pop-up menu. To avoid automatic splitting, choose View ⇨ Snap to Beats to turn off the Snap to Beats feature.

Repositioning a beat marker

To move a beat marker, click and drag it along the clip to its new position.

Deleting a beat marker

To get rid of a beat marker you've placed, click and drag it off the waveform. When you release the mouse button, the beat marker vanishes in a puff of smoke.

If you delete a beat marker that's not associated with an edit, the puff of smoke is the end of the matter. But when you remove a beat marker that you've associated with an edit (as discussed later in this chapter), iMovie displays the Remove Beat Marker dialog box (see figure 7.7) asking you to decide what to do with the associated edit. These are your choices:

7.7 The Remove Beat Marker dialog box enables you to choose whether to extend an edit associated with the beat marker or leave it as it is.

- **Cancel.** Click this button to leave the beat marker in place (and not get rid of it).
- **Extend Left.** Click this button to extend the clip to the left.
- **Extend Right.** Click this button to extend the clip to the right.
- **Leave As-Is.** Click this button to leave the clip at its current length. You'll need to fix any problems that removing the beat marker has caused with the synchronization between the video and the audio.

Genius

You can also wipe out all the beat markers in a clip. Open the clip in the Clip Trimmer, Ctrl+click or right-click in the waveform, and then choose Remove All Beat Markers from the shortcut menu.

Making playback start at the right frame

When you've trimmed a clip, and maybe set beat markers, you can make playback start at exactly the frame you want.

Pinning a background track

To make a background audio item start playing after the beginning of the movie rather than right at the beginning, pin the audio item where you need it.

To pin the background audio item, click it in the Project window and drag it to the right until the Playhead shows the frame at which you want to start playback. As you drag, iMovie changes the item's shading to purple to indicate that it is pinned (see figure 7.8).

Synchronizing a clip with a beat marker

When you've added beat markers to the audio in a project, you can synchronize video clips, titles, and other elements (such as cutaways) with the beat markers.

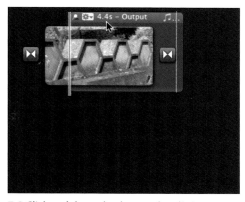

7.8 Click and drag a background audio item to pin it in exactly the right place.

To synchronize a video clip, click and drag it from the Event browser to the Project window so that it overlaps a beat marker. iMovie automatically adjusts the length of the clip so that it runs from that beat marker to the next beat marker. You can do the same thing with a still image by clicking and dragging it from the Photos browser to the Project window so that it overlaps a beat marker.

To synchronize a title, cutaway, or other element that appears above the main line of video clips, click and drag it to align its beginning with a beat marker. The item then starts playing at the beat marker.

You can also use the Precision Editor to synchronize a title, cutaway, or other element with a beat marker like this:

1. **Open the Precision Editor as usual.** For example, click the clip's Action button and choose Precision Editor from the pop-up menu.

2. **Click the Extras button at the left end of the Precision Editor's toolbar.** iMovie displays the extras (titles, cutaways, and so on) at the top of the Precision Editor window and the audio track at the bottom (see figure 7.9).

3. **Click and drag the extra element to align its end with the beat marker on the audio track.**

4. **When you've finished using the Precision Editor, click Done.**

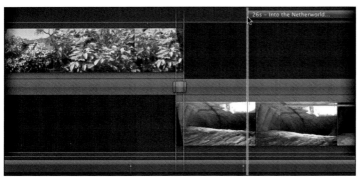

7.9 Display extras in the Precision Editor so that you can synchronize a title or other item with a beat marker.

If Snap to Beats is turned on, and you take an action that will throw your project out of sync, iMovie displays the Snap to Beats is Enabled dialog box (see figure 7.10) to warn you of the problem. Click Continue if you're prepared to rearrange your project as needed; otherwise, click Cancel.

7.10 iMovie warns you if you're about to put your project out of sync.

Adding another piece of background music

If you need to add another piece of background music, click and drag it from the Music and Sound Effects browser to the background well in the Project window, just as for the first piece. When iMovie displays the green border and shading, drop the item.

iMovie automatically sets the second item to play when the first ends and applies a one-second cross-fade between them.

Figure 7.11 shows a project with two pieces of background music set. Each piece shows the length of time for which it will play.

7.11 A movie project with two pieces of background music set to play one after the other.

Rearranging background music clips

If you need to shift your background music clips into a different order, click a clip and drag it to where you want it to appear. iMovie displays a yellow outline and purple shading around the clip you're moving from a floating position to a pinned position (see figure 7.12), so you can easily see what you're doing.

7.12 You can rearrange background music clips by clicking and dragging.

When you're working with a long movie, it can be hard to reposition background audio in the Project window, so iMovie provides the Arrange Music Tracks dialog box as well. Here's how to use this dialog box to rearrange music tracks:

1. **Ctrl+click or right-click the background audio well in the Project window and choose Arrange Music Tracks from the pop-up menu.** iMovie displays the Arrange Music Tracks dialog box (see figure 7.13).

2. **To unpin a pinned track, click it in the Pinned Music Tracks list, and then click Unpin Track.** iMovie transfers the track to the Floating Music Tracks list.

3. **Drag the tracks in the Floating Music Tracks list into the order you want them.**

4. **Click OK.**

Play your movie back and make sure that the audio clips work in their new positions. Often, you'll need to make further adjustments using the techniques described earlier in this chapter.

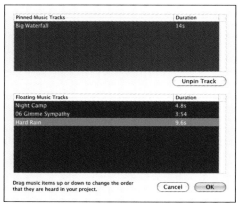

7.13 The Arrange Music Tracks dialog box enables you to unpin pinned tracks and reshuffle the floating tracks into order.

Using only the audio from a video clip

Sometimes you may need to use the audio from a video clip without showing the video — for example, so that you can play one video clip's audio as the soundtrack to another video clip.

iMovie enables you to do this without effort. Just select the clip (or the footage from the clip) in the Event browser, then click and drag the selection to the Project window. Drop the selection on the clip to which you want to add the audio, and then choose Audio Only in the pop-up menu that iMovie displays.

Alternatively, you can detach the audio from a video clip you've placed in the Project window. Ctrl+click or right-click the clip and choose Detach Audio from the shortcut menu. iMovie displays a purple icon below the video clip representing the audio track (see figure 7.14). You can then click this purple icon and drag it to where you need it.

7.14 A detached audio clip appears as a purple icon below the video clip it comes from.

Genius

When you detach the audio from a video clip, iMovie doesn't actually strip out the audio; instead, it sets the video clip's audio volume to zero and gives you a separate icon for handling the audio. If you move the detached audio elsewhere in the soundtrack and need to play the video clip's audio again, you can simply turn the volume back up.

Adding Sound Effects

As you've seen, background music is an audio clip applied to the entire movie. If you move a clip to a different point in the movie, the audio in the background track isn't affected (though it will play along with a different video segment).

By contrast, a *sound effect* is an audio clip that you attach to a particular video clip in the movie. If you move that video clip, the sound effect goes with it.

To add a sound effect to a video clip, follow these steps:

1. **Open the Music and Sound Effects browser.** Press ⌘+1 or click the Music and Sound Effects browser button on the toolbar.

2. **Choose the item that contains the audio file you want to use.** For example, choose GarageBand to see your GarageBand compositions, or choose iLife Sound Effects to see the sound effects.

3. **Click the audio file, drag it to the Project window, and position it over the clip.** Move the Playhead to where you want the sound to start (see figure 7.15), and then drop the audio file.

7.15 To attach a sound effect to a clip, click and drag the audio file over the video clip and move the Playhead to the frame at which you want the sound to start playing.

Narrating with Voiceover

When you need to add spoken narration to a movie, use iMovie's Voiceover feature. Voiceover enables you to quickly add audio to explain what's happening or set the scene.

To add a voiceover to your movie, follow these steps:

1. **Open the Voiceover window (see figure 7.16).** Click the Voiceover button on the toolbar (the microphone button) or press O.

2. **In the Record From pop-up menu, choose the microphone or sound source you want to use.** For example, choose Built-in Microphone if you're recording through your Mac's microphone.

7.16 Choose the recording source and set the input volume in the Voiceover window.

3. **Set the input volume:**

   - Speak into the microphone at the volume you'll use.

   - Drag the Input Volume slider as needed to put the volume bars about three-quarters of the way across to the right, but not so that you're getting the red LEDs at the right end all the time.

4. **If you're recording in a noisy environment, you may need to adjust the Noise Reduction slider to get good results.** This slider enables you to tell the microphone to try to filter out background noises so that it picks up your voice clearly.

5. **Select the Voice Enhancement check box if you want iMovie to try to improve the sound of your voice.** You should experiment with this feature and see if you like the effect; if not, turn it off by clearing the check box.

6. **Select the Play project audio while recording check box if you need to hear the project's audio as you speak your narration.** Hearing the audio can help you get your timing right, but you'll need to listen to it through headphones to prevent your microphone from picking up the audio and recording it into the voiceover.

7. **In the Storyboard, skim to the point at which you want to start recording the voiceover.**

8. **When you're ready to begin, click where you want to start.** The viewer prompts you to get ready and then counts down from 3 to 1, playing the three seconds of footage before the point where you clicked.

9. **Speak the voiceover, and then press Spacebar to stop.** iMovie displays a purple bar called Voiceover Recording under the clips (see figure 7.17).

10. **Repeat Steps 7 to 9 if you need to record more voiceovers.**

11. **When you finish recording, click the Close button to close the Voiceover window.**

7.17 iMovie displays the voiceover as a purple bar under the clips to which it's attached.

Genius

You can make voiceovers overlap if need be. And you can trim a voiceover either by clicking it and dragging one of its end handles or by Ctrl+clicking or right-clicking it, clicking Trim, and working in the Trim Clip pane.

Managing Multi-track Audio Levels

When you have set multiple tracks to play at the same time, you'll need to adjust their audio levels to get the mix right. You can do this in two main ways:

● **Set each track to play at the right level.** By adjusting the playback volume of each clip, you can set the overall audio balance.

Genius

In iMovie, you can't set a custom volume curve on a track — for example, playing it softly at first, then more loudly. To create a volume curve, you must use GarageBand, discussed later in this chapter. But what you can do in iMovie is use the ducking feature to lower the volume of other tracks so that your target audio track is audible.

● **Apply ducking to other tracks.** When you want one particular track to stand out, you can set iMovie to automatically *duck* (lower) the volume of all other audio tracks. This makes your target track stand out against the others. When the target track finishes playing, iMovie removes the ducking from the other tracks, so the sound level comes back up to where you had set it.

Either way, your first step should be to set the volume of the background music so that you can judge the volume of the foreground music against it.

Setting the volume of the background music

Here's how to set the volume of the background music:

1. **Open the Audio pane of the Inspector dialog box (see figure 7.18).** Click the background audio clip's Action button and choose Audio Adjustments from the pop-up menu. Alternatively, click the background audio well (anywhere in the green shading for the clip) and press A.

2. **Click and drag the Volume slider to set the volume for the background audio.**

3. **If you need to adjust the fading settings, do so as discussed earlier in this chapter.**

4. **Click Done to close the Inspector dialog box.**

7.18 Use the Audio pane of the Inspector dialog box to set the volume for the background music.

Note

The Ducking controls aren't available for the background audio track because you can't duck other tracks against the background track.

Setting each track to play at the level you want

Next, set each track's volume so that it plays at the level needed.

1. **Open the Audio pane of the Inspector dialog box.** Click the audio clip's Action button and choose Audio Adjustments from the pop-up menu, or click the clip and press A.

2. **Click and drag the Volume slider to set the volume for the audio track.**

3. **Leave the Ducking controls alone for the time being.** You'll set them in the next section.

4. **Make any adjustments needed to the Fade In settings and Fade Out settings.**

5. **Click Done to close the Inspector dialog box.**

Applying ducking to make one track stand out

Last, use ducking to fade the other tracks behind the track you want to be most audible at any given point.

Where needed, apply ducking like this:

1. **Open the Audio pane of the Inspector dialog box.** Click the audio clip's Action button and choose Audio Adjustments from the pop-up menu, or click the clip and press A.

2. **In the Ducking area, select the Reduce volume of other tracks to check box.**

3. **Drag the Ducking slider to set the volume of the other tracks.** You may need to listen a few times to choose the best level.

4. **Click Done to close the Inspector dialog box.**

Creating a Soundtrack with GarageBand

When you need to compose a score for your movie from scratch rather than build a soundtrack from your existing audio files, bring the movie into GarageBand and work with it there. GarageBand provides all the tools you need to create a soundtrack quickly from prerecorded loops, record your own original performances on either software (virtual) instruments or real (physical) instruments, and mix them down to give exactly the sound you want.

For best results, finish cutting the movie in iMovie first, so you can work smoothly in GarageBand, apply exactly the right timings, and then export the finished product.

Learning the GarageBand '09 Interface

Your first move is to get up to speed with the GarageBand interface. Like iMovie, GarageBand packs a huge amount of power into a streamlined interface with several areas that display different components depending on the task you're performing.

Before you can get started with GarageBand, you need to open a GarageBand project. Just like iMovie, GarageBand enables you to open only one project at a time.

To launch GarageBand, click the GarageBand icon on the Dock; if it's not there, click the Finder icon, choose Go ⇨ Applications, and then double-click the GarageBand icon.

GarageBand displays the opening screen shown in figure 7.19.

7.19 When you open GarageBand, the application prompts you to create a new music project or podcast episode, open an existing project, or use Magic GarageBand.

Create and save your song project like this:

1. **If the New Project button in the left panel isn't selected, click it so that you see the available instruments (such as Piano, Electric Guitar, and Voice) and features (such as Songwriting and Podcast).**

2. **Click the instrument you want to use — for example, Keyboard Collection — and then click the Choose button.** GarageBand displays the New Project from Template dialog box (see figure 7.20).

3. **In the upper part of the dialog box, name your song, and choose where to save it.** As usual, you can click the drop-down arrow to the right of the Save As box to reveal the dialog box's navigation area.

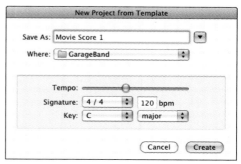

7.20 In the New Project from Template dialog box, name your song, choose where to save it, and set the tempo, signature, and key.

4. **Set the tempo for the song by dragging the Tempo slider to adjust the number in the bpm box.** If you don't know what tempo you want, leave the default tempo — 120 beats per minute — selected; you can change it later if necessary.

5. **Choose the time signature for the song in the Signature pop-up menu.** Again, it's safe to leave the default value if you don't have a firm idea of your needs; you can change this later too.

6. **Choose the key in the Key pop-up menu, and then choose major or minor in the pop-up menu to the right of it.** The same goes for this — you can accept the default value and then change it later if you need.

7. **Click Create.** GarageBand closes the New Project from Template dialog box and displays your project.

Figure 7.21 shows how the GarageBand window looks with a project open.

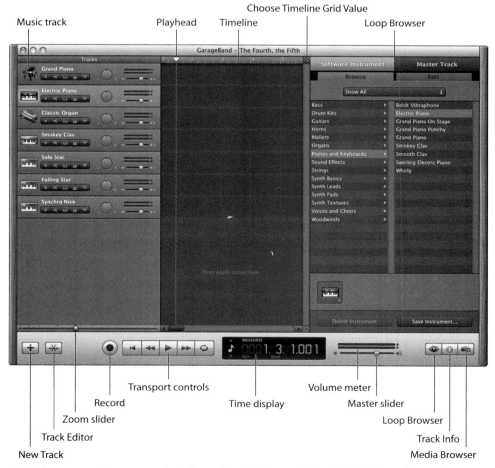

Music track   Playhead   Timeline   Choose Timeline Grid Value   Loop Browser

Transport controls   Volume meter
Record   Time display   Master slider
Zoom slider   Loop Browser
Track Editor   Track Info
New Track   Media Browser

7.21 When you create a song project, GarageBand looks something like this. The track or tracks depends on the instrument or feature you chose in the opening GarageBand screen.

GarageBand starts the project with a track for the instrument you chose (for example, guitar) or a sample selection of tracks, but you can delete any track — or change it to another instrument — as needed.

These are the main elements of the GarageBand window:

- **Tracks column.** You place a track in this column for each Software Instrument or Real Instrument you want to play or record. The track header shows the instrument type and contains controls for recording the track, listening to it, changing its volume, and panning it.

- **Playhead.** The triangle in the Timeline and the red line down across the tracks indicate the current play position. The Playhead moves as you play back the tracks. You can also move it by dragging or by using the Transport controls.

- **Timeline.** This is the area where you arrange loops, tracks, and sounds so that they start when you want them to and play for the required length.

- **Zoom slider.** Drag this slider to zoom in on the Timeline so you can see it in more detail, or to zoom out to see more of your project at once.

- **New Track button.** Click this track to open the dialog box for adding a new Software Instrument track or Real Instrument track.

- **Loop browser.** This pane enables you to pick prerecorded audio loops to place in the song.

Note The Loop browser, Track Info pane, and Media browser share the same area on the right side of the screen, so you can display only one of these items at once. To give yourself more space for the timeline, you can also hide whichever of these three is currently displayed.

- **Loop Browser button.** Click this button to display or hide the Loop browser, which you use to pick prerecorded audio loops.

- **Track Info button.** Click this button to display or hide the Track Info pane, which you use for working with Software Instruments and Real Instruments.

- **Media Browser button.** Click this button to display or hide the Media Browser, which you use to select audio clips, photos, and movies, just like in most of the other iLife applications. You use the Media Browser when creating podcasts rather than when creating songs.

- **Track Editor button.** Click this button to display the Track Editor, which you use to edit the audio in a track.

- **Record button.** Click this button to start or stop recording.

- **Transport controls.** Use these buttons to move the Playhead to where you want it.

- **Time display.** This readout displays details of the time, measures, chord, or project. To switch among the four available sets of information, either click the up and down arrows, or click the icon on the left and choose from the pop-up menu.

- **Master Volume slider.** Drag this slider to control the master volume of the song. (Use the controls in the Mixer column to set the volume level for an individual track.)

- **Volume meters.** These meters display the output level for the song as a whole.

- **Playhead Lock button.** Click this button to lock or unlock the Playhead in the Timeline from the Playhead in the Track Editor. By unlocking the two Playheads, you can work with a different part of the song in the Timeline than in the Track Editor, which can be handy.

- **Choose Timeline Grid Value button.** Click this button to change the note value shown in the Timeline grid. For many projects, it's best to use the default setting, Automatic, which lets GarageBand change the note value automatically as you zoom in and out.

From iMovie to GarageBand

What you need to do now is bring your movie into GarageBand so that you can compose the soundtrack for it. Follow these steps:

1. **In iMovie, share the movie to the Media Browser so that GarageBand can access it:**

   1. Click the movie project in the Project Library or open it in the Project window.

   2. Choose Share ⇨ Media Browser to open the Publish your project to the Media Browser dialog box.

   3. Select the check box for each size you want to publish. For example, select the Large check box.

   4. Click Publish.

Genius

You can also click and drag video clips from your Event Library directly into the Movie Track. This capability is sometimes useful, but GarageBand doesn't provide video-editing tools, so cuts between clips will be straight. Usually, you'll want to create your movie in iMovie and then import the finished video into GarageBand.

1. **In GarageBand, choose Track⇨Show Movie Track to display the Movie Track at the top of the tracks list.** You can also press ⌘+Option+B.

2. **Click the Media Browser button in the lower-right corner of the GarageBand window to display the Media Browser.**

3. **Click the Movies button at the top to display the Movies pane.**

4. **Click the movie and drag it to the Movie Track.** GarageBand converts the movie, creates thumbnails, and then displays the thumbnails and the Movie Sound track (see figure 7.22).

7.22 The Movie Track and Movie Sound track appear at the top of the GarageBand window.

You're now ready to get to work on the soundtrack. Press ⌘+S or choose File⇨Save to save your project with the movie in it. Unlike iMovie, GarageBand doesn't automatically save your changes, so it's a good idea to keep saving them regularly in case you have hardware, software, or power trouble.

Creating a score in GarageBand

The quickest way to create a score in GarageBand is to build it out of the prerecorded loops that GarageBand includes. You can also record your own live performances into GarageBand and edit them there. Either way, you'll need to set volume curves and mix the soundtrack to balance the sounds.

First, though, chances are you'll need to change the way the Movie Sound track plays so that you can hear what you're doing.

Setting the volume for the Movie Sound track

When you import your movie, GarageBand places its audio in the Movie Sound track, which appears below the Movie Track at the top of the GarageBand window.

GarageBand plays the Movie Sound track at normal volume at first, but you'll often need to change it. These are your three options:

- **Increase or decrease the volume.** Drag the volume slider in the Movie Sound track header to the right or to the left.

- **Mute the track.** Click the Mute button (the button with the speaker icon) in the Movie Sound track header so that it turns blue. Click it again when you need to unmute the sound.

- **Delete the track.** If you don't need the movie's sound (because you'll record a whole new sound track), click the track, and then choose Track⇨Delete Track or press ⌘+Delete.

Adding loops to a track

To create a soundtrack for your movie quickly, build it out of the audio loops that come with GarageBand. Most of the loops are sections of music designed to fit together, but others are sound effects.

Here's how to add a Software Instrument loop to a project:

1. **Open the Loop browser (see figure 7.23) by clicking the Loop Browser button in the lower-right corner of the window.** You can also press ⌘+L.

2. **Find the loop you want to add:**

   - Click the button for the type of instrument or sound you want. For example, click All Drums to see the list of drum loops.

   - To search by a keyword, type it in the search box and press Return. For example, type **modern** and press Return to see only the drum loops with "modern" in their name.

   - Double-click a loop to audition it.

3. **Click the loop and drag it to the track to which you want to add it.**

   - To add the loop to an existing track, drag the loop to that track. If the loop is the wrong type for the track (for example, a Software Instrument loop and a Real Instrument track), GarageBand warns you.

   - To create a new track for the loop, drag the loop to open space below the track list. GarageBand creates a new track for you.

   - Either way, GarageBand adds the loop as a *region*, a copy of the loop that you can adjust without changing the original version of the loop.

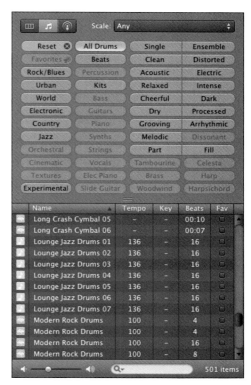

7.23 The Loop browser open in Musical Button view with the All Drums button selected.

4. **Play back the region and see how it sounds in the soundtrack.** Move the Playhead to where you want to start playback, and then click Play.

5. **Repeat or shorten the region if needed:**

   ● **Repeat the region.** To play the region more than once, position the mouse pointer over the upper part of the region's right border so that the pointer changes to a curling arrow. Drag the border to the right as far as you want the region to repeat. GarageBand shows a notch at the end of each full repetition (see figure 7.24).

   ● **Shorten a region.** To play only part of the region, position the mouse pointer over the lower part of the region's right border so that the pointer changes to a bracket with two arrows. Drag to the left to shorten the region (see figure 7.25).

7.24 Drag the upper part of a region's right border to the right to repeat the region. The notches at the top and bottom indicate complete repetitions of the loop.

7.25 Drag the lower part of a region's right border to the left to shorten the region.

Recording an instrument

GarageBand's wide selection of Software Instruments enables you to play everything from grand piano to bass and drums straight into your soundtrack using a physical keyboard. Alternatively, you can connect a guitar, bass, or miked instrument and record what you play in your soundtrack.

Here's how to record an instrument.

1. **Connect your instrument to your Mac in one of two ways:**

   ● **Software Instrument.** Connect a musical keyboard to your Mac via USB or MIDI.

   ● **Real Instrument.** Connect the instrument or mike to your Mac via an audio interface (for example, one of the USB audio interfaces available on the Apple Store).

2. **Click the + button in the lower-left corner of the GarageBand window to display the New Track dialog box (see figure 7.26).**

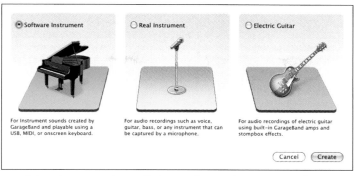

7.26 Select the appropriate radio button for your instrument in the New Track dialog box.

3. **Select the appropriate radio button:**

   - **Software Instrument.** Select this radio button if you're using a USB or MIDI keyboard.

   - **Real Instrument.** Select this radio button for a microphone or for any physical instrument except an electric guitar.

   - **Electric Guitar.** Select this radio button for an electric guitar. (This option gives you access to GarageBand's special guitar amps and effects.)

4. **Click Create.** GarageBand adds a new track, assigns it to the default instrument for that track type, and displays the Track Info pane.

5. **In the left column, click the instrument category you want — for example, Synth Leads for a Software Instrument.** GarageBand displays the list of available instruments (or kits, for drums) in the right column (see figure 7.27).

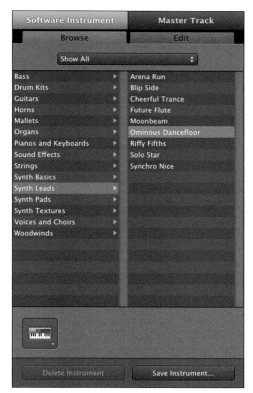

7.27 Choose the instrument category and the specific instrument for the track on the Browse tab of the Track Info pane.

6. **In the right column, click the instrument you want — for example, Ominous Dancefloor.** GarageBand applies the instrument.

7. **Test the instrument's sound by playing your keyboard.** If you don't like the sounds, you can choose another instrument by repeating Steps 4 and 5.

8. **If you want to change the icon for the instrument, click the instrument icon near the bottom of the Track Info pane, and then choose an icon on the pop-up panel.**

9. **Click the Track Info button if you've finished using the Track Info pane.**

10. **Make sure the dot on the Record button for the track is red to indicate that the track is set for recording.** If the dot is gray, click it to turn it red.

11. **Position the Playhead where you want to start playing.** For example, click the Go to Beginning button to move the Playhead to the beginning of the song.

12. **Click the Record button to start recording.** Alternatively, press R.

13. **Play your part on the keyboard (for a Software Instrument) or on the musical instrument (for a Real Instrument).**

14. **Click the Record button to stop recording, or click the Play button to stop both recording and playback.**

Muting and soloing tracks

When working on your soundtrack, you'll often need to focus on a single track or just a handful of tracks. You can do this by using GarageBand's Mute and Solo controls, which appear in the track header (see 7.28).

To mute a track so that you hear the other tracks without it, click the track's Mute button once to turn on muting. Click a second time to turn muting off again.

To solo a track so that you hear that track without the others, click the Solo button. Click the Solo button a second time to turn soloing off.

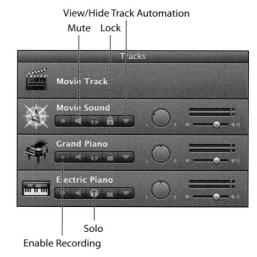

7.28 Use the buttons in the track header to mute and solo tracks so that you can hear exactly what you need to.

Creating a volume curve for a track

One of GarageBand's neatest tricks is letting you create a volume curve for each track. This means you can not only set the volume for a track overall, but you can also create a *volume curve* that changes the level automatically as the track plays.

By creating the right volume curve for each track, you can bring different parts of the audio to the foreground as needed throughout your soundtrack.

Here's how to create a custom volume curve for a track:

1. **Click and drag the Track Volume slider to set the relative volume of the track.**

   When you add the track, GarageBand sets the slider to 0 decibels (dB), which means the track's loudness is not increasing or decreasing.

   Drag the slider to the left to reduce the track's volume. Drag the slider to the right to increase the volume.

   GarageBand displays a tooltip show-ing the decibel measurement you're setting (as shown in figure 7.29).

2. **If the Automation track isn't dis-played, click the View/Hide Track Automation button on the track header to display it.** Figure 7.30 shows the Automation track with the Track Volume automation curve displayed and turned on.

7.29 Changing a track's volume using the Track Volume slider.

3. **In the Automation Parameters pop-up menu, choose Track Volume if it's not already selected.**

   The line along the Automation track shows the volume level. Unless you've set a vol-ume curve already, this line will be horizontal, maintaining a steady volume.

   You can increase the volume by dragging the first control point up or decrease it by dragging down. This first control point controls the overall volume of the track until you create a volume curve, so dragging it has the same effect as moving the Track Volume slider for the track.

4. **To create the volume curve, place control points on the volume line like this:**

   Set the song to cycle through the section you're working with so that you can hear the effects of the changes you make. Start playback.

- Click where you want to place a control point. Each control point appears as a blue dot for a Real Instrument track or a green dot for a Software Instrument track (see figure 7.30).

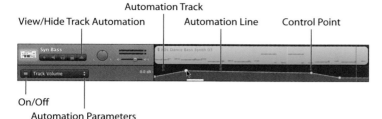

7.30 Dragging a control point to create a volume curve on an Automation track.

- Drag a control point up to increase the volume at that point, or drag it down to decrease the volume.

- To change when a control point alters the volume, drag the control point to the left or right along the volume curve.

- To get rid of a control point, drag it along to the next control point, which consumes it.

5. **When you finish setting the volume curve, click the View/Hide Track Automation button to hide the Automation track again.** If you're going to change panning (discussed next), you may want to leave the Automation track displayed.

Genius

You can also create a volume curve for the master track, the track that controls all the others. Choose Track ↔ Show Master Track to display the master track at the bottom of the track list, and then use the same techniques to create a suitable volume curve. For example, you may want to fade the master track in at the beginning and out at the end.

Setting the panning for a track

To control the left-right placement of the sound on a track, use the panning controls. These enable you to position different tracks where you want them around the panorama of the soundtrack, so that the tracks sound as though they're coming from different directions.

GarageBand automatically pans the Movie Sound track to the left to give you space in the middle and right of the track for adding music and sounds, so you'll normally want to pan your other tracks to these areas. If this panning doesn't suit you, drag the panning knob in the Movie Sound track header. Or mute or delete the Movie Sound track if you want to have the whole panorama for the tracks you add in GarageBand.

To set a track panning position for the track as a whole, click and drag the Track Pan knob downward to pan to the left or upward to pan to the right.

Genius

You can create a custom panning curve that moves the track to different pan positions at different points. For example, you can bring in a sound effect on the left and then move it across to the right. Click the View/Hide Track Automation button, choose Track Pan in the pop-up menu, and then create a custom curve using the same techniques as for the custom volume curve in the previous section.

Watching the movie preview

To watch your movie in its current state, click the movie picture at the right end of the Movie Track to display the Movie Preview window (see figure 7.31). Now drag the Playhead on the scrubbing bar to where you want to watch, and press Spacebar to start playback. Press Spacebar again to stop.

Creating chapter markers

GarageBand also enables you to add markers to your movie, breaking the Movie Track into marker regions that show you how long each section lasts. You can move marker regions or

7.31 Open the Movie Preview window and press spacebar to see how your movie's soundtrack is coming along. Drag the lower-right corner if you want to resize the window.

resize them using the same techniques you use for audio clips, or you can simply use the marker regions for navigation.

Here's the easiest way to add a marker:

1. **Position the Playhead where you want the marker region to start.** Either drag the Playhead or play through the movie to reach the right point, and then stop playback.

2. **Click the Add Marker button, press P, or choose Edit ⇨ Add Marker.** GarageBand adds a marker to the Track Editor (see figure 7.32).

7.32 Markers make your movie easier to navigate and let you add URLs the viewer can reach.

3. **Add artwork for the marker by dragging it from the Photos tab of the Media Browser to the marker's placeholder in the Artwork column in the editing area.** If you need to edit the photo, double-click it in the Artwork column to open it in the Artwork Editor, and then resize it and select the part you want as described earlier in this chapter.

Genius

You can also create a new region and add artwork to it by dragging a photo from the Photos tab of the Media Browser to the appropriate point on the Movie Track.

4. **Click in the marker's row in the Chapter Title column in the editing area, type the title, and then press Return to apply it.**

5. **If you want to add a URL to the marker, click in the URL Title column in the marker's row, and then type the text you want to display for the URL.** Then click in the URL column and type the URL itself. The URL title can be the same as the URL itself if you want, but often it's helpful to display a URL title that's shorter than the URL, more descriptive, or both.

Exporting your finished movie project

When you've finished creating the score for your movie project in GarageBand, export your final movie like this:

1. **Choose Share ⇨ Export Movie to Disk.** GarageBand displays the Export your movie to disk dialog box where you can choose the quality for your exported movie.

2. **In the Video Settings pop-up menu, choose the quality you want to create:**

   - For general use, choose Full Quality.

   - For a specific use, choose Email, Web, Web Streaming, iPod, or Apple TV.

   - If you want to hone the settings manually, choose Expert Setting. You'll get the chance to choose exactly the settings you want in a moment.

3. **Click Export.** GarageBand prepares the movie for export, and then displays the Export to Disk dialog box (for all Video Settings options except Expert Setting) or the Save exported file as dialog box (for Expert Setting).

4. **Type the name you want to give your movie, and choose the folder in which to store it.** GarageBand suggests the ~/Music/GarageBand folder (where ~ represents your home folder), but you'll probably want to change to one of your movie folders (for example, ~/Movies).

5. **If you chose Expert Setting, choose the details in the Save exported file as dialog box (see figure 7.33):**

   - In the Export pop-up menu, choose the format — for example, Movie to QuickTime Movie or Movie to MPEG-4. See Chapter 10 for details on the formats.

   - If the Options button is available, click it to open a dialog box for choosing further options.

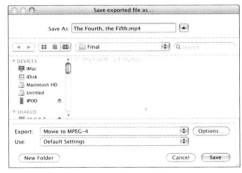

7.33 The Save exported file as dialog box enables you to choose from a wide range of formats for your movie file.

6. **Click Save.** GarageBand exports the movie file.

What's the Best Way to Manage My Video?

Some clips used in the project 'PF Project 1' are not on the hard disk 'PostFlop'.

Copy the events (1.1 GB)

Copy the clips (88 MB)

Move the events (1.1 GB)

Cancel

Modern Macs have huge hard drives, but vast video files can quickly eat through them. To manage video efficiently, you must first understand the smart way in which iMovie handles your video footage and movie projects. You can then sort your footage neatly into suitable Events, mark footage as favorites or rejects, and reclaim valuable space by getting rid of the footage you don't want to keep. To make video clips easier to find, you can give them keywords, no matter which Events they're in. To keep your projects together, you can consolidate a project's files on a single drive or even move a project to a different drive.

Understanding How iMovie Handles Your Video Footage

Stuffed with high-definition video and high-quality audio, video files can quickly chew up all the free space on even the largest hard disk. To make sure you're not the loser in video's war on terabytes, Apple has designed iMovie to handle video footage in the smartest way possible.

Here's what happens:

1. **Video footage goes into the library once — and once only.** When you import video from a camcorder, iMovie divides it up into clips. If the video comes from a tape, iMovie automatically creates the separate clips by using the timecode marked on each frame; when there's a gap in the timecode, iMovie starts a new clip. If the camera records onto memory such as memory cards or a hard disk, the camera stores the video clips in separate files anyway, and iMovie preserves those separate files when you import the video.

2. **iMovie stores each video clip in an Event.** Each video clip you import belongs to an *Event*, a storage container for sorting and manipulating your video footage. When you import video, you choose whether to assign it to an existing Event or a new Event that you name. After that, you can create new Events as needed, and move or copy a clip from one Event to another.

3. **iMovie treats your edits as a filter.** In most applications, when you make a change, you're actually changing the file you're working on. For example, if you open a document in Microsoft Word and delete parts of it, those parts are really gone (unless you're using revision marks). With iMovie, though, you're usually working with your video clips but not changing them — instead you're changing the way you look at them. It's as if Word were able to say "Okay, that first paragraph — take the first two words out, make the second sentence italic, and then delete the last line." But all the while, the paragraph's text was kept secure somewhere you couldn't touch it.

4. **iMovie saves changes automatically.** In most applications, you need to manually save any changes you want to keep; for example, if you change a text file in TextEdit, you must save the changes when you close the file, or else you'll lose them. But the way that iMovie handles video clips, movie projects, and edits tends to be confusing until you've worked with iMovie for a while. So iMovie automatically saves changes for you as you work. You can quit iMovie at any point, and it will save your latest changes without prompting you.

5. **Project files are really small.** When you create a file in most applications, whatever you put into that file is saved in that file. For example, if you put 500 pictures in a PowerPoint presentation, you end up with a huge presentation. But an iMovie project file is just a description of the files the project uses and the effects you apply to them — for example, "Take the clip called Sunrise Disaster, play the first five seconds and ten frames, and apply the Sepia video effect." The project file draws on the clips in the iMovie library, but it doesn't save them in the project file.

6. **You create new video files when you export a movie.** The point at which you actually create new video files is when you export a movie for use in another application. At this point, iMovie gives up on showing you what you want to see and creates a file that the other application can use. For example, when you export a movie to iTunes, iMovie creates QuickTime files for the sizes you specify (such as Medium and Large).

Genius iMovie protects your video clips from you changing them — all the while allowing you to play them back almost exactly as you want. Given the constraints of working with video on a computer, this is a really smart way to handle video footage. But it has several side-effects, as you'll see later in this chapter.

Sorting Your Footage among iMovie Events

As you've seen earlier in this book, the Event is the iMovie tool you use to separate your footage into different bins.

Every clip must belong to an Event. As soon as you bring a clip into your video library, you must assign it to an Event: You can't have a clip floating around freely in your library. You can move the clip to another Event afterward if you want, or you can copy it to another Event so that it is in two or more Events.

Creating a new Event

You can create a new Event three ways:

- **When you import video.** In whichever Import dialog box you're using (for example, the Import dialog box for importing from a tape camcorder), click the Create new Event option button. Type the name for the Event in the text box, and then click the Import button.

- **At any time in the Event Library.** Click the year inside which you want to create the new Event and choose File⇨New Event. iMovie creates a new Event, gives it a default name based on the current date, and displays an edit box around it. Type the name you want the Event to have, and then press Return to apply the name.

- **By splitting an existing Event.** See the discussion on splitting an Event a little later in this chapter.

Moving a clip from one Event to another

Creating a new Event, or choosing an existing Event when you import video, ensures that each clip is assigned to an Event. But to keep your Event Library organized, you'll often need to move a clip from one Event to another.

Here's how to move a clip from one Event to another:

1. **Option+click the clip to select all of it.** iMovie displays a yellow outline around the clip.

2. **Click and drag the clip to the Event in which you want to place it.** iMovie displays the Move Clip to New Event dialog box (see figure 8.1).

3. **Click OK.** iMovie moves the clip to the Event you chose.

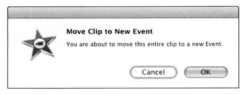

8.1 iMovie double-checks that you want to move the clip to another Event.

Merging iMovie Events

If you find that iMovie has split up clips that belong together into separate Events, you can easily merge the Events. Follow these steps:

1. **Click the Event whose name you want to lose and drag it on top of the Event whose name you want to keep.** iMovie displays the renaming sheet shown in figure 8.2.

8.2 You can merge two Events into a single Event to pool their clips.

2. **If necessary, type a new name for the merged Event.** If you simply want to use the name of the second Event you used, you can just accept iMovie's suggestion.

3. **Click OK.** iMovie merges the Events and puts the merged Event in the appropriate place in the Events list.

Splitting iMovie Events

Here's how to split an Event into two events:

1. **Click the Event in the Event Library to display its clips.**

2. **Ctrl+click or right-click the clip before which you want to split the Event, and then choose Split Event Before Clip from the shortcut menu.** iMovie creates a new Event containing the clip you clicked and those clips that follow it. iMovie gives the new Event the existing Event's name with 1 added to the end. For example, if the existing Event is named Tour, iMovie names the new Event Tour 1.

3. **Double-click the default name for the new clip, type the new name, and then press Return.**

Sorting and grouping Events

You can view your Events in the Event Library several ways. The default view — Last Import and iPhoto Videos at the top, followed by Events organized by year — works well for light use, but you may also want to view Events by month or day, or arrange the Events by the drives on which they're stored.

Viewing Events by month or day

If you want to see the Events listed by month in the Event Library, choose View ⇨ Group Events by Month. iMovie adds a separate category for each month that has footage; figure 8.3 shows an example. Choose the same command again if you want to hide the months again.

If you want to see Events broken out by day, choose View ⇨ Show Separate Days in Events. Give the same command again if you want to hide the days.

8.3 You can set iMovie to display the Event Library with Events grouped by month for easy navigation.

Viewing Events and folders by drives

If you want to see the Events and folders listed by the drives on which they're stored (see figure 8.4), click the Group Events by Disk button in the upper-right corner of the Event Library. Alternatively, open the View menu and click Group Events by Disk; iMovie places a check mark next to the menu item to indicate that this feature is switched on.

To return to the reverse date order, just click the Group Events by Disk button again. Alternatively, choose View⇨Group Events by Disk again; iMovie removes the check mark from the menu item.

8.4 Viewing Events by disk enables you to tell easily which drive an Event's clips are stored on.

Marking Video Footage

As you've seen earlier in this book, you can simply select the video footage you want from a clip and add it to a movie project without needing to rate your clips. But to save time in the long run, you'll often want to go through your clips, mark the sections you want to keep as favorites and the sections you want to get rid of as rejects, and leave the so-so footage in limbo.

Marking the clips in this way has two benefits. First, you can choose Favorites Only in the Show pop-up menu to restrict the Event browser to only your good footage. And second, you can delete the rejected footage to unclutter your video library and reclaim some disk space from it.

iMovie provides two ways to mark your favorites and rejects — the normal way (as described next) and the Advanced way (described after that).

Marking video as favorite or rejected

Once you've selected the footage you want, you can quickly mark it as a favorite. Similarly, you select footage you don't want to keep and mark it as a reject:

8.5 Use these toolbar buttons to quickly mark favorites and rejects.

- **Mark as a favorite.** Click the Mark Selection as Favorite button on the toolbar (see figure 8.5) or press F. iMovie puts a green bar across the top of the selected part of the clip.

- **Mark as rejected.** Click the Reject Selection button or press R. iMovie puts a red bar across the top of the selected part of the clip.

- **Remove the marking.** Click the Unmark Selection button or press U. iMovie removes the green bar or red bar.

After marking favorites and rejects, you can narrow down the clips displayed by clicking the Show pop-up menu and choosing Favorites Only, Favorites and Unmarked, or Rejected Only, as appropriate. When you want to see all the clips again, click the Show pop-up menu once more and choose All Clips from it.

Marking using the Advanced Tools

When you need to work fast on a project, you can display the Advanced Tools and use their swift means of marking favorites and rejects. Instead of selecting the footage you want and then clicking a button to tell iMovie whether it's a favorite or a reject, you activate a favorite-marking pointer or a reject-marking pointer, quickly mark the clips with it as if you were using a colored highlighter, and then deactivate it.

Genius

Whether the Advanced Tools method of marking suits you may depend on how steady your hand is and what type of footage you're working with.

First, turn on the Advanced Tools. Choose iMovie➪Preferences, click the General tab, select the Show Advanced Tools check box, and then click the Close button (the red button on the title bar) to close the Preferences window.

When you turn on the Advanced Tools, the behavior of the Mark as Favorite button, Unmark button, and Mark as Reject button changes. When you click one of these buttons, the mouse pointer takes on the symbol from the button, and becomes a tool for marking across a clip.

Using the Advanced Tools, you can mark up your footage like this:

161

1. **In the Event Library, click the Event you want to work with.**

2. **On the toolbar, click the marking button you want to use.** For example, click the Mark as Favorite button if you want to mark the footage you want to use (often the best way to start when rating your clips). iMovie adds the marking button's symbol to the mouse pointer — a green star for Mark as Favorite, a white star for Unmark, or a red cross for Mark as Reject.

3. **Move the mouse pointer over a clip, and then move the Playhead to where you want to start marking.**

4. **Click and drag with the mouse pointer to mark the footage you want.** Figure 8.6 shows the Mark as Favorite pointer marking a clip.

5. **Repeat Steps 3 and 4 for each clip you want to mark.** You can change from one Event in the Event Library to another without turning off the marking pointer.

6. **When you've finished marking the footage, click the marking button again to turn off marking.** Alternatively, click another marking button — for example, the Mark as Reject button — and mark some more footage.

8.6 Click and drag with an Advanced Tools pointer to quickly mark footage as a favorite, to unmark it, or to mark it as a reject.

Genius

When you've turned on Advanced Tools, the marker buttons look the same until you select some footage in the Event browser. When you do this, each of the buttons adds a + sign to indicate that it's *not* acting in its Advanced Tools mode — it's just acting normally.

Retrieving rejected footage

When you're working quickly, it takes only the blink of an eye to reject some footage by accident. If this happens, you can retrieve it easily like this:

1. **In the Event Library, click the Event that contains the rejected footage.**

2. **In the Show pop-up menu, choose Rejected Only.** iMovie restricts the display to the clips you've marked as rejected.

3. **Unmark each clip you want to keep:**

   • **Using Advanced Tools.** To unmark an entire clip, click the Unmark button, and then Option+click each clip in turn. To unmark a portion of a clip, click and drag across the part you want to unmark. When you've finished unmarking, click the Unmark button again to turn the tool off.

   • **Using regular tools.** To unmark an entire click clip, select all the clips, and then click the Unmark button. To unmark a portion of a clip, select the part you want to unmark, and then click the Unmark button.

Deleting rejected footage from an Event

When you've marked all the unwanted footage in an Event as rejected, you can tell iMovie to get rid of it.

Caution Before you delete the rejected footage from an Event, make sure that any movie project that uses clips from the Event has enough spare frames at the ends of clips for you to adjust transitions. You may sometimes need to add frames to a clip so that you can lengthen a transition without obscuring essential frames. If you've deleted the extra frames, you can't lengthen a transition.

To delete the rejected footage from an Event, follow these steps:

1. **In the Event Library, click the Event from which you want to remove the footage.** You can select several Events if necessary. For example, select a month (or even a year) to work with all the Events it contains.

2. **Click on the Show pop-up menu and choose Rejected Only to make iMovie display only the rejected clips (see figure 8.7).**

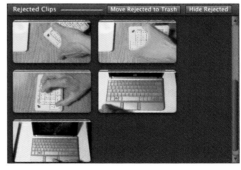

8.7 Review your rejected clips before clicking the Move Rejected to Trash button.

3. **Review the clips to make sure there's nothing valuable.** Depending on how many clips are involved, you may want to play them all or simply glance at the filmstrips and skim any clips you don't recognize.

4. **Click the Move Rejected to Trash button in the Event browser or choose File ⇨ Move Rejected Clips to Trash.** iMovie displays the Move Rejected Clips to Trash dialog to make sure you understand what's happening.

5. **Click the Move to Trash button to move the clips to the Trash.** iMovie changes the selection in the Show pop-up menu to Favorites and Unmarked.

6. **When you're ready to empty the Trash, click the Trash icon on the Dock, and then click the Empty Trash button.**

Running Space Saver to Reclaim Drive Space

If you deleted your rejected footage (as described earlier in the chapter), but you need to free up more space, try the Space Saver feature. Space Saver provides a way to grab all the frames that you haven't used or made into favorites — and then delete them.

Here's how to run Space Saver:

1. **Select the Event from which you want to delete all unused video.** You can select several Events if you want — click the first Event, and then ⌘+click each of the others.

2. **Choose File ⇨ Space Saver.** iMovie displays the Space Saver dialog box (see figure 8.8).

3. **Make sure that only the check boxes you need are selected:**

   • **Not added to any project.** Select this check box if you want iMovie to get rid of any clips that you haven't made part of any project.

8.8 Use Space Saver to reclaim your Mac's disk space by disposing of clips you haven't used from an Event.

   • **Not marked as Favorite.** Select this check box if you want iMovie to dispose of any clips you haven't marked as favorites.

   • **Not marked with a keyword.** Select this check box if you want iMovie to throw out any clips you haven't marked with one or more keywords.

4. **Click Reject and Review.** iMovie closes the dialog box and switches the Show pop-up menu to Rejected Only, marking the clips with the red bar across the top that means they're rejected (see figure 8.9).

5. **Skim or play the clips to make sure there's nothing you want to keep.** This step is optional, but it's usually a good idea to make sure Space Saver hasn't scooped up any vital clips.

6. **Click the Move Rejected to Trash button at the right end of the Rejected Clips bar.** iMovie displays the Move Rejected Clips to Trash dialog box (see figure 8.10) to confirm the decision.

7. **Click the Move to Trash button to move the clips to the Trash.** iMovie changes the selection in the Show pop-up menu to Favorites and Unmarked.

8. **When you're ready to empty the Trash, click the Trash icon on the Dock, and then click the Empty Trash button.**

8.9 Normally, you'll want to review your rejected clips before moving them to the Trash.

8.10 iMovie double-checks that you want to get rid of the rejected clips.

If you've emptied the Trash, your files are gone. The only way to recover them is to use a third-party application such as VirtualLab Mac OS X (www.binarybiz.com/vlab/mac.html). This application has a free trial that enables you to see files you'll be able to recover before you pay to actually recover them.

Assigning Keywords to Video

To make your video clips easier to sort and to find, you can add keywords to them. A *keyword* is simply a tag that you add to footage to make it easier to access. iMovie includes a handful of built-in keywords, but you can edit them as needed and also create new keywords of your own.

Note

Before you can assign keywords to clips, you must display iMovie's Advanced Tools. Choose iMovie ⇨ Preferences, click the General tab, select the Show Advanced Tools check box, and then click the Close button (the red button on the title bar) to close the Preferences window.

Before you apply keywords to your clips, spend a few minutes customizing the list of keywords in the Keywords dialog box. Here's what to do:

1. **Option+click a clip to select it.**

2. **Press K or click the View Keywords for Selection button — the button with the key icon — that appears in the middle of the toolbar.** iMovie displays the Keywords dialog box. This dialog box has two panes, the Auto-Apply pane and the Inspector pane.

3. **Change the list of keywords to suit your needs.** You can perform all these actions in the Auto-Apply pane, but you can also perform most of them in the Inspector pane:

    • **To change an existing keyword, double-click it.** Type the replacement word in the edit box (see figure 8.11), and then press Return.

    • **To remove a keyword, click it, and then click Remove.** This works only in the Auto-Apply pane.

    • **To add a keyword in the Auto-Apply pane, type it in the box in the lower-left corner of the dialog box, and then click Add.** In the Inspector pane, type the word in the same box, but click Add to Clip to add it to the selected clip as well as to the list of keywords.

    • **To rearrange the list of keywords, drag them up and down the list.** iMovie automatically assigns the numbers 1 to 9 to the first nine keywords so that you can apply them quickly.

8.11 You can easily edit the list of keywords to match your needs.

Applying keywords manually

When you've set up your list of keywords, you can apply them to your clips either manually (as described here) or using the Auto-Apply feature (as described next).

Here's how to apply keywords manually:

1. **Press K or click the View Keywords for Selection button on the toolbar to display the Keywords dialog box.**

2. **If the Auto-Apply pane is displayed, click the Inspector button to display the Inspector pane.**

3. **In the Event browser, select the clip or part of a clip to which you want to apply the keywords.** Use normal selection techniques — for example:

   - Click a clip to select iMovie's preset amount, such as 4 seconds. Click and drag the selection handles to adjust the selection.

   - Option+click a clip to select all of it.

   - Click and drag through a clip to select just part of it.

4. **Select the check box for each keyword you want to apply.** You can also press the 1 through 9 keys to apply the keywords currently assigned those numbers.

5. **Repeat Steps 3 and 4 as needed to add keywords to your clips, and then press K or click the Close button to close the Keywords dialog box.**

Using the Auto-Apply feature

To apply keywords to video even more quickly, use the Auto-Apply feature. This feature enables you to choose a keyword, or group of keywords, and then apply it, or them, to the footage you choose.

Here's how to use Auto-Apply:

1. **Click the View Keywords for Selection button on the toolbar to display the Keywords dialog box.**

2. **Click the Auto-Apply button at the top to display the Auto-Apply pane (see figure 8.12).** This pane contains the same list of keywords as the Inspector tab — it just gives you a different way to apply them.

3. **Select the check box for each keyword you want to apply, either by clicking or by pressing the appropriate number key.** You can also add or remove keywords, just as you can in the Inspector pane.

4. **Drag across each section in the filmstrip that you want to give the keywords.** As you drag, iMovie displays an orange key icon on the mouse pointer to indicate that you're applying keywords (see figure 8.13).

5. **When you release the mouse button, iMovie flashes a balloon showing the keywords you've applied (see figure 8.14).** iMovie then shrinks the balloon till it disappears in the blue bar across the top of the selected footage.

8.12 Use the Auto-Apply pane of the Keywords window to instantly tag the footage you select.

8.13 The orange key icon on the mouse pointer indicates that you're applying keywords to the section you select.

8.14 iMovie briefly displays a balloon showing the keywords you've just applied.

Note To apply the keywords to a whole filmstrip, Option+click it. To cancel applying keywords while you're dragging, press Esc. To remove keywords after you've applied them, press ⌘+Z or choose Edit ⇨ Undo Apply Keywords.

6. **Keep marking footage with keywords as needed.** iMovie keeps displaying the orange key icon on the mouse pointer, so you can just keep on selecting footage. Change the selection of keywords when you need to.

7. **Close the Keywords dialog box.** Press K or Esc, click the View Keywords for Selection button on the toolbar, or click the Close button on the dialog box.

Filtering clips according to keywords

After you've applied keywords to your clips, you can use the keywords to filter the clips so that you see only the clips with the keywords you choose. This is an easy way of viewing only the clips you're interested in.

To filter clips by keywords, follow these steps:

1. **In the Event Library, select the event you want to work with.** You can also select a folder of Events to collect clips from all the Events it contains.

2. **Click the Keyword Filtering button to display the Keyword Filter panel (see figure 8.15).** The panel appears to the left of the Event browser; if the Event Library is displayed, the Keyword Filter panel appears between the Event Library and the Event browser.

3. **Click the green (right-hand) side of a keyword's button to display clips marked with that keyword.** iMovie illuminates the green button to show that you're using that keyword, and displays matching clips in the Event browser.

4. **Click the red (left-hand) side of a keyword's button to exclude clips marked with that keyword.** iMovie illuminates the red button to show that you're excluding that keyword, and removes clips tagged with that keyword from display in the Event browser.

5. **If you need to turn one of the red or green buttons off, click it again.**

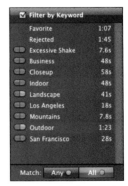

8.15 Use the Keyword Filter panel to display only the clips that match the keywords of your choice.

169

6. **In the Match area at the bottom, click the Any button if you want to see clips that have any of the keywords you've selected.** Click the All button if you want only clips that have all the keywords.

7. **Work with the clips you've found.** For example, select footage to add to your movie project.

8. **When you've finished using the Keyword Filter panel, click the Keyword Filtering button to close the panel again.**

Consolidating All of a Project's Files on the Same Drive

If you run iMovie with its default settings, it stores both your video clips and your movie projects on your Mac's hard drive. In most cases, this is the best place for them, as it ensures they're always present and correct when you're at your Mac. And if you run iTunes with its default settings, your song files will also be on your Mac's hard drive, enabling you to use them easily in iMovie projects.

But if you work extensively with video, chances are you'll run out of drive space sooner or later. At this point, you may need to store files on a different drive. Or you may have so many songs that you keep them on a separate hard drive anyway.

When a project uses files stored on different drives, things can get confused, especially when you need to move a project to a different drive (see the next section). To avoid problems, iMovie provides a command for "consolidating" all of a project's files — in other words, putting them all on the same drive.

Here's how to consolidate all of a project's files on the same drive:

1. **Click the project in the Project Library.** If the project is open in the Project window, it's already selected, so you're good to go.

2. **Choose File ⇨ Consolidate Media.** iMovie displays the Consolidate Media dialog box (see figure 8.16).

8.16 When consolidating a project, you can copy the Events, copy the clips, or move the Events.

If the Consolidate Media command on the File menu is grayed out and unavailable, the project doesn't use any files stored on another drive, so you can't consolidate it.

3. **Click the button for the type of consolidation you want to perform:**

   • **Copy the Events.** Click this button to make iMovie copy every clip in every Event that the project uses to the hard drive on which the project is stored. Use this option when you need to be able to work further on the project from the other drive but don't want to remove the clips from their current drive (because other projects need them).

   • **Copy the clips.** Click this button to copy only the actual clips the project uses to the hard drive on which the project is stored. Use this option when you've added all the clips the project needs.

   • **Move the Events.** Click this button to make iMovie move every clip in every Event the project uses to the hard drive on which the project is stored. Use this option when you want to be able to work further on the project from the other drive and no longer need any of the clips for other projects on the current drive.

iMovie displays a progress readout as it copies or moves the files. If the project contains many gigabytes of data, it will take several minutes to copy.

Moving a Project to Another Drive

Sometimes you may need to move a movie project to another hard drive, either so that you can take it to another Mac and work on it there or simply to store it safely while freeing up space on your Mac's hard drive. Or you may want to copy a project to another hard disk while leaving it on your Mac's hard drive.

With iMovie, you can both move and copy projects as long as you use a FireWire or USB 2.0 drive (you can't use a DVD or a network drive). You can move or copy either just a project file — a project without the media files it uses — or a project and its Events, which includes all the video clips and other media files.

Connect this drive to your Mac as usual, and it will appear as an icon at the bottom of the Project Library. You can then move or copy the project to the drive like this:

● **Move the project and its Events.** In the Project Library, ⌘+click the project and drag it to the external drive. iMovie displays the Move Project dialog box (see figure 8.17). Click the Move project and events button.

● **Move only the project file.** In the Project Library, ⌘+click the project and drag it to the external drive. In the Move Project dialog box, click the Move project button.

● **Copy the project and its Events.** In the Project Library, click the project and drag it to the external drive. iMovie displays the Copy Project dialog box (see figure 8.18). Click the Copy project and events button.

● **Copy only the project file.** In the Project Library, click the project and drag it to the external drive. In the Copy Project dialog box, click the Copy project button.

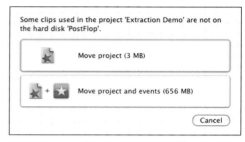

Some clips used in the project 'Extraction Demo' are not on the hard disk 'PostFlop'.

Move project (3 MB)

Move project and events (656 MB)

Cancel

8.17 When moving a project, you will normally want to move its Events as well.

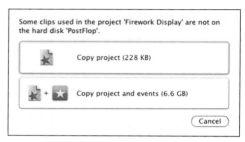

Some clips used in the project 'Firework Display' are not on the hard disk 'PostFlop'.

Copy project (228 KB)

Copy project and events (6.6 GB)

Cancel

8.18 When copying a project to an external hard drive, include its Events unless they are already stored on that drive.

Caution

Use the Move project or Copy project command only when you will edit the project on another Mac connected to the hard disk that contains the project's video and media files. For example, if the video and media are already on an external hard disk, use the Move project command to move the project's details to that disk as well. You can then move the disk to another Mac and edit the project.

Whichever option you choose, iMovie shows a progress readout of what it's doing (see figure 8.19. As you'd imagine, moving or copying a project along with several gigabytes of events will take much longer than copying only the project file, which is minute by comparison.

Moving files to PostFlop
clip-2008-08-18 15:32:52.dv

Cancel

Time remaining: less than a minute

8.19 Moving or copying a project with its files takes several minutes, depending on how big the files are.

Keeping Your Project Library Organized

If you create stacks of movie projects, the Project Library can get crowded. To ease the congestion, you can use folders within the Project Library to organize your movie projects.

Here's how to work with folders:

- **Create a folder.** Ctrl+click or right-click in the Project Library window, choose New Folder from the shortcut menu, type the name in the New Folder dialog box (see figure 8.20), and then press Return.

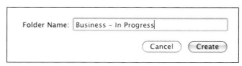

8.20 Create folders to organize your movie projects in the Project Library.

- **Create a subfolder.** Ctrl+click or right-click the existing folder in which you want to create the subfolder, and then create the folder as described previously.

- **Create a project within a folder.** Click the folder, and then create the new project (for example, click the New Project button or press ⌘+N).

- **Move a project to a folder.** Click the project and drag it to the folder. iMovie highlights the folder in which the project will land (see figure 8.21).

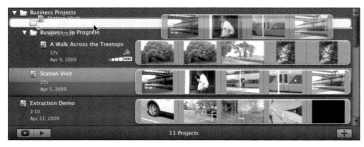

8.21 Click a project and drag it to the folder you want to keep it.

- **Move a folder to within another folder.** Click the folder and drag it to the folder in which you want to put it.

- **Delete a folder.** Ctrl+click or right-click the folder and choose Move Folder to Trash from the shortcut menu. Alternatively, click the folder and choose File ⇨ Move Folder to Trash or press ⌘+Backspace.

- **Expand and collapse folders.** Click the disclosure triangle to the left of a folder to expand it or collapse it.

How Can I Use Still Photos in My Movies?

Most of the time you'll probably want to use video clips in your movies, but iMovie makes it easy to add photos as well — either from iPhoto or from your Mac's file system. Not only can you change the length of time a photo plays back in your movie, but you can also pan and zoom over it to add movement and interest, or use an image as an overlay for video. Finally, you can snap still frames from your movies for use in other projects.

Understanding the iPhoto Workflow

You can make your images look great in iPhoto and then add them to your movie projects in iMovie, but first, take a quick look at the iPhoto workflow. Here's how it goes:

1. **You import photos from your digital camera into iPhoto.**

2. **You use iPhoto to sort the images, rate them, and improve them.**

3. **iPhoto adds the images to the iLife Media Browser.** The Media Browser is the tool that makes the photos available to iMovie, iWeb, and iDVD.

4. **In iMovie, you open the Photos browser pane, choose the photo you want, and then drag it to the Project window to add it to your movie project.**

Exploring the iPhoto Interface

Because you're familiar with the iMovie interface, you'll find iPhoto a snap to use. Like iMovie, iPhoto hides plenty of power behind a deceptively simple interface — so I'll start by going over what's what in iPhoto.

Launch iPhoto by clicking the iPhoto icon on the Dock or (if it doesn't appear there) double-clicking the iPhoto icon in the Applications folder. The easiest way to open the Applications folder is to click the desktop and choose Go ➪ Applications or press ⌘+Shift+A. Once you've launched iPhoto, Ctrl+click or right-click the Dock icon and choose Keep in Dock if you want to keep the icon there.

Figure 9.1 shows the main iPhoto window with the key elements labeled. When you're working in iPhoto, you'll spend most of your time in the main window, but you can also open a photo for editing in full screen so that you can see as much of a photo as possible.

Source list

The Source list pane on the left of the main iPhoto window shows the different sources of photos available to you:

- **Your iPhoto library.** iPhoto puts all your photos into the library, and the Library category in the Source list gives you four different views:
  - **Events.** Like iMovie with its video clips, iPhoto uses Events as the main means of dividing your photos into different groups. A photo can belong to only one Event, but you can move a photo from one Event to another as needed. iPhoto can automatically create Events for you when you import photos, but you can also create Events manually if you prefer.

Source list

Information pane

Viewing area

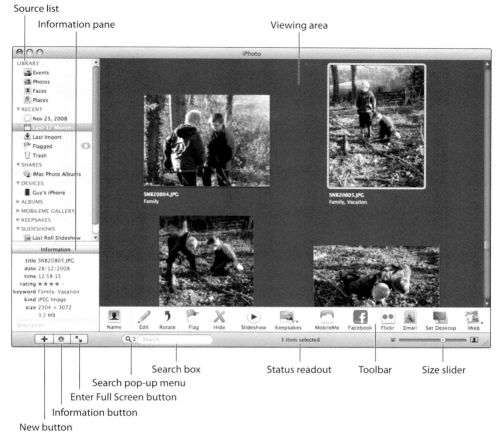

Search box

Search pop-up menu

Enter Full Screen button

Information button

New button

Status readout

Toolbar

Size slider

9.1 The main iPhoto window.

Photos. The Photos view shows you all the photos in the library. This view is useful when you lose a photo, but normally it shows you too many photos to handle sensibly at once.

Faces. The Faces view enables you to view the photos you've assigned to a named face. Once you teach iPhoto the name for a face (for example, a family member), iPhoto uses its face-recognition technology to show you all the other photographs in which a matching face appears. Faces is over-ambitious and tends to find false positives, so you need to approve every match to avoid getting surprises.

Places. The Places view enables you to sort your photos by their geographical location — either from the coordinates recorded by a camera that has GPS built in or from the information that you add to the photo manually.

- **Recent items.** The Recent category in the Source list gives you access to items you've worked with recently. The most important items here are as follows:

  - **Last 12 Months.** This item contains all the photos you've added in the last 12 months.

Genius

The Last 12 Months item can be a great way to find your recent photos — but you may find it contains far too many. If so, choose iMovie ➪ Preferences, click the General button, and change the *number* setting on the "Show last *number* months album" line. For example, make it Show last 2 months album if you want to see only the last two months.

  - **Last Import.** This item contains the last set of photos you imported from your digital camera or by dragging in graphics files.

  - **Flagged.** This item contains all the photos on which you've set a flag, a marker indicating that you want to be able to find the photo easily. Flagging photos is a great way of keeping tabs on the photos you're working with, no matter which Event they're stored in.

- **iPhoto libraries other people are sharing on your network.** Just as you can share your own music and browse other people's music in iTunes, you can browse other people's shared photos and share your own photos with them in iPhoto.

- **Any connected devices.** Your digital camera or a memory card containing photos appears in the Devices category. From here, you can import the photos into iPhoto.

- **Items you've created and published.** In iPhoto, you can create albums, slide shows, and keepsakes (such as photo books), and can publish photo albums to your MobileMe Gallery, to the Facebook social-networking site, or to the Flickr photo-sharing Web site.

Information pane

The Information pane in the lower-left corner of the iPhoto window shows information about the photo, photos, or other item you've selected.

You can show or hide the Information pane by clicking the Information button (the *i* button) in the lower-left corner of the window.

Toolbar

The toolbar across the bottom of the iPhoto window contains buttons for manipulating the photo or photos you've selected.

Viewing area

The viewing area — the main area of the iPhoto window — is where you view your photos, either as small thumbnail versions or large, taking up the whole area. Drag the Size slider to change the size of the thumbnails. From here, you can open a photo for viewing or editing.

Importing Photos into iPhoto

Your first step is to import photos to build your library. You can import them from a digital camera, a memory card, a folder, or even an e-mail message.

Importing photos from your digital camera

Here's how to import photos from your digital camera:

1. **Connect the digital camera to your Mac using the camera's USB cable.**

Genius

If your Mac doesn't recognize your digital camera, and the camera stores its photos on a memory card, remove the memory card from the camera and insert it in a memory card reader connected to your Mac. Most digital cameras use standard storage formats that Mac OS X can recognize easily when they're connected as a drive like this.

2. **Turn the camera on.** This should make Mac OS X detect the camera. When it does, it launches or activates iPhoto and prompts you to import the photos on the camera (see figure 9.2).

3. **Type a descriptive name for the Event in the Event Name text box.**

4. **If you want, type a generic description for the photos in the Description text box.** You can give each photo its own description later, but often it's good to have a basic description that you can then adapt for each photo.

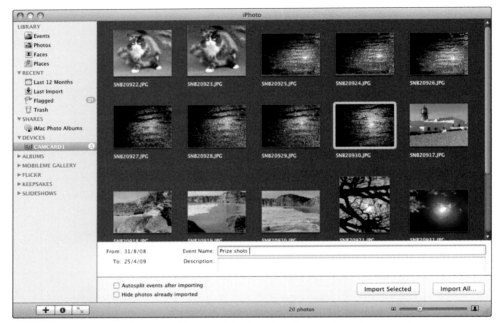

9.2 Mac OS X automatically opens iPhoto and displays thumbnails of the photos on the camera or storage card you've connected.

5. **If you want iPhoto to split the photos into different Events by date and time, select the Autosplit events after importing check box.**

Genius

When you're importing photos, iPhoto uses the Event length set in the Events pane of the iPhoto Preferences window: One event per day, One event per week, Two-hour gaps, or Eight-hour gaps. To set your preference, choose iPhoto ⇨ Preferences, click the Events button, click on the Autosplit into Events pop-up menu, and then choose your setting.

6. **If the camera or memory card contains photos you've imported before, select the Hide photos already imported check box to make iPhoto hide these photos so you don't try to import them again.** Hiding the photos you've already imported also enables iPhoto to show you the new photos on the camera or memory card more quickly.

7. **Choose which photos you want to import:**

   ● To import all the photos shown, click Import All.

To import only some of the photos, select them by dragging across a range or by clicking the first photo and then holding down ⌘ while you click each of the other photos. Then click Import Selected.

If iMovie displays the Duplicate Photo dialog box (see figure 9.3) to ask if you want to import a photo you've imported before, decide what to do. Select the Apply to all duplicates check box if you want to make the same choice for all photos you've imported before, and then click the Don't Import button or the Import button, as appropriate.

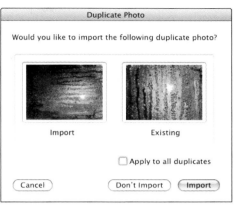

8. **iPhoto imports the photos you chose, and then prompts you to delete the photos from the camera or memory card (see figure 9.4).**

9. **Click the Eject button next to the camera's or memory card's icon in the Source list to eject it.** When iPhoto removes the camera or memory card from the Source list, you can safely unplug it.

9.3 iPhoto makes certain you know you're importing a duplicate photo. In this example, the version that's already in the library has been rotated and cropped.

9.4 Choose whether to have iPhoto delete or keep the photos from the camera or memory card.

Importing photos from a folder or disc

If your photos are in a folder or on a CD or DVD rather than on a camera or a memory card, you can bring them into your library using the Import command.

1. **Choose File ➪ Import to Library or press ⌘+Shift+I to open the Import Photos dialog box.**

2. **Select the photos you want to import.** You can import either an entire folder or one or more photos from within a folder.

3. **Click Import.**

Importing photos from the Finder or e-mail

When the photo you want to import is in a folder, you can just select it and drag it to the viewing area in iPhoto to add the photo or photos to your library.

If you receive a photo in the body of an e-mail message, you can drag the photo from your e-mail application (such as Mail or Entourage) to the viewing area in iPhoto.

If you receive a photo as an attachment in Mail, click and hold down the Save button on the attachment line, and then choose Add to iPhoto from the menu that appears. In other e-mail applications, you may need to save the attached photo to a folder, and then drag the photo from a Finder window to the viewing area in iPhoto.

Editing Photos in iPhoto

Once you've brought your photos into iPhoto, you can use its powerful tools to edit and improve them. This section shows the editing maneuvers you'll use most of the time.

To open a photo for editing, click it in the viewing area, and then click the Edit button on the toolbar. iPhoto displays editing buttons on the toolbar in place of the regular buttons (see figure 9.5).

Rotating photos

If you've turned your camera vertically to take a photo, you'll need to rotate the photo after importing it into iPhoto.

To rotate a photo, click the Rotate button on the toolbar. The Rotate button shows the direction set in iPhoto's General preferences: clockwise or counterclockwise. To rotate the photo in the opposite direction, Option+click the Rotate button.

Genius

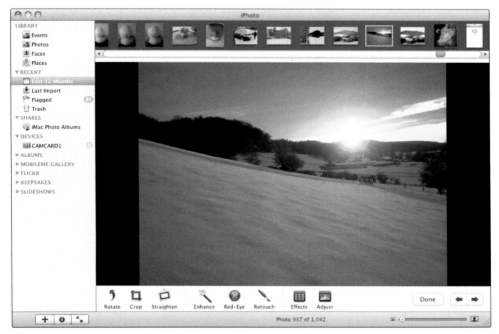

9.5 Click the Edit button on the toolbar to open a photo for editing. iPhoto displays the editing buttons, as shown here.

Straightening photos

After you've fixed the rotation, you can apply any straightening needed. To straighten a photo, click the Straighten button, and then drag the slider to the left or right (see figure 9.6). Use the gridlines that iPhoto displays to align horizontal or vertical features in the photo. Click the X button when you want to hide the slider.

Cropping photos

To give your photos maximum impact and make them fit in your movies, you'll often need to crop them. iPhoto enables you to crop either to a specific size or aspect ratio — for example, so that a photo is the right aspect ratio for a wide-screen movie — or to whatever custom dimensions the photo's subject needs.

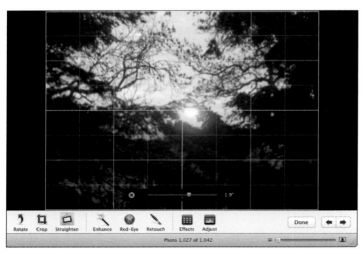

9.6 iPhoto enables you to quickly straighten a photo taken with the camera off the horizontal.

Here's how to crop a photo:

1. **Open the photo for editing.**

2. **Click the Crop button on the toolbar.** iPhoto displays the cropping tools, as shown in figure 9.7.

9.7 iPhoto enables you to quickly crop a photo to exclude parts you don't want and emphasize those you do want.

3. **If you want to constrain the crop area to a particular size or aspect ratio, open the Constrain pop-up menu and choose it.** For example, choose the size marked 16 x 9 (HD) to constrain the crop area to the 16:9 aspect ratio.

4. **Set the size of the crop area.** Drag one of the corner handles to change the cropping area in two dimensions, or drag an edge of the crop area to change the area in only one dimension (if you're not using a constraint). To temporarily override the constraint without turning it off, Shift+drag a corner handle or an edge. iPhoto displays a grid across the photo to help you judge the cropping (see figure 9.8).

9.8 iMovie displays a grid to help you judge the composition of the cropped area.

5. **Reposition the crop area as needed by clicking in it and dragging it to where you want it.** Again, iPhoto displays the grid as you click and drag.

6. **Click Apply to apply the cropping to the photo.**

7. **If you've finished editing the photo, click Done.** Otherwise, leave the photo open for further editing.

Adjusting colors, highlights, and shadows

Like iMovie, iPhoto provides a full set of tools for adjusting colors, highlights, and shadows. You can make a quick change with the Enhance tool, adjust colors manually in the Adjust dialog box, and change the white point of a photo to remove an unwanted color cast.

Giving a photo a quick boost with the Enhance tool

When you need to improve a photo quickly, try clicking the Enhance button on the toolbar. The Enhance tool makes iPhoto automatically adjust the exposure, contrast, and saturation of the photo, and attempt to fix any problems with the white balance and the distribution of black and white tones.

Figure 9.9 shows a photo that needs drastic changes. The subject (a window in a ruined church) has visual appeal, but the backlighting has confused the iPhone's sensor, and the image is severely underexposed. As a result, most of the picture is a dark, muddy mess.

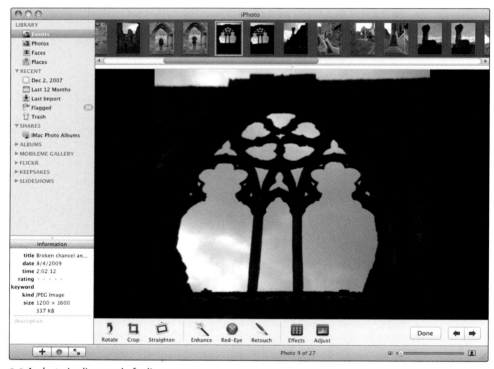

9.9 A photo in dire need of adjustment

See what effect clicking the Enhance button produces, and then decide what to do:

- **If you like the effect, keep it.**

- **If the effect is an improvement but not enough, click the Enhance button again.**
  Alternatively, open the Adjust dialog box and work on the colors manually, as discussed next.

- **If you don't like the effect, undo it.** Press ⌘+Z or choose Edit ➪ Undo Enhance Photo to restore the photo to how it was before.

Figure 9.10 shows the result of clicking the Enhance button for the sample photo. There's some improvement — in particular, you can now see some of the stonework at the sides of the picture. But the photo can be better, so it gets the ⌘+Z key press.

Opening the Adjust dialog box

To change the colors, highlights, and shadows in a photo manually, work in the Adjust dialog box. Click the Adjust button on the toolbar to open the Adjust dialog box (see figure 9.11), and then use the controls to change the color balance.

If you've worked with iMovie's color adjustments (see Chapter 5 for details), you'll see close similarities in the controls in the Adjust dialog box. But even if you haven't adjusted colors in iMovie, you'll find the Adjust dialog box easy to use.

At the top of the Adjust dialog box is the *histogram*, a graphical diagram that shows how the colors in the selected photo are distributed between pure black (at the left end, 0 percent) and pure white (at the right end, 100 percent).

9.10 The same photo after clicking the Enhance button once.

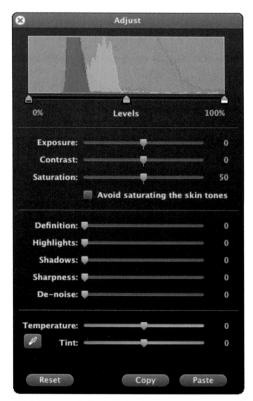

9.11 iPhoto's Adjust dialog box contains some of the same color adjustments as iMovie's Video pane in the Inspector dialog box.

187

Using the Eyedropper to remove unwanted color casts

First, if the color balance of the photo is wrong, correct it using the Eyedropper tool.

You'll often get the wrong color temperature in your photos because of the lighting conditions under which you've shot them. For example, sunlight tends to give a warm, almost golden color temperature, while fluorescent lights give a much cooler, blue-tinged color temperature.

To help you get the white balance right, many digital cameras include white-balance controls. These can make a huge difference, but it's all too easy to forget to change the white balance the next time you pick up the camera in a hurry.

If the areas of the photo that should be pure white appear a tinged white, use the Eyedropper tool to remove it like this:

1. **In the Adjust dialog box, click the Eyedropper tool — the button to the left of the Tint slider at the bottom.** iPhoto changes the mouse pointer to a crosshair cursor and displays a message ban telling you to pick a *neutral grey* or white point in the photo. "Neutral grey" means a grey that's not suffering from the color cast.

2. **Click a white point or grey point in the photo.**

   - Zoom in on the photo if that helps you find the color you need.

   - White is usually easier to judge than grey — provided your photo contains some white.

   - When you click, iPhoto moves the Temperature slider and the Tint slider to reflect the color you chose. You'll see the whole photo change with the new settings, and the histogram at the top of the Adjust dialog box alters to show the photo's new color balance.

   - Click again if you need to. Often, you'll need to click various different white or off-white spots before you find a suitable color balance.

If you can't find a suitable color point in the photo, click Reset to reset the photo to its previous white balance. You'll lose any other changes you've made in the Adjust dialog box — that's why you're changing the white point first.

3. **If you need to tweak the color balance more, click and drag the Temperature slider or the Tint slider.**

   You'll see the peaks in the histogram change positions as you drag to match the color change in the photo.

Genius

The Temperature slider changes the color temperature — the feeling the color gives. The left end gives a cool blue effect, and the right end gives a warm golden effect. The Tint slider changes the amount of green and red tones in the photo. Drag to the left to add red and reduce the green; drag to the right to reduce the red and add green.

Normally, you'll need to make only very small adjustments on these sliders when correcting the white balance.

4. **When you've finished correcting the white balance, click the Eyedropper tool again or the Close button on the message bar to turn off the Eyedropper.**

Changing the exposure

If a photo is underexposed (too dark overall) or overexposed (too light overall), click and drag the Exposure slider in the Adjust dialog box. The scale goes from 0 percent to 100 percent, but generally you'll need to make only small changes to improve the photo's look considerably.

Figure 9.12 shows the result of increasing the exposure for the sample photo. This has brightened the picture a bit more than the Enhance tool did, enabling you to see more of the walls. A side-effect is that all detail is lost from the sky — at least, for the moment.

9.12 After increasing the exposure, the sample photo is noticeably brighter.

Changing the black and white tones and gray levels

After you correct any exposure problems in the photo, see if you need to change the black and white tones and gray levels. Follow these steps in the Adjust dialog box:

1. **If the data in the histogram doesn't reach all the way to the left side, try adding black tones to the photo.** Click the black slider and drag it to the right, toward where the histogram's data starts.

2. **If the data in the histogram doesn't reach all the way to the white side, try adding white tones to the photo.** Click the white slider and drag it to the left, toward where the histogram's data starts. Figure 9.13 shows the sample photo after adding white tones.

3. **If you want to adjust the gray balance of the photo, click and drag the Levels slider to the left or the right.** Figure 9.14 shows the sample after adjusting the gray balance.

9.13 With white tones added, the photo is lighter overall.

9.14 Adjusting the gray balance evens out the distribution of light and dark in the photo.

Changing the contrast

If the photo lacks difference between the light and dark tones, increase the contrast by clicking and dragging the Contrast slider in the Adjust dialog box to the right. Likewise, if the difference between the light tones and dark tones is too harsh, click and drag the Contrast slider to the left to tone down the difference.

Adjusting the color saturation

If you need to give the colors in a photo more punch, you can increase the color saturation. Similarly, if you find the colors too bright, you can decrease the saturation.

Click and drag the Saturation slider in the Adjust dialog box to the right to boost the colors, or drag it to the left to produce a calmer effect. Unless you're trying to produce a drastic effect, you'll normally need to make only small changes to improve a photo. When the photo includes people, select the Avoid saturating the skin tones check box if you want iPhoto to leave their skin colors unchanged as far as possible.

Adjusting the definition

If the photo lacks definition in the mid tones, click the Definition slider and drag it to the right to increase the clarity.

Genius The Definition slider is a contrast control that changes only the mid tones in the photo. The Highlights slider is a contrast control that's restricted to the lighter tones. And — you've guessed it — the Shadows slider is a contrast control that works only with the darker tones.

Recovering contrast in highlights and shadows

Now look at the highlights in the photo. If your changes to the exposure, light tones, or contrast have *blown out* the highlights, making the details disappear (as has happened with the clouds in the sample photo), click the Highlights slider and drag it to the right to recover the highlights.

Next, look at the darker areas. If your changes have cost you detail here as well, click the Shadows slider and drag it to the right to add contrast to the shadows and make the detail visible again.

Figure 9.15 shows the sample photo after some delicate work with the Definition, Highlights, and Shadows sliders. As you can see, the clouds are now visible again.

9.15 After adjustments to definition, highlights, and shadows, the clouds are visible again in the background.

Reducing the noise in a photo

If the photo suffers from *noise* — random variations in the color or brightness caused by the camera's sensor — try to remove it. Click the De-noise slider and drag it to the right to see if iPhoto can remove the noise.

Caution   Don't drag the De-noise slider too far, as you may lose detail in the photo.

Increasing the sharpness of a photo

Finally, make any change needed to the sharpness of the photo by clicking the Sharpness slider and dragging it to the right.

Sharpness changes the photo by increasing the difference between adjacent pixels that already have a marked difference in color. For example, if your photo shows sunlight and shadows, increasing the sharpness makes the borders between the two stand out more.

Figure 9.16 shows the sample photo after all the adjustments. As you can see, there's a considerable improvement over the original.

Copying and pasting adjustments to other photos

When you've worked out exactly which fixes a photo needs, you can quickly apply those same fixes to other photos that need similar treatment. So if you shoot ten photos of a breathtaking sunset that don't come out quite

9.16 After all the adjustments, the sample figure is worth keeping, though still no masterpiece.

right, you need to spend time fixing the first; you can then quickly copy those fixes to the others.

To copy the adjustments from the current photo, click the Copy button in the Adjust dialog box. Then click the photo to which you want to apply the adjustments, and click the Paste button in the Adjust dialog box.

Applying effects to photos

You can also change a photo by applying one of iPhoto's eight visual effects — for example, blurring the photo's edges, reducing it from color to black and white, or making it a vignette in a black oval frame.

Here's how to apply a visual effect to a photo:

1. **Open the photo for editing.**

2. **Click the Effects button on the toolbar to open the Effects window (see figure 9.17).**

3. **Click the effect you want and adjust it as needed:**

   - The B & W and Sepia effects can only be On or Off.

   - The Antique, Fade Color, Boost Color, Matte, Vignette, and Edge Blur effects have various settings. Click the effect to apply level 1, then click the right arrow to increase the effect or the left arrow to reduce it.

   - Click Original in the middle of the window to restore the original look.

4. **Close the Effects window when you're satisfied with the result.**

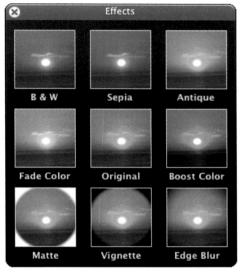

9.17 Applying one or more effects quickly changes a photo's look and feel.

Exporting a still from iPhoto for video use

When you're creating your movies on the Mac that contains your iPhoto library, you can simply pull a photo into iMovie from the library by using the Media Browser (see the next section). But when you need to get a photo out of your iPhoto library so that you can use it elsewhere, export it like this:

1. **Select the photo or photos you want to export.**

2. **Choose File ➪ Export to open the Export Photos dialog box, then click the File Export tab (see figure 9.18) if it's not displayed.**

3. **In the Kind pop-up menu, choose the format to use for the exported files:**

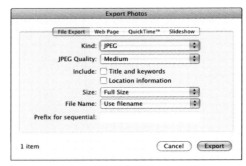

- **Original.** The format in which you imported the files (typically JPEG or RAW).

- **Current.** The format in which iPhoto is storing the photo. iPhoto uses JPEG unless you've selected the Save edits as 16-bit TIFF files check box in the Advanced pane in the iPhoto Preferences window. (The advantage of saving edits to RAW files in TIFF format is that you get higher quality than from JPEG format.)

9.18 In the File Export tab of the Export Photos dialog box, you choose the format, size, and naming convention for the photo files you export.

- **JPEG.** The best choice for general use, although you lose quality. Choose the quality in the JPEG Quality pop-up menu: Low, Medium, High, or Maximum.

- **TIFF.** A good choice for use in publishing.

- **PNG.** The high-quality choice for general computer use.

4. **Select the Titles and keywords check box and the Location information check box if you want to include these details in the files.** These options aren't available for PNG files.

5. **In the Size pop-up menu, choose the size: Small, Medium, Large, Full Size, or Custom.** For Custom, an extra section of the dialog box appears that enables you to choose the maximum dimension and the orientation.

6. **In the File Name pop-up menu, choose how to name the files: Use title, Use file-name, Sequential, or Use Album.** If you choose Sequential, type the text in the Prefix for sequential box. For example, type **Family** to get files named Family 01, Family 02, and so on.

7. **Click Export, choose the folder in which to save the photos, and then click OK.** iPhoto exports the files and then closes the Export Photos dialog box.

Importing Photos into iMovie

When you've edited your photos to your satisfaction in iPhoto, they're ready for importing into your movie projects. This takes only moments:

1. **Click the Photos browser button to open the Photos browser pane (see figure 9.19).** You can also press ⌘+2 to display the Photos browser pane.

2. **In the Albums lists at the top of the Photos browser pane, choose the album that contains the photo you want.** For example, if the photo is in the last set of photos you imported, choose the Last Import item. If you want to see the last year's worth of photos, choose the Last 12 Months item.

9.19 Use the Photos browser pane to insert a photo from your iPhoto library in your movie.

Genius

Alternatively, click in the Search box and enter a search term. You can click the pop-up menu at the left end of the Search box and choose Keywords from it to restrict the search to items you've tagged with a particular keyword in iPhoto.

3. **Select the photo or photos you want.** If necessary, click and drag the Thumbnails Size slider in the lower-right corner of the Photos browser pane to zoom in on the thumbnails (or zoom out so that you can see more at once).

4. **Click and drag the photo or photos to the Project window.** iMovie displays a vertical green line to show where they'll land.

Genius

If you find the Photos browser pane too small for comfort, use iPhoto instead. Simply open iPhoto, click the photo you want, and then drag it to the Project window in iMovie. Drop the photo when the vertical green bar appears between the right clips. You can also drag in a graphics file from a Finder window if you prefer not to add it to your iPhoto library.

Note

If you get an error message when importing a particular photo file into iMovie, see Chapter 12 for a solution.

Changing the Duration a Photo Plays

When you add a photo to the Project window, iMovie automatically assigns it the default duration set in the project's properties — for example, four seconds.

Nine times out of ten, you'll need to change the duration. Play back the part of the movie that contains the photo and decide whether this time is the exception.

Changing the duration of a single photo

If you do need to change a photo's duration, you can either trim it to a shorter length or use the Clip pane of the Inspector dialog box to increase or decrease the duration.

Trimming a photo's duration the quick way

If you need to shorten the duration rather than lengthen it, you can use the quick way: Click the photo in the Project window, and then drag either the right selection handle to the left or the left selection handle to the right. Figure 9.20 shows an example of dragging the right selection handle. iMovie displays a readout in either seconds and tenths of seconds or, if you've chosen to display frames, seconds and frames (as in the figure).

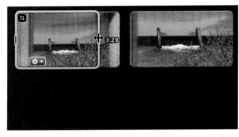

9.20 You can shorten the duration of a photo by dragging either the left or right selection handle.

When you've reached the right point, Ctrl+click or right-click and choose Trim to Playhead from the shortcut menu. iMovie shortens the duration of the photo.

Shortening the duration like this is easy and quick. But if you need to make the photo play for longer — as you probably will need to do around half the time — you have to use the Inspector dialog box instead.

Changing the duration with the Clip pane

The more formal way of setting the duration of a photo is to use the Clip pane of the Inspector dialog box. Follow these steps:

1. **Click the photo to select it.**

2. **Press the letter I or click the Inspector button in the toolbar to open the Inspector dialog box with the Clip pane at the front (see figure 9.21).** You can also double-click the photo to open the dialog box.

3. Type the duration in the Duration box.

○ If you've selected the Display time as HH:MM:SS:Frames check box in the General pane of the iMovie Preferences window, type the time in seconds and frames — for example, 2:15 represents two seconds and 15 frames, or two and a half seconds in the NTSC video format.

9.21 Set the duration (in seconds and tenths of seconds, or in seconds and frames) for iMovie to display the photo.

○ Otherwise, type the time in seconds — for example, 2.5 for two and a half seconds.

4. If you want iMovie to apply this duration to all the photos in the project, select the Applies to all stills check box. Normally, you will not want to do this, as it makes iMovie override any custom timings you've set.

5. Click Done to close the Inspector dialog box. Try playing back the movie around the photo, and make sure the setting is suitable.

Changing the default duration for photos

As you've just seen, you can change the default duration of a movie project's photos directly from the Inspector dialog box for photos (by selecting the Applies to all stills check box). You can also change the default duration by moving the Photo Duration slider in the Timing pane of the Project Properties dialog box (see figure 9.22), which you open by pressing ⌘+J or choosing File ⇨ Project Properties. The Photo Duration slider enables you to set the default duration to anywhere from one second to ten seconds.

The advantage to making the duration change in the Timing pane is that you can choose how to apply the change:

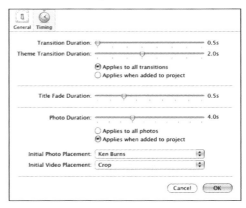

9.22 In the Timing pane of the Project Properties dialog box, you can change the default duration for photos but choose to apply the new default duration only from now on.

- **Applies to all photos.** Select this option button to play each of the photos in the movie project to the time the Photo Duration slider is showing. All the existing photos get this duration, as do all photos you add from now on.

Caution Select the Applies to all photos option button only if you're prepared to have iMovie automatically change the length of every photo you've already added to your movie project. Unless you're creating a regular and strictly choreographed movie — for example, a yearbook movie with a fixed time slot for each person's photo — this is not a good idea.

- **Applies when added to project.** Select this muddily-named option button to apply the duration only to photos you add from now on. Any photos already in the movie project keep their current durations. This is usually what you want.

Choosing the default placement for photos

While you've got the Timing pane of the Project Properties dialog box open, take a minute to make sure that the Initial Photo Placement setting is what you want. You have three choices:

- **Fit to Frame.** This placement makes iMovie add letterboxing (horizontal bars on the top and bottom) or pillar-boxing (vertical bars on the left and right) to photos that are the wrong aspect ratio for the project. Use this placement when you want to make sure that the whole photo appears — that is, when it's vital that nothing be cut off the photo.

- **Crop.** This placement makes iMovie enlarge the photo so that it occupies the full aspect ratio, cropping off parts of the dimension that was already fitting. For example, if a photo's aspect ratio makes it too wide and short for the frame, Crop increases the photo's height to match the frame, and then crops off the extra parts of the width.

- **Ken Burns.** This placement applies a small Ken Burns effect to the photo — just enough zooming and panning to hold the audience's attention longer than a still photo would. You can change any of the details of the Ken Burns effect, as discussed later in this chapter.

Choose the placement you'll want most often for the photos you add to your movie projects. You can change a photo's placement at any time, but setting the right default placement will save you time and effort.

Creating Moving Photos

A still photo can make an effective contrast to the rest of your movie, especially when you create a freeze-frame effect (as discussed later in this chapter) to stop the action for a moment before picking it up again at the same point. But if you simply use many still photos in a movie — or build a movie only out of still photos — there's every chance that it will appear unappealingly static.

To add life and movement to your still photos, you can use iMovie's Ken Burns effect. This effect, which is named after the famous documentary director Ken Burns, consists of panning and slowly zooming across a photo. For example, if you have a photo showing a group of people, you can start by showing the whole group, and then slowly pan across the photograph and zoom in on a single face.

Creating a Ken Burns effect is easy, as iMovie does most of the work. You simply choose the area of the picture at which you want to start the effect, choose the area at which you want to end the effect, and let iMovie figure out the direction of the pan and zoom.

Editing the Ken Burns effect

With its default settings, iMovie automatically applies a small Ken Burns effect to each still photo you add to a movie project. You can change this default setting by choosing either Fit to Frame or Crop in the Initial Photo Placement pop-up menu in the Timing pane of the Project Properties dialog box, as discussed earlier in this chapter.

Play back the photo and see how the effect works. Most likely, you'll need to customize it. To do so, follow these steps:

1. **Click the photo in the Project window to display it in the viewer.**

2. **Click the Crop button on the toolbar (or press C) to display the cropping tools and Ken Burns Effect tools for still photos in the viewer (see figure 9.23).** If you've changed your Initial Photo Placement setting, click the Ken Burns button near the upper-left corner of the viewer.

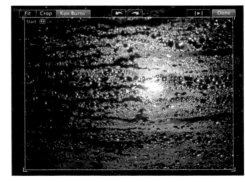

9.23 The cropping tools and Ken Burns Effect tools for still photos.

3. Choose the starting rectangle for the Ken Burns effect:

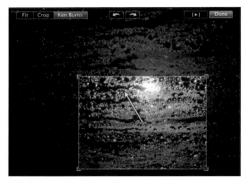

- Click the green Start rectangle to select it. (The rectangle may be selected already.)

- Click and drag a corner or side of the rectangle to resize it (see figure 9.24). iMovie automatically constrains the rectangle to the aspect ratio for the project, so you can't drag the rectangle to the wrong aspect ratio.

9.24 Resize the green Start rectangle to choose how much of the photo to display at first.

- If necessary, click within the Start rectangle and drag it to select a different area of the picture.

Note

When you're editing a Ken Burns effect, the green cross shows you where the middle of the green Start rectangle is. The red cross shows you where the middle of the red End rectangle is. The yellow arrow shows you the direction and extent of the pan you'll get from the green cross to the red cross.

4. Choose the ending rectangle for the Ken Burns effect:

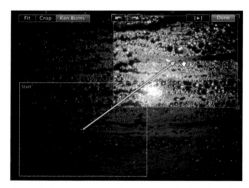

- Click the red End rectangle to select it.

- Click and drag a corner or side of the red End rectangle to resize it.

- If necessary, click within the End rectangle and drag it to select a different area of the picture. Figure 9.25 shows the sample picture with the End rectangle in place.

9.25 Resize and reposition the red End rectangle to choose where the effect will end.

5. **Click the Play button (or press Spacebar) to view the effect and judge how well it works**. If necessary, adjust the Start rectangle or the End rectangle.

6. **Click Done to apply the Ken Burns effect to the photo.**

Applying effects to multiple photos

When you need to make exactly the same adjustment to two or more photos at the same time, add the photos to your project, select them, and then make the adjustments. iMovie applies the adjustments to all the photos at once, even though the Viewer shows only the last photo you selected.

When you've made one or more adjustments to one photo, you can copy an adjustment and paste it to other photos. Follow these steps:

1. **Ctrl+click or right-click the adjusted photo in the Project window, and then click Copy on the shortcut menu.**

2. **Also in the Project window, click the first photo to which you want to apply the adjustment.** If you want to apply it to multiple photos, ⌘+click each of the others.

3. **Choose Edit ➪ Paste Adjustments, and then choose the adjustment type from the Paste Adjustments submenu.** For example, choose Edit ➪ Paste Adjustments ➪ Crop to crop the selected photos the same way as the one you copied.

Using Images as Overlays for Video

Instead of inserting a photo or image as a stand-alone item in a movie (and perhaps jazzing it up with the Ken Burns effect), you can use an image as an overlay for video: The image appears on top of the video, and you see the video clip through the transparent areas of the image.

To create this effect, which iMovie treats as a cutaway, follow these steps:

1. **Create a PNG image that shows the image you want to overlay on the video.** Make the background of the image transparent; if it's opaque, you won't see any of the video.

Genius

To get your overlay to appear exactly as you need it, export a still photo from the video clip, as discussed later in this chapter. Open the still photo in your graphics application so that you can see exactly where your overlay elements must appear. When you have finished creating and positioning the overlay, delete the photo layer from the file.

2. **Add the image to your iPhoto library if you need to manipulate it.** If you prefer not to add the image to your iPhoto library, you can drag it into iMovie from a Finder window instead.

3. **In iMovie, make sure that the Advanced Tools are displayed.** Choose iMovie ➪ Preferences, select the Show Advanced Tools check box in the General pane, and then close the Preferences window.

4. **Click the image in the Photos browser pane in iMovie, drag it to the Project window, and then drop it on the clip on which you want to overlay it.** If your image is not in your iPhoto library, click it in a Finder window and drag it to the Project window from there.

5. **When iMovie displays the pop-up menu of actions, choose Cutaway.** iMovie positions the icon for the image above the host clip (see figure 9.26).

6. **Preview the effect in the viewer.** Figure 9.27 shows the example image overlaid on the video.

7. **Edit the overlay as needed.** For example, you can crop it or add a Ken Burns effect to it.

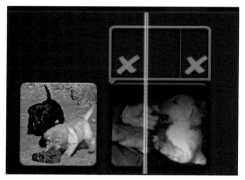

9.26 How an overlay image appears in the Project window.

9.27 The overlay as it appears in the viewer.

Adjusting the Crop or Fit of a Photo

To make a photo fit your movie project, you'll often need to change its dimensions. You can choose between cropping the photo so that only part of it appears or having the entire photo appear but with black bars above and below, or to the left and right, if the photo's aspect ratio doesn't match the movie's aspect ratio.

Here's how to crop or fit a photo:

1. **Click the photo in the Project window to display it in the Viewer.**

2. **Click the Crop button on the toolbar (or press C) to display the cropping tools and Ken Burns Effect tools for still photos in the Viewer.**

3. **Choose whether to display the whole photo or part of it:**

   - To display the whole photo, click the Fit button. iMovie displays the photo with any black bars it needs to fill the rest of the frame. Figure 9.28 shows an example. Go to Step 6.

   - To crop the photo, click the Crop button. iMovie displays a green cropping frame around the suggested part of the photo (see figure 9.29).

4. **Click and drag one or more corners of the green cropping frame to select the crop size you want.**

5. **If necessary, click and drag the cropping frame so that it contains the right part of the photo.**

6. **Click Done.**

9.28 Fitting a photo with black bars so that the whole photo appears.

9.29 Cropping a photo so that only part of it appears.

Creating Still Images and Freeze Frames from Video

Being able to turn your photos into movies is great, but what if you want to do things the other way around and get a still photo from a video clip?

iMovie makes it easy to create a still image from a video clip and add it automatically to a movie project. You can then use it there to create a freeze-frame effect in your movie. But you can also import the still image into iPhoto, which is handy when you want to use the still image elsewhere — for example, in posters or other promotional material for your movie.

Creating a still image and adding it to a movie project

The first way of creating a still image from a video clip is to use a video clip in your Event Library. Use this method except for when you want the still image to create a freeze-frame scene. Follow these steps:

1. **In the Event Library, click the event that contains the clip from which you want to grab the still image.**

2. **In the Event browser, skim to the frame you want.**

3. **Ctrl+click or right-click that frame and choose Add Still Frame to Project.** iMovie creates a still image from the frame and adds it to the end of the movie project that's open in the Project window. iMovie automatically applies a small Ken Burns effect to the image.

4. **If you want to add the still image to iPhoto, do so as described at the end of the chapter.**

5. **If you want to use the still image in your movie project, click and drag it in the Project window to where you want it.** You can then set its duration and effects as described earlier in this chapter. If you want the still image only for iPhoto and not in your movie, click it in the Project window, and then press Backspace to delete it.

Creating a freeze-frame scene

When you create a still image from a video clip you've already placed in the Project window, iMovie automatically creates a freeze-frame scene for you. At the frame you choose, iMovie splits the clip into two separate clips, and inserts the still frame between them.

The effect is that the movement or action stops, pauses for the default duration set in the project's properties, and then resumes seamlessly. You can enliven the freeze frame by applying the Ken Burns effect (or other effects) if you want.

To create the kind of freeze-frame scene I've just described, follow these steps:

1. **In the Project window, move the Playhead to the right frame.** Figure 9.30 shows an example.

2. **Ctrl+click or right-click and choose Add Freeze Frame.** iMovie creates a still image from the frame, splits the clip, and inserts the frame. Figure 9.31 shows the same project with the clip split.

3. **If you want to crop the image or apply a Ken Burns effect, click the image, and then press C to display the cropping tools.** Use them as described earlier in this chapter, and then click Done.

4. **If you want to change the image's display time or add an effect, double-click the image, and then work in the Inspector dialog box.**

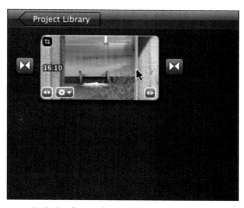

9.30 Pick the frame from which you want to create a still image.

9.31 iMovie automatically splits the clip so that it can place the still image at the frame you chose.

Genius iMovie's trick of creating a freeze-frame scene automatically from a clip in the movie project is great when you want to create a freeze frame. But when you simply want to create a still image that you can use elsewhere, you'll do better to create the image from the same clip in the Event browser.

Importing the still image into iPhoto

If you create a still image using either of the two previous techniques, you can quickly bring it into iPhoto like this:

1. **In the Project window, Ctrl+click or right-click the still image and choose Reveal in Finder.** iMovie opens a Finder window to the folder that contains the still image.

205

Genius

iMovie saves the still images for a movie project inside the package file that contains the movie's files. To see the package file's contents, open a Finder window to the ~/Movies/iMovie Projects folder (where ~ represents your Home folder). Ctrl+click or right-click the package file with the movie's name, and then choose Show Package Contents. You'll find the still images in the Stills folder.

2. **Open iPhoto and position it so that you can see both it and the Finder window.**

3. **Click and drag the still image file into the main part of the iPhoto window.** You can then access it from the Last Import item in the Recent category in the Source list.

How Can I Share My Movies?

You Tube™ Publish your project to YouTube

Account: [▼] (Add...) (Remove)

Password: [   ]

Category: [Comedy ▼]

Title: Vacation Fun

Description: [   ]

Tags: [   ]

	iPhone	átv	Computer	YouTube		
Size to publish: ⦿ Mobile	●		●	●	480x360	ⓘ
◯ Medium		●	●	●	640x480	ⓘ
◯ Large		●	●	●	720x540	ⓘ
◯ HD			●	●	1280x720	ⓘ

☑ Make this movie personal

(Cancel) (Next)

Once you've finished your movie and played it back on your Mac to check it's just right, you'll probably want to share it with your family, friends, or the whole world. iMovie makes it easy for you to share a movie to an iPod (or iPhone) or Apple TV, but you can also publish a movie straight to the YouTube video-sharing site on the Web or place it in your Gallery on Apple's MobileMe service. If you want to place a movie on your iWeb Web site, you can publish the movie to the Media Browser from iMovie and then pull it into iWeb from there. For other types of sharing, you can create a file of your movie.

Sharing a Movie to iTunes

The easiest way to share a movie is to add it to iTunes. This creates one or more versions of the movie that you can watch in iTunes itself, on an iPod or iPhone, or on an Apple TV.

Sharing the movie

Here's how to share the movie to iTunes:

1. **Select the movie project you want to share.** If the movie project is already open in the Project window, you're all set. Otherwise, click the movie in the Project Library.

2. **Choose Share ➪ iTunes.** iMovie displays the Publish your project to iTunes dialog box (see figure 10.1).

3. **Choose the sizes you want to create.** iMovie enables you to export a movie to iTunes using any or all of four video sizes. Table 10.1 explains the sizes, their resolutions, and the devices on which they work.

10.1 When you publish a project to iTunes, you can create multiple sizes to ensure the movie looks good on different devices.

   - Usually you'll want to select the Mobile check box, the Medium check box, and the Large check box so that you can watch the movie on an iPod or iPhone, an Apple TV, or your Mac.

   - iMovie creates a separate movie file for each type of device, adding the size to the project's name — for example, "Our New Arrival – Mobile" and "Our New Arrival – Medium" — so that you can distinguish the files. Each file takes up space, so unless your Mac has a ton of hard disk space free, create only the sizes you need.

4. **Click Publish.**

The more sizes you choose, the longer the publishing takes. When iMovie has finished creating the files, it automatically launches or activates iTunes so that you can check out the movies. Click the Movies item in the Sidebar to see the list of movies.

Table 10.1 Sizes and Resolutions to Export to iTunes

	Tiny	Mobile	Medium	Large
Resolution (Standard)	176×144	480×360	640×480	720×540
Resolution (Widescreen)	176×144	480×272	640×360	960×540
iPod			✓	
iPhone	✓	✓		
Apple TV			✓	✓
Computer		✓	✓	✓

Removing a shared movie from iTunes

Normally, when you've shared a movie with iTunes, you'll want to leave it there so you can watch it whenever you want to. But if you need to remove it, here's what to do:

1. **Click the movie in the Project Library.** If you've already opened the movie in the Project window, you can simply work from there.

2. **Choose Share ⇨ Remove from iTunes.** iMovie removes all the versions of the movie project from iTunes without confirming your request or telling you that it has completed it.

Sharing a Movie to the Media Browser

When you want to be able to use a movie in iWeb or iDVD, publish it to the iLife Media Browser. Once you've done this, you can quickly pull the movie from the Movies pane of the Media Browser into iWeb or iDVD.

Adding a movie to the Media Browser

Here's how to share a movie to the Media Browser:

1. **Click the project in the Project Library.** If you've already got the movie open in the Project window, you're good to go.

2. **Choose Share ➪ Media Browser.**
   iMovie displays the Publish your project to the Media Browser dialog box (see figure 10.2).

3. **Choose the sizes you want to create.**
   Table 10.2 summarizes your options. For the Media Browser, it's usually worth selecting the Mobile, Medium, Large, and HD check boxes. Selecting the Tiny check box is seldom worthwhile, unless you're determined to spread low-quality versions of your movies as widely as possible.

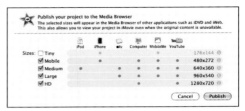

10.2 When you publish a movie to the Media Browser, you can choose among the Tiny, Mobile, Medium, Large, and HD formats.

4. **Click Publish.**

Table 10.2 Sizes and Resolutions to Export to Media Browser

	Tiny	Mobile	Medium	Large	HD
Resolution (Standard)	176×144	480×360	640×480	720×540	N/A
Resolution (Widescreen)	176×144	480×272	640×360	960×540	1280×720
iPod			✓		
iPhone	✓	✓			
Apple TV			✓	✓	
Computer		✓	✓	✓	✓
MobileMe	✓	✓	✓	✓	
YouTube		✓	✓	✓	✓

Using a movie project in iWeb

After adding a movie project to the Media Browser, you can use the movie in iWeb like this:

1. **Click the Web page to which you want to add the movie.** If necessary, add a new page to the Web site by clicking the Add Page button, selecting the template you want in the Template Chooser window, and then clicking the Choose button.

2. **Click the Movies button to display the Movies pane of the Media Browser.**

3. **Drag the movie to the Web page.** You can then resize and reposition it as needed.

Removing a movie project from the Media Browser

If you need to remove a movie project from the Media Browser, you can choose which versions to remove. Here's how:

1. **Click the project in the Project Library.** If the movie is open in the Project window, you don't need to return to the Project Library.

2. **Choose Share ⇨ Remove from Media Library.** iMovie displays the Remove rendered movies from the Media Browser dialog box (see figure 10.3).

3. **Select the check box for each size you want to remove.** As you'd expect, the only check boxes available are for the sizes you've added to the Media Browser.

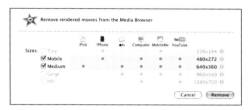

10.3 You can remove just some sizes of a movie from the Media Browser or remove them all at once.

4. **Click Remove.** iMovie removes the versions you chose.

Publishing a Movie to Your MobileMe Gallery

If you have a MobileMe subscription, you can easily publish a movie to your MobileMe Gallery, the area in which you can share photos, movies, and other items with either a limited audience or everyone on the Web.

First, if you're not currently signed in to your MobileMe account, you should sign in before publishing your movie. Click System Preferences in the Dock, click MobileMe, click Sign In, and then enter your MobileMe credentials if Mac OS X prompts you to do so.

Now follow these steps in iMovie:

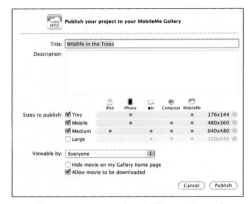

1. **Select the movie project in the Project Library.** If the movie project is already open in the Project window, you don't need to go back to the Project Library.

2. **Choose Share ⇨ MobileMe Gallery.** iMovie displays the Publish your project to your MobileMe Gallery dialog box (see figure 10.4).

3. **Improve the title in the Title box if necessary.**

10.4 You can put up to four different sizes of movie on your MobileMe Gallery. This enables visitors to download the size they want.

4. **Type a description of the movie in the Description box.** Make the description pithy rather than rambling — you want to grab a visitor's attention right away.

5. **In the Sizes to publish area, select the check box for each size you want to publish.** Table 10.2, earlier in this chapter, gives the details on the sizes you can use on MobileMe (Tiny, Mobile, Medium, or Large).

6. **In the Viewable by pop-up menu, choose who may view the movie:**

   ● **Everyone.** Anyone on the Web can view the album.

   ● **Only me.** You keep the album to yourself — good for personal or work photos.

   ● **(An existing name.)** If you've already set up a person or group for sharing, choose the name from the pop-up menu.

   ● **Edit Names and Passwords.** To add the name of a person or group and assign a password, click this item, and work on the sheet that appears. Click OK when you finish.

7. **If you want to hide the movie on your Gallery page, select the Hide movie on my Gallery home page check box.**

Genius

Hiding a movie so that it doesn't appear on your MobileMe Gallery page is good for when you need to share different movies with different people. Instead of needing to password-protect a movie to keep out people you don't want to see it, you can simply prevent the movie from appearing, and give the movie's URL to the people you want to watch it.

8. **Select the Allow movie to be downloaded check box if you want people to be able to download the movie rather than just watch it online.**

9. **Click Publish.** iMovie prepares the movie sizes you chose and publishes them to your Gallery, then displays a dialog box telling you it has done so (see figure 10.5).

10.5 After you publish a movie to your MobileMe Gallery, you can view it yourself or tell a friend about it.

10. **Click Tell a Friend to start an e-mail message announcing your movie, click View to view your Gallery, or click OK to close the dialog box.**

If you need to remove a movie from your MobileMe Gallery, follow these steps:

1. **Select the movie project in the Project Library.** If the movie project is already open in the Project window, just start from there.

2. **Choose Share ⇨ Remove from MobileMe Gallery.** iMovie displays the Unpublish from your MobileMe Gallery dialog box (see figure 10.6).

3. **Click Continue.** iMovie communicates with MobileMe and removes the movie from your Gallery.

10.6 When you remove a movie from your MobileMe Gallery, iMovie warns you that the action is not undoable. This is fine because you can publish the movie project again with a couple of clicks.

Publishing a Movie to YouTube

If you want to share your movie with the world, you can export it easily to YouTube as described in this section. Here's how to publish a movie project to YouTube:

1. **In the Project Library, select the project you want to export.** As before, if you've opened the project in the Project window, you're ready to publish it.

2. **Choose Share ⇨ YouTube.** iMovie displays the Publish your project to YouTube dialog box (see figure 10.7).

3. **In the Account pop-up menu, choose the account from which you want to post the movie.** The first time you add a video to YouTube, you need to add the account to iMovie's list. Here's what to do:

- **Click the Add button.** iMovie displays the Add Account screen (see figure 10.8).
- **Type your YouTube username in the box.**
- **Click Done.** iMovie adds the name to the Account pop-up menu and selects it.

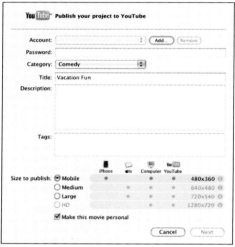

10.7 Getting ready to publish a movie project to YouTube.

10.8 Adding a YouTube user name to iMovie.

Note

If you have multiple YouTube accounts, you can also use this process to add another YouTube account after the first. If you need to remove an account, select it in the Account pop-up menu and click Remove.

4. **Type your password in the Password box.** Rather than display the characters you type, iMovie displays dots in case someone's snooping over your shoulder.

5. **Open the Category pop-up menu and choose the YouTube category into which you want to put the movie.** The categories are largely self-explanatory. For example, if your movie is a demonstration of cooking, you might choose Howto & Style or Education. If it's a travelog, Travel & Events is usually the best bet.

6. **Type the movie's title in the Title box.** iMovie enters the project's title for you, but you'll often need to choose a more descriptive, snappier, or more memorable title to get the most hits on YouTube.

Caution Keep the title to 63 characters or fewer. Otherwise, YouTube may simply truncate the title after the 63rd character when you upload the movie or may fail to accept the movie even though iMovie doesn't report any problem.

7. **Type a description of the movie in the Description box.**

8. **In the Tags box, type the tags you want to give the movie.** Tags are the words with which YouTube matches people's searches, so put in a variety of related terms. Separate each tag from the next with a comma.

9. **In the Size to publish area, choose the size you want to publish (you can choose only one).** Refer to Table 10.2 for the details on the sizes.

   - Normally, you'll want to publish either the Mobile size or the Medium size. The Mobile size works on the iPhone, on computers, and in browsers on YouTube, so it's a good bet. The Medium size works on Apple TV, computers, and YouTube, but not on the iPhone.

   - iMovie doesn't offer the Tiny size for YouTube.

10. **Select the Make this movie personal check box if you want to share it only with people on your lists — either the Friends list and the Family list that YouTube automatically gives you, or lists you've set up yourself.**

11. **Click Next.** iMovie displays the YouTube Terms of Service screen, which covers copyright concerns.

12. **Click Publish.** iMovie creates the movie at the size you chose, uploads it to YouTube, and then displays the dialog box shown in figure 10.9.

Your video has been uploaded to YouTube. It may be several minutes or hours before your video is processed and viewable, depending on YouTube's server load.

Your video can be viewed at: http://www.youtube.com/watch?v=J_993K1rBi8

(Tell a Friend)   (View)   (OK)

10.9 Once your movie is safely on YouTube, you can view it or tell your friends about it.

Genius Sometimes, when you try to publish a movie to YouTube, iMovie displays an error message recommending that you decrease the amount of metadata in the movie. Before you cut down the description or tags, try publishing the movie again as it is because this error can occur when metadata isn't the problem. If you get the error persistently for the same project, try reducing the metadata.

13. **Choose what to do next:**

   ● **Click Tell a Friend to have iMovie start an e-mail message giving the movie's name and URL.** You can then address the message, edit it as needed, and send it on its way.

   ● **Click View to open a browser window to the URL.** Often YouTube won't have processed the video yet, so you'll see the message "This video is not yet processed." If so, keep the window or tab open and refresh it later to view the video.

   ● **Click OK to close the dialog box without telling your friends or viewing the video.**

Removing a Movie from YouTube

If you decide you no longer want one of your movies to be on YouTube, you can remove it easily enough. Follow these steps:

1. **In iMovie, click the project in the Project Library.**

2. **Choose Share ⇨ Remove from YouTube.** iMovie displays the dialog box shown in figure 10.10.

3. **Click Go to YouTube.** iMovie opens or activates your Web browser and displays your My Videos page on the YouTube site.

10.10 You can easily remove one of your movies from YouTube if it has passed its sell-by date.

4. **Select the check box for the movie or movies you want to delete.**

5. **Click Delete, and then click OK in the confirmation dialog box (see figure 10.11).**

10.11 Confirm the deletion in your Web browser.

6. **Close the browser tab or window, return to iMovie, and click Done.** iMovie removes the YouTube sharing from the movie's details.

Exporting a Movie as a File

As you've seen so far in this chapter, iMovie makes it easy to use your movie projects in a variety of ways. But other times, you may simply want to create a file that contains the movie. iMovie enables you to do this too — in many different file formats.

Exporting a movie quickly to an MPEG-4 file

If you want to export a movie quickly to a Tiny-, Mobile-, Medium-, or Large-sized MPEG-4 (Moving Pictures Experts Group-4) file using iMovie's preset settings, creating a file that will play on almost any type of computer, follow these steps:

1. **Select the movie project in the Project Library.** Alternatively, open the project in the Project window.

2. **Choose Share⇨Export Movie or press ⌘+E.** iMovie displays the Export As dialog box shown in figure 10.12.

3. **In the Export As box, iMovie enters the project's name.** Edit this name or type a new name as necessary.

4. **In the Where pop-up menu, choose the folder in which to store the exported file.** If necessary, expand the dialog box so that you can see the Sidebar.

10.12 The quick way to create a file containing a movie is to use the Share⇨Export Movie command.

5. **In the Size to Export area, select a radio button — Tiny, Mobile, Medium, Large, or HD — as appropriate.** Table 10.2 (earlier in this chapter) explains the sizes.

6. **Click Export.** iMovie exports the movie to the file and saves it in the folder you chose.

Exporting to another file format

When you need a file format other than MPEG-4, or when you need to control exactly how iMovie exports the file, you can export to a QuickTime file instead. Here's how:

1. **Select the movie project in the Project Library.** Alternatively, open the project in the Project window.

2. **Choose Share ⇨ Export using QuickTime.** iMovie displays the Save exported file as dialog box shown in figure 10.13.

10.13 The Export using QuickTime command enables you to choose from a wide variety of export formats.

3. **In the Save As box, iMovie enters the project's name.** Edit this name or type a new name as necessary.

4. **In the Where pop-up menu, choose the folder in which to store the exported file.** If necessary, expand the dialog box so that you can see the Sidebar.

5. **In the Export pop-up menu, choose the format you want.** Table 10.3 explains your options.

Table 10.3 Export Options Using QuickTime

Export Format	Explanation
Movie to 3G	Creates a movie in the 3GP format, streaming the movie to 3G mobile phones.
Movie to Apple TV	Creates a movie in the MPEG-4 format. This gives you the same result as choosing Share ⇨ Export Movie and choosing the Medium size (which is easier). The movie's resolution is 640×480 pixels (standard aspect ratio) or 640×360 pixels (widescreen aspect ratio).
Movie to AVI	Creates a movie in the AVI format, which is widely used on Windows. You can choose the quality and compression (which is optional but usually a good idea to keep the file size down).
Movie to DV Stream	Creates a movie in a DV format. You can choose whether the movie is formatted for NTSC or for PAL.
Movie to FLC	Creates a movie in the FLIC animation format. You can choose the frame rate and whether the movie uses Windows Colors or Mac Colors.
Movie to Image Sequence	Creates an image file for each frame of the movie. You can choose from various image formats (such as JPEG).
Movie to iPhone	Creates a movie in the MPEG-4 format suitable for viewing on the iPhone or iPod touch. This gives you the same result as choosing Share ⇨ Export Movie and choosing the Small size. The movie's resolution is 480×360 pixels (standard aspect ratio) or 480×270 pixels (widescreen aspect ratio).

Export Format	Explanation
Movie to iPhone (Cellular)	Creates a movie in the 3GP format suitable for watching as a stream on the iPhone. The movie's resolution is 176×132 pixels (standard aspect ratio) or 176×99 pixels (widescreen aspect ratio).
Movie to iPod	Creates a movie in the MPEG-4 format suitable for viewing on any iPod or on a TV to which it's connected. The movie's resolution is 640×480 pixels (standard aspect ratio) or 640×360 pixels (widescreen aspect ratio). These resolutions are the same as the Movie to Apple TV export format, but Movie to iPod uses a lower bitrate and so has a smaller file size.
Movie to MPEG-4	Creates a movie in the MPEG-4 format. This is the same as choosing Share ➪ Export Movie, except you can click the Options buttons to set a wide variety of movie options, including the image size, frame rate, and audio format.
Movie to QuickTime Movie	Creates a movie in the QuickTime format. You can choose from a wide variety of settings to get the resolution and quality you need.
Sound to AIFF	Exports the sound track from the movie to a file in the AIFF format, an uncompressed, full-quality format used widely on the Mac.
Sound to AU	Exports the sound track from the movie to a file in the AU format. This file format is less widely used than AIFF or WAV.
Sound to WAV	Exports the sound track from the movie to a file in the WAV format, an uncompressed, full-quality format used widely on Windows.

Genius

QuickTime's "Sound To" export formats are great for grabbing the audio from a movie so that you can use it elsewhere. Choose the Sound to AIFF format if you plan to use the audio only on Macs; for Windows, the Sound to WAV format is a better choice.

6. **If the Options button is available rather than dimmed, you can click it to choose options for the export format.** For example, if you choose the Movie to QuickTime Movie export format, you can choose options like this:

   • **Click the Options button to display the Movie Settings dialog box (see figure 10.14).**

- **To change the video settings, click the Settings button in the Video box, and then choose compression, motion, data rate, and encoding settings in the Video Compression Settings dialog box.**

- **To apply a special effect such as Lens Flare, click the Filter button, and then choose settings in the Filtering dialog box.**

- **To change the resolution of the video, click the Size button, and then choose settings in the Export Size Settings dialog box.**

- **To use a different sound format or quality, click the Settings button in the Sound box, and then choose settings in the Sound Settings dialog box.**

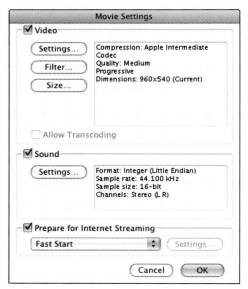

10.14 Use the Movie Settings dialog box and its ancillary dialog boxes when you need full control over the movie file you're exporting.

- **If you want to be able to stream the movie across the Internet, select the Prepare for Internet Streaming check box, and then choose Fast Start, Fast Start – Compressed Header, or Hinted Streaming.** Fast Start is usually the best choice for general use. Hinted Streaming is for use with QuickTime Streaming Server.

- **Click OK to close the Movie Settings dialog box and return to the Save exported file as dialog box.**

7. **Click Save.** iMovie exports the file in the format you chose.

Exporting to a Final Cut XML file

If you have Final Cut Express or Final Cut Pro, Apple's more powerful video-editing applications, you may want to bring movies that you've created in iMovie into Final Cut so that you can develop them further.

To do this, you can use iMovie's Export Final Cut XML command. But before you do, it's vital that you're clear on what you get and what you don't get:

- **Video.** You get the video footage, but iMovie removes any color adjustments you made.

- **Audio.** You get the audio tracks, but iMovie removes any voiceovers, sound effects, and music tracks.

- **Transitions.** iMovie replaces all your custom transitions with Cross Dissolves.

- **Titles.** You lose all the titles.

- **Cropping and Ken Burns Effects.** iMovie removes these as well.

- **Picture-in-picture clips and green-screen clips.** iMovie removes these effects too.

That may sound as though there's not much left. But if what you're looking to do is get your edited video into one of the Final Cut applications so that you can re-edit it there, you get just about enough.

Here's how to export your movie project to a Final Cut XML file:

1. **Click the movie project in the Project Library.** You can also start from the Project window if you already have the movie project open.

2. **Choose Share ➪ Export Final Cut XML.** iMovie displays the Export FCP XML dialog box (see figure 10.15).

3. **In the Save As box, type the name you want to give the file.** iMovie suggests XML File, which isn't helpful.

4. **In the Where pop-up menu, choose the folder in which to store the exported file.** If necessary, expand the dialog box so that you can see the Sidebar.

10.15 When you export a movie to Final Cut XML, you lose transitions, voiceovers, cropping, and more — but you do transfer the footage.

5. **Select the Use flattened audio from thumbnail movies check box if you want to include the rendered audio.** Clear this check box if you plan to render the audio in Final Cut (which gives you more control over how it sounds).

6. **Click Save.** iMovie exports the file. You can then import it into Final Cut.

223

Using iDVD?

iDVD gives you the power to make professional-quality DVDs from your movies, photos, and more. In this chapter, you'll learn about iDVD's workflow, meet its interface, and set vital preferences. Then you'll create a DVD, apply a theme to make it look right, add content to it, and customize it. I'll also show you how to make DVDs quickly with iDVD's OneStep DVD and Magic DVD features, how to burn a DVD to disc, and how to shift a whole DVD project to another Mac.

Understanding the iDVD Workflow

Even with all the help that iDVD provides, creating a DVD normally takes several steps, so it helps to understand the workflow.

First, iDVD enables you to create DVDs in three ways:

- **Manually.** This is the way you'll create most projects. Creating a DVD manually gives you full control over what goes on the DVD, how the content is arranged, and how the DVD's interface looks. The only disadvantage is that you must put in more time and effort.

- **Magic iDVD.** The Magic iDVD feature enables you to create a DVD the quick and easy way. Magic iDVD gives your DVD project a kick start by automatically arranging the elements in the project for you. You still get to choose the content, and you can customize the iDVD's contents, menus, and appearance by building on the project that Magic iDVD creates.

- **OneStep DVD.** The OneStep iDVD feature enables you to import video footage from the tape on your DV camcorder and drop it directly onto a DVD instead of importing the footage into iMovie and turning it into a movie there. Use OneStep DVD for content that's either final (for example, a movie project someone has exported to the DV camcorder) or that you don't need to edit (for example, when you need to provide someone with raw footage you've shot so that she can watch it or edit it).

With those three ways of creating DVDs in mind, here's the iDVD workflow:

1. **Create suitable content in the other iLife applications:**

   - **Movies.** Create movies in iMovie, as discussed in this book, and export them to the Media Browser. If you have movies already prepared in other folders, you can use them directly from there.

   - **Photos.** If you want to create slideshows in iDVD, prepare the photos in iPhoto. For example, put your edited photos in a photo album so that you can grab them all at once.

   - **Music.** Compose songs in GarageBand and save previews of them in the Media Browser so that iDVD can access them. You can also export the finished songs to iTunes and use them from there. And you can use any song or playlist from your iTunes library — so you may want to assemble a suitable playlist for a DVD.

2. **Start creating a DVD project in iDVD.** Normally you'll create a regular DVD project so that you can add content manually (see Step 3), but you can also get moving quickly by using Magic iDVD. If you use Magic iDVD, you avoid Step 3 altogether, and Magic iDVD takes care of Step 4 for you.

3. **Add content to the DVD.** Next, you add your movies, photos, and music to the DVD. You may need to add chapter markers to a movie that doesn't have them.

4. **Customize the menu screen for the DVD.** The menu screen is the background on which the various buttons for controlling the DVD appear. You can add movies and slideshows to the menu screen to give it more impact.

5. **Check the DVD's status and inspect the items it contains.**

6. **When the DVD project is ready, burn it to DVD.**

I'll show you how to go through the workflow later in this chapter. First, though, I'll show you the iDVD interface and make sure you've got iDVD's preferences set suitably.

Opening iDVD and Meeting the Interface

Let's get started by launching iDVD and starting a DVD project so that you can see iDVD's interface.

Opening iDVD

If the iDVD icon appears in the Dock, click it to launch iDVD. Otherwise, click the desktop, choose Go⇨Applications, and then double-click the iDVD icon; if you want to keep iDVD in the Dock so you can launch it more easily in future, Ctrl+click or right-click the iDVD icon in the Dock and choose Keep in Dock from the shortcut menu.

The first time you launch iDVD, the application displays the iDVD opening screen shown in figure 11.1.

11.1 On the iDVD opening screen, choose the type of DVD project you want to create.

Creating a new DVD project

To reach the iDVD interface, create a new DVD project like this:

1. **Click the Create a New Project button from the iDVD opening screen.** iMovie displays the Create Project dialog box (see figure 11.2).

2. **Type the name for the project in the Save As box.** iDVD suggests My Great DVD as a name, but you'll almost certainly want to change this to something more specific.

11.2 When you create a new DVD project, you name it, choose its aspect ratio, and decide where to save it.

3. **In the Where pop-up menu, choose the folder in which to save the DVD project.**

   - iDVD suggests the Documents folder, but it's better to use a different folder so that your Documents folder doesn't get cluttered. For example, create a new folder for your DVDs inside the Documents folder.

   - If necessary, expand the Create Project dialog box so that you can see the Sidebar and create a new folder.

Caution Make sure the drive you use has at least 8GB to 10GB for burning a full single-layer disc and 15GB to 20GB for burning a full double-layer disk. These amounts of space are larger than the DVD itself because iDVD has to assemble the files, create a disc image, and then burn it to the DVD.

4. **In the Aspect Ratio area, choose the aspect ratio for your project:**

   - Select the Standard radio button if you're creating a DVD for standard-format screens.

   - Select the Widescreen radio button if your audience will use wide screens.

Genius When choosing the aspect ratio for your DVD project, consider both your content and your intended audience. If your content is wide-screen movies, a wide screen DVD enables the audience to see the movies in full — but only if they have wide screens (either TVs or computers) to watch the DVD on. You can change the aspect ratio of a project later if necessary.

5. **Click Create.** iDVD creates the project and displays it in the main iDVD window.

Meeting the iDVD interface

At this point, you should be seeing the main iDVD window with a project open, as in figure 11.3.

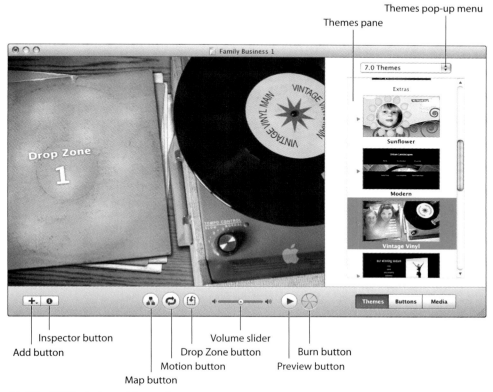

11.3 The iDVD window with a project open.

These are the main items in the iDVD interface:

- **Themes pane.** In this pane, you choose the theme (the predefined look) that you want to give the DVD as a whole.

- **Themes pop-up menu.** This pop-up menu enables you to choose which set of iDVD themes appear in the Themes pane.

- **Drop zones.** These are areas to which you can click and drag items (for example, photos or movies) from the Media Browser to add them to the menu screen.

- **Add button.** Click this button to display a menu for adding a submenu, movie, or slide-show to the project.

- **Inspector button.** Click this button to display the Inspector dialog box for the current item. For example, clicking this button from the menu screen displays the Menu Info dialog box.

- **Map button.** Click this button to display the DVD map, a diagram that shows you the DVD's contents and how they are laid out. Click this button again to return to the menu display.

- **Motion button.** Click this button to play through the movies in your drop zones so that you can see how they look. Click this button again to stop playback.

- **Drop Zone button.** Click this button to display the Drop Zone editor, which enables you to see all your drop zones at once and rearrange them. Click this button again to return to the menu display.

- **Preview button.** Click this button to make iDVD display a preview of the project in the iDVD Preview window, so that you can see how the project looks in its current state.

- **Burn button.** Click this button to start burning the open project to DVD.

- **Themes button.** Click this button to display the Themes pane on the right of the iDVD window.

- **Buttons button.** Click this button to display the Buttons pane on the right of the iDVD window. This pane gives you a choice of control buttons for adding to your DVD's menus.

- **Media button.** Click this button to display the Media pane on the right of the iDVD window. This pane provides access to your audio files in GarageBand and iTunes, the photos in your iPhoto library, and the movies you've added to the Media Browser from iMovie.

Note The Themes pane, Buttons pane, and Media pane share the area on the right of the iDVD window. To switch from pane to pane, click the Themes button, the Buttons button, or the Media button.

Setting the iDVD Preferences

Now that you've got iDVD open and you know what the main parts of the iDVD interface are, take a few minutes to set preferences. The preferences settings enable you to tell iDVD how you want to work and how it should encode your video.

To open the iDVD preferences window, choose iDVD⇨Preferences or press ⌘+, (comma). If the preferences window doesn't show the General pane at first, click the General button on the toolbar to display this pane.

Setting the General preferences

The General preferences (see figure 11.4) contain the following settings:

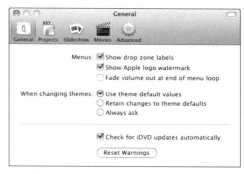

- **Show drop zone labels.** Select this check box to have iDVD label the areas on the menu screens where you can drop background music, photos, or movies. These labels are usually helpful.

- **Show Apple logo watermark.** Select this check box if you want to make an Apple logo appear as a watermark on the menu backgrounds of your DVD. Apple selects this check box by default to increase brand awareness.

11.4 The General preferences include settings for fading out audio on menu loops and choosing how to handle theme changes.

- **Fade volume out at end of menu loop.** Select this check box if you want iDVD to gradually fade out the volume at the end of each loop.

- **When changing themes options.** In this section, choose how to handle changes you've made to a theme when you switch a DVD project from one theme to another. Select the Use theme default values radio button if you want to use the values in the new theme. Select the Retain changes to theme defaults radio button if you want to keep your changes. Select the Always ask radio button if you want iDVD to prompt you to decide at the time.

- **Check for iDVD updates automatically.** Select this check box if you want iDVD to automatically look for its own updates. Deselect the check box if you prefer to check manually by choosing iDVD ⇨ Check for Updates or by using Software Update.

- **Reset Warnings.** As you'll see later in this chapter, you can turn off many of iDVD's warnings by selecting a Don't ask me again check box in them. Click this button if you need to reset all iDVD's warnings.

Setting the Projects preferences

The Projects preferences (see figure 11.5) enable you to choose the following settings:

- **Video Mode.** NTSC is the format generally used in North America, whereas Europe is PAL territory. The two formats use different numbers of frames per second of video and different numbers of horizontal lines, so a DVD in one format won't play properly on a TV that uses the other format.

231

Encoding. This is a vital setting. In the pop-up menu, choose Best Performance if you want iDVD to encode movies for DVD as you work so that they're ready to burn when you finish the project. Choose High Quality to encode at higher quality when you start to burn your project. Choose Professional Quality to encode at the highest quality available, again when you start to burn your project.

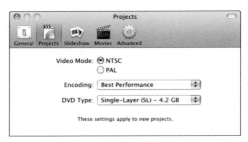

11.5 Choose the video mode (NTSC or PAL), encoding type, and DVD type in the Projects preferences.

DVD Type. In the pop-up menu, choose whether to create Single-Layer or Dual-Layer discs. If your Mac's SuperDrive can burn only Single-Layer discs, this pop-up menu is unavailable.

Genius

The High Quality and Professional Quality settings in the Encoding pop-up menu in the Projects preferences give visibly better results than the Best Performance setting. The disadvantage is that, because neither of them starts encoding until you start burning the DVD project, burning takes longer. Professional Quality takes about twice as long as High Quality to encode the video, so plan ahead if you intend to use it.

Setting the Slideshows preferences

The Slideshow preferences (see figure 11.6) enable you to choose the following settings for slideshows you add to your DVDs:

Always add original photos to DVD-ROM contents. Select this check box if you want to include original, full-size photos on the DVD as well as the smaller versions used for the slideshows. This setting is helpful if you distribute the photos. If you just want the audience to view the photos via the DVD's menus, deselect this check box.

11.6 The Slideshow preferences enable you to add original photos to the DVD, stay in the TV Safe Area, fade the volume out, and include titles and comments.

• **Always scale slides to TV Safe Area.** The TV Safe Area is that part of a widescreen project that will appear on a standard-format TV screen (whose aspect ratio is 4:3 rather than 16:9). Select this check box if you want to make sure the full photo always appears on the TV screen. This is a good idea unless you're certain the DVD will be viewed only on widescreen monitors.

• **Fade volume out at end of slideshow.** Select this check box if you want iDVD to fade the volume out at the end of a slideshow. This effect can be useful with music, but you won't usually want to make voiceovers trail away.

• **Show titles and comments.** Select this check box if you want to include the titles and comments with the photos. Having the titles and comments can be useful when you make DVDs for yourself, but you'll probably want to omit them when you make DVDs for other people.

Setting the Movies preferences

The Movies preferences (see figure 11.7) enable you to choose how to handle movies you import into iDVD:

• **When importing movies.** Select the Create chapter submenus radio button if you want iDVD to automatically create a submenu screen that enables the viewer to access the chapters (the scenes) in the movie. This setting works well for many movies, so you'll probably want to leave this radio button selected. If you don't want chapter menus, select the Do not create chapter menus radio button instead; if you want iDVD to prompt you to decide each time, select the Always ask radio button.

11.7 In the Movies preferences, choose whether to create chapter submenus. You can also add folders iDVD should scan automatically for movies.

• **Look for my movies in these folders.** If you want iDVD to look for movies in other folders than your ~/Movies folder, your iTunes Movies, and the Media Browser, add the folders to this list like this:

1. **Click the Add button to display the Open dialog box.**

2. **Select the folder that contains the movies.**

3. **Click Open.** iDVD adds the folder to the Look for my Movies in these folders box.

Setting the Advanced preferences

The Advanced preferences (see figure 11.8) enable you to choose the following settings:

- **Look for my themes in these folders.** iDVD automatically searches your Mac's /Library/Application Support/iDVD/ Themes folder for themes. If you have themes in another folder, add that folder by clicking the Add button.

- **OneStep DVD capture folder.** The read-out shows the folder iDVD is using to store the data it captures from your camcorder for creating OneStep DVDs. If you're running out of space on your Mac's hard drive, you may need to switch to a folder on an external drive. Click the

11.8 The Advanced preferences enable you to add themes, change your OneStep DVD capture folder, and set your preferred DVD burning speed.

Change button, select the folder in the Open dialog box, and then click the Open button.

- **Preferred DVD Burning Speed.** In this pop-up menu, choose the DVD burning speed you want to use. Usually, it's best to choose Maximum Possible and let iDVD handle the speed. But if you find that full-speed burning produces DVDs containing errors, choose a lower speed here.

Closing the Preferences window automatically saves your new preferences settings.

Applying a Theme to the DVD

A *theme* is a complete set of formatting for the DVD, including the layouts, background, fonts, and background music. You can apply a theme at any point during a project, so you can change from one theme to another if you need to. But usually you'll want to start by choosing the theme for your project up front so that you can see how the content you add will work with it.

Here's how to apply a theme to your DVD project:

1. **If the Themes pane isn't displayed at the moment, click the Themes button in the lower-right corner of the iDVD window to display it.** Figure 11.9 shows the Themes pane.

2. **In the Themes pop-up menu at the top of the Themes pane, choose the category of themes you want to see:**

- **All.** All the themes installed on your Mac.

- **7.0 Themes.** Themes from iDVD '08 and iDVD '09.

- **6.0 Themes.** Themes from iDVD '06.

- **5.0 Themes.** Themes from iLife '05.

- **Old Themes.** Themes from earlier versions of iLife.

- **Favorites.** Themes you've marked as your favorites.

3. **To see the other screens a theme includes, click the disclosure triangle next to it.**
   Figure 11.10 shows the available screens for the Vintage Vinyl theme.

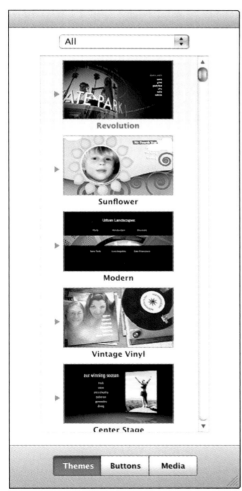

11.9 Use the Themes pane to quickly select the overall look and feel for your DVD.

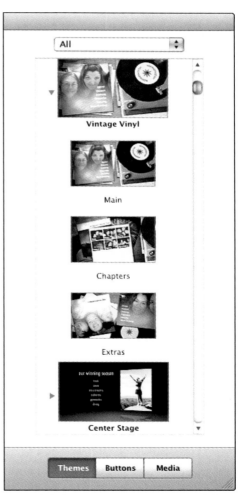

11.10 Click the disclosure triangle to reveal the other screens for a theme. Click the triangle again to hide the other screens.

4. **Click the theme you want.** iDVD applies the theme to the project. Figure 11.11 shows the Center Stage theme applied.

11.11 The DVD screens take on the look of the theme you apply.

If you're creating a standard-format project and choose a widescreen-format theme, iDVD displays the Change Project Aspect Ratio dialog box (see figure 11.12) asking if you want to change aspect ratio and giving you three choices:

- **Cancel.** Click this button to cancel applying the theme. You can then pick another theme that uses the right aspect ratio.

11.12 You may need to decide whether to change the project's aspect ratio to match the ratio of the theme you applied.

- **Keep.** Click this button to maintain the aspect ratio. This is usually the best choice because changing the aspect ratio gives the DVD the wrong aspect ratio for your movie.

- **Change.** Click this button to change the project to the theme's aspect ratio.

After applying the theme, save your project by pressing ⌘+S or choosing File ⇨ Save.

Genius

Unlike iMovie, iDVD doesn't automatically save changes for you, so save the project whenever you've made a change you don't want to have to make again. iDVD does prompt you to save unsaved changes when you quit, but you'll lose unsaved changes if iDVD crashes or your Mac suffers a power outage.

Preparing Your Content for iDVD

The next step is to get your content ready for use in the iDVD project. Once it's ready, you can place it in your project as discussed in the next section.

You can bring in content from six main sources:

- **Movies from iMovie '09.** The easiest way is to share movies to the Media Browser, but you can also pick a movie project in iMovie and launch a new iDVD project directly from it.

- **Movies from iMovie HD.** If you still use iMovie HD, or if you have old iMovie HD projects, you can export them to QuickTime files so that you can add them to your iDVD project.

- **Movies from Final Cut Express or Final Cut Pro.** If you create movies in either of the Final Cut applications, you can export a movie (or part of it) to a QuickTime file and then bring it into an iDVD project.

- **Photos from your iPhoto library.** You can create slideshows in iDVD with photos from your iPhoto library. Sadly, you can't use slideshows that you've created in iPhoto in your DVDs.

- **Songs from your iTunes library.** You can add songs from your iTunes library either as background music for the DVD's menus or as music for a slideshow you've created in iDVD.

- **Compositions from GarageBand.** If you compose original music in GarageBand, you can use it in iDVD either as the music for a slideshow or as background music for the DVD's menus.

Importing a movie from iMovie '09

Being siblings in the iLife '09 family, iDVD '09 and iMovie '09 know how to play well together. You can get a movie from iMovie into iDVD by sharing it to the Media Browser or creating a DVD project based on the movie.

Share a movie to the Media Browser

Sharing a movie to the Media Browser is the normal way of transferring a movie to iDVD. Once you've shared the movie to the Media Browser from iMovie, the movie appears in the Movies pane of the Media Browser in iDVD, and you can easily add it to a project.

Here's how to share a movie to the Media Browser from iMovie:

1. **Click the movie project in the Project Library or open it in the Project window.**

2. **Choose Share ⇨ Media Browser to open the Publish your project to the Media Browser dialog box.**

3. **Select the check box for each size you want to publish.** For example, select the Medium check box and the Large check box.

4. **Click Publish.**

Create a DVD project based on a movie

The other way of transferring a movie from iMovie to iDVD is to create a DVD project based on the movie. This creates a new DVD project with the movie's name. You can then customize the DVD project as needed. This method is most useful when you want to create a DVD project based on one particular movie rather than a group of movies (or other content).

In iMovie, select the movie in the Project Library (or open it in the Project window), and then choose Share ⇨ iDVD. There are no options to choose; iMovie exports the movie and launches or activates iDVD, which displays the DVD project.

If iDVD is running, and the open project contains unsaved changes, iDVD prompts you to save them (see figure 11.13). Normally you'll want to click Yes, but if you've done something regrettable to the DVD project and want to lose the changes, click No.

11.13 When you create a new DVD project from iMovie, iDVD prompts you to save any unsaved changes to your current DVD project.

Importing content from iMovie HD or Final Cut

If you use iMovie HD, Final Cut Express, or Final Cut Pro, getting your content into iDVD is a two-stage process:

- First, export the movie to a QuickTime file, as discussed in this section.

- Second, import the QuickTime file into iDVD, as discussed later in this chapter.

Exporting a QuickTime file from iMovie HD

To use iMovie HD projects in your DVDs, export them to QuickTime files like this:

1. **Choose File ⇨ Share or press ⌘+Shift+E.** iMovie HD displays the Sharing dialog box.

2. **Click the QuickTime button to display the QuickTime pane (see figure 11.14).**

3. **In the Compress movie for pop-up menu, choose Full Quality.** You can also choose Expert Settings and then choose exactly the settings you need after you click the Share button — but in most cases, you'll want to ship the movie out to iDVD at full quality.

4. **Click Share.** iMovie HD displays the Save dialog box.

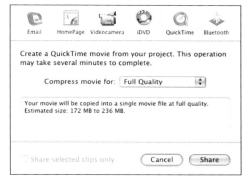

11.14 To use an iMovie HD movie in an iDVD project, export it to a QuickTime file.

5. **Choose the folder for the exported file, and type the filename you want to give the file.**

6. **Click Save.** iMovie HD exports the movie, showing you its progress as it does so.

Caution

If you open the iDVD pane in iMovie HD's Sharing dialog box, you'll see a Share button that looks like exactly what you need. But it doesn't work with iDVD '09, so don't use it; instead, use the QuickTime pane to export the movie to a QuickTime movie.

Exporting a QuickTime file from Final Cut

From Final Cut, export your movie to a QuickTime file like this:

1. **Select the movie sequence you want to export.**

2. **Choose File ▷ Export ▷ QuickTime Movie to open the Export dialog box.**

3. **In the Markers pop-up menu, select Chapter Markers if you've inserted chapter markers in your movie sequence.**

4. **In the Settings pop-up menu, choose the format you want to use: NTSC or PAL.** If you're creating a DVD for North America, you'll typically want NTSC; for Europe, PAL is the normal choice.

5. **Choose the folder in which to save the exported movie.** For example, you can use a folder within your ~/Movies folder to keep your exported movie files separate from your Final Cut files.

6. **Clear the Make movie self-contained check box.** Because you're going to import this movie into iDVD, all you need to create is a QuickTime file that references the content in Final Cut, not an actual movie file.

Genius

If you need to create a QuickTime file from Final Cut that you will use on another Mac, select the Make movie self-contained check box. The export produces a full-blown QuickTime movie rather than a file that contains references to the project components needed to create the movie. You can than transfer this movie to which-ever Mac needs it.

7. **Click Save.** Final Cut creates the file containing the references to the movie.

Preparing your photos for use in iDVD

To prepare your photos for use in iDVD, add them to your iPhoto library and make any edits they need. For example, rotate a photo to the right orientation, crop it to show the subject prominently, and adjust the colors so that it looks great.

iPhoto automatically adds each photo in your library to the Media Browser, so you don't need to take any action to make a photo available to iDVD. But to make photos easier to find, you may want to flag them or add them to an album.

Preparing your iTunes songs for use in iDVD

iTunes automatically adds every song in your library to the Media Browser, so they're available to iDVD without you needing to take any action.

If you need to use several songs in sequence, add them to a playlist. Click the New Playlist button (the + button) in the lower-left corner of the iTunes window, type the name for the playlist in the edit box, and then press Return to apply the name. You can then click and drag songs to the playlist, and click and drag them into the order in which you want them to play.

Preparing your GarageBand compositions for use in iDVD

You can make your GarageBand compositions available to iDVD either by saving them with an iLife preview (which enables you to browse them in the Media Browser) or by exporting them to iTunes.

Saving a project with an iLife preview

GarageBand gives you the choice of saving each project with an iLife preview automatically or saving a project with a preview when you close it.

To save each project with an iLife preview automatically, choose GarageBand ➪ Preferences, select the Render an audio preview when saving check box in the General pane, and then close the Preferences window.

If you don't select the Render an audio preview when saving check box, GarageBand displays the Do you want to save your project with an iLife preview? dialog box (see figure 11.15) each time you close a project. Click Yes to create the preview; click No to skip creating it; and select the Do not ask me again check box if you want to apply your decision to all projects from now on.

11.15 GarageBand prompts you to save a project with an iLife preview so that you can use it from the Media Browser in iDVD or other applications.

Exporting a song to iTunes

When you've finished a song in GarageBand, you can export it to iTunes like this:

1. **Choose Share ➪ Send Song to iTunes to open the Send your song to your iTunes library dialog box shown in figure 11.16.**

2. **Change the text in the iTunes Playlist, Artist Name, Composer Name, and Album Name boxes as needed.**

   GarageBand uses the details stored in the My Info preferences (choose GarageBand ➪ Preferences), so set the details you normally use in the fields there.

   If you want to give the song different artist and composer credits, or put it in a different album, change the information in this dialog box.

11.16 Exporting a song from GarageBand to iTunes makes the song appear in the Media Browser in iDVD.

3. **If you want to compress the song to reduce the file size, select the Compress check box and choose the compression method:**

- Select AAC Encoder or MP3 Encoder in the Compress Using pop-up menu. AAC gives marginally higher quality than MP3 and is great for iDVD, iPods, iPhones, and iTunes. MP3 files are playable in more hardware and software players than AAC files.

- Choose the quality from the Audio Settings pop-up menu. Higher Quality is usually the best choice for use with iDVD.

4. **Click Share.** GarageBand mixes down the song and adds it to your iTunes library. iTunes starts playing the new song automatically, no matter if you were listening to something else at the time.

Adding Content to Your DVD Project

With your content all lined up to go as described in the previous section, you can now add movies and slideshows to the DVD project and place them where you want them to appear in the DVD's menu screens.

Adding a movie from the Media Browser

Here's how to add a movie to your DVD project:

1. **Click the Media button in the lower-right corner of the iDVD window to display the Media pane.**

2. **Click the Movies button at the top of the Media pane to display the Movies pane (see figure 11.17).**

11.17 The Movies pane in the Media Browser provides access to your movies in iMovie, iPhoto, Photo Booth, and iTunes.

3. **In the box at the top of the Movies tab, choose the source of the movies:**

- **Movies.** These are the movies you've added to the Media Browser from iMovie.

- **iPhoto.** These are movies you've imported to iPhoto from your digital camera.

- **Photo Booth.** These are video clips you've shot in Photo Booth.

- **iTunes.** These are movies you've exported to iTunes from iMovie or otherwise added to iTunes. Click the disclosure triangle to display the Movies category within iTunes.

- **Folders.** These are movies in the folders you've told iDVD to search for movies. You can add other folders in the Movies preferences, as described earlier in this chapter.

4. **Click the thumbnail for the movie you want to add, and then drag it to the menu in the main part of the iDVD window.** You can drop it anywhere that the mouse pointer includes a green circle containing a + sign (see figure 11.18).

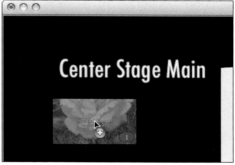

11.18 Adding a movie to the menu screen.

Caution

Make sure you don't drop the movie in one of the drop zones — if you do, iDVD makes it part of the menu screen rather than a separate movie.

5. **iDVD creates a button bearing the movie's name on the menu background.**

6. **If you want to change the button's text, click the button once, and then click it again to display the text-editing controls (see figure 11.19).** Edit the text as needed, choose the font, style, and size, and then click elsewhere to apply the changes.

11.19 You can easily change the text or formatting of a menu button.

243

Adding a movie that isn't in the Media Browser

When you need to add a movie that's not in the Media Browser (for example, a movie you've exported from Final Cut), import it like this:

1. **Choose File ➪ Import ➪ Video to open the Import dialog box.**

2. **Navigate to the folder that contains the exported movie, and then click it.**

3. **Click Import.** iDVD imports the movie and adds a button for it.

Adding chapter markers to a movie

If you import a movie that already contains chapter markers (such as those you can insert by using iMovie's Advanced Tools), iDVD automatically creates chapters for the movie as long as you've selected the Create chapter submenus radio button in Movies preferences. The chapter submenu enables the viewer to move quickly through the movie from one scene to another.

If your movie doesn't have chapter markers, you can add basic markers in iDVD. The limitation is that the markers can only be at regular intervals — for example, every two minutes. This gives the user quicker navigation than fast-forward or rewind, but it doesn't let a user jump to the beginning of a scene, which is what you normally want (and what the audience expects).

Here's how to add chapter markers in iDVD:

1. **Click the movie's button on the menu screen.**

2. **Choose Advanced ➪ Create Chapter Markers for Movie.** iDVD displays the dialog box shown in figure 11.20.

3. **Set the number of minutes in the Create marker every box.**

4. **Click OK.** iDVD adds the markers to the movie.

11.20 iDVD can add chapter markers to a movie, but they can only be at regular intervals.

Adding a slideshow

Here's how to add a slideshow to your DVD project:

1. **Make sure you're on the main menu for your DVD project.**

2. **In the lower-left corner of the iDVD window, click the Add button, and then choose Add Slideshow.** iDVD adds a button named My Slideshow to the menu (see figure 11.21).

3. **With the My Slideshow button still selected, click the button to select the text, and then type the name you want to give the slideshow.** You can also change the font, style, and size if you want. Click outside the button when you finish.

11.21 The first step in adding a slideshow to a DVD project is to add a button for it.

4. **Double-click the slideshow button you just created.** iDVD opens the slideshow editor and selects the Photos tab in the Media pane.

5. **In the Photos pane, select the Event, category, or album that contains the photos you want.** For example, select the Flagged category if you want to use photos you flagged.

6. **Click and drag one or more photos — or an album — to the slideshow editor to add them to the slideshow (see figure 11.22).** To select multiple photos at once, click the first, and then ⌘+click each of the others.

   - If you add a photo you don't want, click it and press Delete to delete it.

   - To view more photos at once, click the Grid View button in the upper-right corner of the slideshow editor.

7. **When you've added all the photos you want, click and drag them into the order you want.** You can play back your slideshow at any point by clicking the Play button. Click the Stop button to exit the preview window and return to the slideshow editor.

8. **If you want to add a song as the soundtrack for the slideshow, click the Audio tab at the top of the Media pane.** Locate the song in either GarageBand or your iTunes library, click it, and then drag it to the slideshow. Drop it anywhere, and iDVD applies it to the whole slideshow.

9. **Set the duration for each slide in the Slide Duration pop-up menu.** iDVD applies this duration to each slide; you can't set different numbers of seconds for different slides.

11.22 Adding a group of photos to a slideshow in the slideshow editor in iDVD.

Genius

If you added a song in Step 8, iDVD automatically sets the Slide Duration pop-up menu to Fit to Audio. This setting automatically divides the length of the song equally among the slides. You can choose another setting if you want to end the slideshow earlier or make it carry on longer.

10. **In the Transition pop-up menu, choose the transition to use for the slides, or choose None if you want no transition effect.** If the direction button to the right of the Transition pop-up menu is available, select the direction in which you want the transition to move — for example, a Cube transition going up, down, to the right, or to the left.

11. **Set the volume for the slideshow by dragging the Slideshow Volume slider.**

12. **To choose other settings for the slide-show, click the Settings button, select the appropriate check boxes in the Settings dialog box (see figure 11.23), and then click OK.** Your options are:

   ● **Loop slideshow.** Select this check box to make the slideshow repeat itself until the viewer stops it.

11.23 Slideshow options include looping the slideshow, displaying navigation arrows, and including titles and comments.

● **Display navigation arrows.** Select this check box to display forward and back arrow buttons on the slides.

● **Add image files to DVD-ROM.** Select this check box if you want to include original, full-size photos on the DVD as well as the smaller versions used for the slideshows. This check box will be selected if you've selected the Always add original photos to DVD-ROM contents check box in Slideshow preferences.

● **Show titles and comments.** Select this check box if you want to include the titles and comments with the photos. This can be useful for your personal DVDs — for example, if you're reviewing the photos to pick the best ones.

● **Duck audio while playing movies.** Select this check box if you want iDVD to lower ("duck") the volume on the slideshow when the viewer is playing a movie. This is almost always a good idea.

13. **When you finish setting up your slideshow, click the Return button to go back to the main menu screen.**

Adding menus

If you want to arrange your DVD with content at different levels, you can create submenus. Follows these steps:

1. **Make sure you're on the main menu for your DVD project.**

2. **In the lower-left corner of the iDVD window, click the Add button, and then choose Add Submenu.** iDVD adds a button named My Submenu to the menu.

3. **Click the My Submenu button, and then click it again to start editing it.** Type the text you want, and change the font, style, and size if necessary. Click outside the button to apply your changes.

4. **Double-click the submenu button to open the submenu's screen.** You can then add items to this screen using the techniques described earlier in this chapter.

5. **Click the Back button to return from the submenu to the main menu.** The back button appears as a left-arrow button or < less-than symbol, depending on the theme.

Genius iDVD enables you to create multiple levels of menus, but it's best to stick to one or two levels of submenus. If you create a morass of different levels, the viewer can easily get bogged down in them.

Editing drop zones

Each menu screen includes one or more *drop zones*, marked areas in which you can place movies, photos, or slideshows. Some menu screens display all their drop zones at once, but others play the drop zones in sequence, with only one appearing at a time.

To see all the drop zones in the menu screen you're using, click the Drop Zone button on the toolbar at the bottom of the iDVD window. iDVD displays the Drop Zone Editor (shown in figure 11.24 with content added).

To add an item to a drop zone, click and drag it from the Media Browser. For example:

Drop zone

- **Still image.** Click and drag a photo from the Photos pane.

- **Slideshow.** Click and drag a group of photos from the Photos pane.

- **Movie.** Click and drag a movie from the Movies pane (see the next section).

When you've finished editing the drop zones, click the Drop Zone button again to hide the drop zone editor and return to the normal display of the menu screen.

Motion Playhead
Intro Movie section
Show/Hide Intro
Movie check box

Show/Hide Outro
Movie check box
Outro Movie section

11.24 Use the drop zone editor to see all the drop zones a menu screen contains.

Note

If you drop the wrong item in a drop zone, just click the drop zone and press Delete to delete the item.

Using motion in menus

To add motion to a menu screen, you can place one or more movies in the screen's drop zones. These movies then play when the menu screen is displayed.

Here's how to add a movie to a drop zone and choose which part to play:

1. **If the Drop Zone Editor isn't open, click the Drop Zone button.**

2. **Click the Media button to display the Media pane, and then click the Movies tab.**

3. **Click the movie you want to add, and then drag it to the drop zone in which you want to place it.** iDVD displays a thumbnail of the movie in the drop zone.

4. **Add movies to any other drop zones in which you want to use movies rather than photos.**

5. **Click the Drop Zone button to return to the main menu, which now shows the movies you added in the drop zones.** Figure 11.25 shows an example in which only the first movie appears.

6. **Set the start point and end point of each movie you added:**

   If your menu screen plays movies in a single drop zone, drag the Motion Playhead along the playback bar across the bottom of the menu screen to make the drop zone display the right movie.

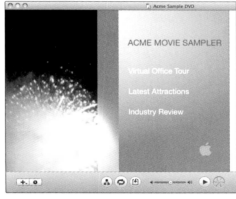

11.25 The movies you added appear in the drop zones. This menu screen has only one drop zone (on the left), in which the movies play in succession.

   Click the drop zone. iDVD displays a yellow-and-black border around it and opens the Movie Start/End panel (see figure 11.26).

   Drag the start marker to select the starting frame. The movie scrubs through the frames as you drag.

   Drag the end marker to select the ending frame.

   Click elsewhere to close the Movie Start/End panel and apply your changes.

   Repeat the procedure for each of the other movies.

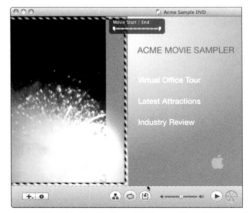

11.26 Use the Movie Start/End panel to choose the frames at which to start and end the movie in the drop zone.

7. **If you want to turn off the movie intro, deselect the Show/Hide Intro Movie check box.** Likewise, if you want to turn off the outro, deselect the Show/Hide Outro Movie check box.

8. **Click the Motion button to loop through the movies in your drop zones and see how they look.** Click this button again to stop the playback.

Customizing iDVD Themes

Each iDVD theme gives you a great start for a DVD, but you'll often want to customize a theme so that it looks and behaves exactly the way you want. You can edit the text format, edit buttons, change the backgrounds to menu screens, and apply background music.

Editing the text format

To edit the text format for an item quickly, click the item to select it, then click again to display the text controls, which you met earlier in this chapter. These enable you to change the font (for example, Helvetica Neue), the font style (for example, Italic), and the font size (for example, 24 points).

For more options, click the text item to select it, and then click the Inspector button to display the Text Info dialog box (see figure 11.27). As well as the font, font style, and font size controls, this dialog box enables you to change the text color; apply or remove a shadow; and choose among left, center, and right alignment.

11.27 Use the Text Info dialog box to change text color, apply or remove shadow, and alter alignment.

Editing buttons

To change the text of a button, click the button, then click again to display the text controls. You can then change the text, font, font style, and font size.

As with editing text, you can reach more options for buttons by clicking the button and then clicking the Inspector button to display the Button Info dialog box (see figure 11.28). This dialog box provides the following controls:

- Font, font style, and font size.
- Text color, shadow, and alignment.
- The transition the button uses and (if there's a choice of direction) which direction the transition uses.

11.28 Use the Button Info dialog box to format the button's text and choose its transition effect.

Changing backgrounds and applying background music

To change the background and audio of a menu screen, follow these steps:

1. **Click the Inspector button on the toolbar or choose View⟿ Show Inspector to open the Menu Info window (see figure 11.29).** If iDVD displays a different Inspector dialog box, it's because you've got a different object (such as a button) selected; click the background of the menu screen to display the Menu Info window.

2. **To change the background image for the menu screen, click a photo in the Photos pane and drag it into the center well in the Background area.**

3. **To change the duration of the loop, drag the Loop Duration slider.**

4. **To add audio to the menu, click a song in the Music pane and drag it into the Audio well.** Drag the Menu Volume slider to set the volume.

5. **If necessary, change the menu's button:**

11.29 Use the Menu Info window to change the background of a menu and add audio.

- If you want to reposition the menu's buttons freely, select the Free positioning radio button instead of the Snap to grid radio button. You can then drag the menu buttons to where you want them.

- To change the highlight color, click the Highlight button, and use the Colors window to choose the color you want. For example, choose a color that works better with the new menu background you've applied.

6. **Deselect the Show drop zones and related graphics check box if you want to hide these items from view.** Temporarily hiding these items can be helpful when you're designing a menu screen.

7. **When you finish making changes, click the Inspector button on the toolbar again to close the Menu Info window.**

Saving custom themes

When you've customized a theme and want to use it again, you can save it as a favorite. Follow these steps:

1. **Choose File ▷ Save Theme as Favorite.** iDVD displays the dialog box shown in figure 11.30.

2. **Type the name you want to give the theme.** Make it descriptive so you'll be able to identify the theme easily.

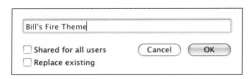

Bill's Fire Theme

☐ Shared for all users   (Cancel) (OK)
☐ Replace existing

11.30 You can save a custom theme as a favorite so that you can reuse it for other DVD projects.

3. **If you want to share your theme with other users of your Mac, select the Shared for all users check box.**

4. **If you want to replace the existing theme you customized, select the Replace existing check box.** Deselect this check box if you want to create a new theme.

5. **Click OK.**

Making a OneStep DVD

Sometimes you may want to put a movie on a DVD without any muss or fuss. You can do so with iDVD's OneStep DVD feature. This is great for times like these:

● You have finished content on your DV camcorder (for example, a movie that you've stored on tape).

Caution OneStep DVD works only with tape camcorders that connect to your Mac via FireWire, not with camcorders that use memory cards or hard disks and connect to your Mac via USB.

● You need to create a DVD containing unedited footage from your DV camcorder.

● You need to burn a movie from iMovie to DVD right this moment.

Genius

iDVD automatically gives the disc the name iDVD_ONESTEP_DVD. This can make it hard to tell one OneStep DVD from another unless you label the DVDs.

Creating a OneStep DVD from a tape camcorder

To create a OneStep DVD from a tape camcorder, follow these steps.

1. **Open iDVD if it's not already running:**

   If iDVD displays the iDVD opening screen, leave it there for the moment.

   If iDVD opens your last project, that's fine too.

   If iDVD is already open, save the project you're currently working on.

2. **Load the tape containing the movie footage in the camcorder.**

3. **Choose the starting point if necessary:**

   If you want to capture only part of the footage on the tape, wind or play the tape until that point is ready to play.

   If you want to capture all the footage on the tape, either rewind the tape or just leave it in its current position — iDVD will rewind the tape for you.

4. **Connect the DV camcorder to your Mac via a FireWire cable, just as you would for importing into iMovie.** Usually, you'll need a four-pin (small) plug at the camcorder end and a regular, six-pin plug at the Mac's end.

5. **Move the camcorder's switch to VCR mode, Playback mode, or whatever the camera calls the mode for playing back footage.**

6. **In iDVD, give the command for creating the OneStep DVD:**

   If you're at the iDVD opening screen, click the OneStep DVD button.

   If you're in the iDVD interface, choose File ➪ OneStep DVD.

7. **iDVD notices the camcorder and prompts you to insert a recordable DVD disc.**

8. **Insert a disc in your Mac's DVD drive.**

9. **iDVD displays the Creating your OneStep DVD screen (see figure 11.31).**

10. **iDVD winds the camcorder's tape back to the beginning.** If you want to start playback from the point you chose, press the Play button on the camcorder immediately to prevent iDVD from winding the tape back.

Creating your OneStep DVD

⊖ Capture Movie
● Prepare DVD
● Process Movie
● Burn

00:05:38:02 captured, 11:57 available

Time remaining : ---

Stop

11.31 OneStep DVD automatically captures the footage from your DV camcorder and burns it to DVD.

Genius

You can also stop iDVD's capture at any point by clicking the Stop button in the Creating your OneStep DVD screen. If you let the capture run, it continues until it finds a ten-second blank section of tape or (if there isn't such a blank section) until the end of the tape.

11. **Wait while iDVD captures the video from the camcorder's tape, prepares the DVD, processes the movie, and then burns the DVD.** iDVD shows you its progress.

12. **When iDVD finishes the burn, it ejects the DVD and prompts you to insert another DVD if you want to burn another copy.**

13. **Insert a blank DVD and repeat the recording process, or click Done to close the OneStep DVD window.**

Creating a OneStep DVD from an iMovie movie

You can also use iDVD's OneStep feature to burn a movie to DVD. This capability is great when you need to distribute a movie on a physical disc.

Here's how to burn an iMovie movie to DVD:

1. **In iMovie, prepare the project for sharing:**

   ● Click the project in the Project Library, or open it in the Project window.

   ● Choose Share ⇨ Media Browser to display the Publish your project to the Media Browser dialog box.

   ● Select the sizes at which you want to publish it — for example, Medium and Large.

   ● Click Publish.

2. **Launch iDVD and open a DVD project.** For example, iDVD opens the project on which you were working when you last quit the application, or you click the Open an Existing Project button on the iDVD opening screen, choose a project in the Open dialog box, and then click Open.

Genius

You must open a project to create a OneStep DVD from a movie. This is because the iDVD opening screen doesn't include a button for creating a OneStep DVD from a movie.

3. **Choose File ⇨ OneStep DVD from iMovie.** iDVD displays the Open dialog box.

4. **Navigate to the iMovie project and select it.**

5. **Click Import. iDVD prompts you to insert a blank DVD.**

6. **Insert the DVD.** iDVD imports the movie and starts burning it to DVD (see figure 11.32).

7. **When iDVD finishes the burn, it ejects the DVD and prompts you to insert another DVD if you want to burn another copy.**

8. **Insert a blank DVD if you want to repeat the recording process, or click Done to close the OneStep DVD window.**

11.32 You can also create a OneStep DVD from an iMovie project that you've published to the Media Browser.

Using Magic iDVD

Magic iDVD enables you to create a customized DVD with as little effort as possible, while providing you with control over the DVD's contents, menus, and appearance. This makes Magic iDVD a great way to save time but still retain creative control (unlike OneStep DVD).

Here's how to create a DVD using Magic iDVD:

1. **Open iDVD if it's not already running.**

2. **Open the Magic iDVD window (see figure 11.33):**

   - If you're looking at the iDVD opening screen, click the Magic DVD button.

   - If you have a project open in iDVD, choose File ⇨ Magic iDVD.

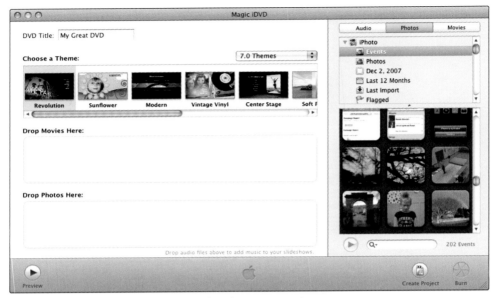

11.33 The Magic iDVD window looks like this when you open it.

3. **Select the default title (*My Great DVD*) in the DVD Title box and type the title you want.**

4. **In the Choose a Theme box, click the theme for the overall look of the DVD.**

   - To see a different selection of themes, open the pop-up menu above the right end of the Choose a Theme box and choose the theme category you want.

   - See the discussion later in this chapter for an explanation of the various categories of themes.

5. **Click and drag one or more movies from the Movies pane on the right to the wells in the Drop Movies Here box.**

   - Click the Movies button in the upper-right corner of the Magic iDVD window to show the Movies pane.

   - You can click and drag movies from either of the Movies folders shown in the Movies pane (see figure 11.34).

   - You can also click and drag movies from the Movies folder in iTunes.

If your movies are in another folder, open a Finder window to that folder, and then click the movie and drag it to the well in iMovie.

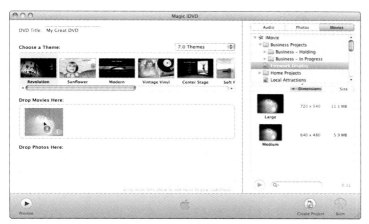

11.34 To add a movie to the Magic iDVD, click and drag it from the Movies pane to a well in the Drop Movies Here area.

Genius

6. **If you want to add one or more slideshows to the DVD, follow these steps:**

   Click the Photos button in the upper-right corner of the Magic iDVD window to display the Photos pane.

   Select the photos you want. You can select an Event, an album, a group of photos you've selected, or a single photo.

   Click and drag your selection to a photo well in the Drop Photos Here box (see figure 11.35). If you drag a single photo, you'll probably want to add others to its photo well; otherwise, it won't make much of a slideshow.

11.35 To add a slideshow to the Magic iDVD, click and drag one or more photos from the Photos pane to a well in the Drop Photos Here area.

257

- To add audio to a slideshow, click the Audio button in the upper right corner of the Magic iDVD window to display the Audio pane (see figure 11.36). Click the song or playlist you want, and then drag it to the photo well for the slideshow.

7. **Click the Preview button.** iDVD assembles a preview of the project and displays it in the iDVD Preview window, together with an on-screen remote control (see figure 11.37). Use the controls on the remote to navigate the DVD. Click the Exit button to return to the Magic iDVD window, where you can add or delete content as needed.

8. **When your project has the contents you want, click Create Project.** Magic iDVD creates the project and then displays it in a window. You can now perfect the project, burn it to DVD, or simply leave it until later.

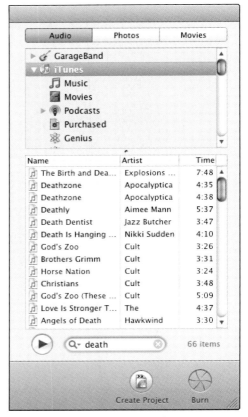

11.36 Use the Audio pane to add a song or composition to a slideshow.

258

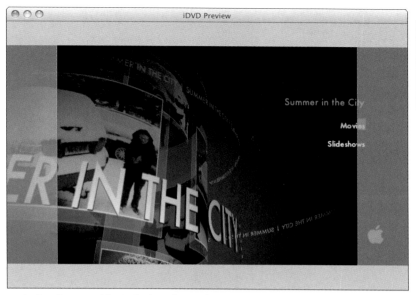

11.37 Preview your Magic iDVD and see what adjustments it needs.

Burning and Archiving DVDs

When you have previewed the DVD project and found it satisfactory, you're ready to burn it to disc or to file. You may also need to archive it so that you can move it to another Mac.

Burning a DVD

To burn the open project to DVD, follow these steps:

1. **If your DVD project contains unsaved changes, press ⌘+S or choose File ⇨ Save to save them.**

2. **Click the Burn button on the toolbar.** iDVD prompts you to insert a recordable DVD.

3. **Insert a disc in your Mac's DVD drive.** If it's a drawer-style drive, close the drawer.

4. **Wait while iDVD burns the disc.** When it has finished, test the disc, remove it, and label it.

Creating a Disc Image or a VIDEO_TS File

Instead of burning your DVD project to a DVD, you can save it as a disc image or as a VIDEO_TS file.

- **Disc image.** If you create a disc image, you then have a file containing the completed DVD that you can burn to multiple DVDs using Disk Utility without having to encode it each time. This is much quicker than encoding the same DVD multiple times.

- **VIDEO_TS folder.** A VIDEO_TS folder contains the video files for the DVD but not the DVD menus. You can play the contents of the VIDEO_TS folder using either DVD Player or third-party software such as the free VLC Media Player (www.videolan.org).

To create a disc image, choose File ➪ Save As Disc Image. In the Save Disc Image As dialog box (see figure 11.38), type the filename, choose the folder in which to save it, and then click Save.

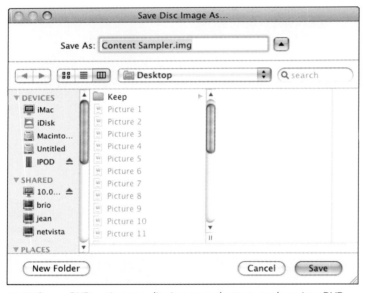

11.38 Save a DVD project to a disc image so that you can burn it to DVD multiple times using Disk Utility.

To create a VIDEO_TS folder, choose File ➪ Save as VIDEO_TS Folder. In the Save VIDEO_TS folder As dialog box, type the filename, choose the folder in which to save the folder, and then click Save.

Archiving your DVD projects

To avoid consuming all your Mac's hard disk space, iDVD keeps your project files small by including in them only the details of the movies, photos, audio, and so on needed to make the DVD, not the files themselves. So when you add a 2GB file to a DVD project, the project file doesn't suddenly increase in size by 2GB; instead, it adds a reference to where the file is, so that it knows where to find it.

This works well until you need to move a DVD project to another Mac. At that point, you need to collect all the files the project needs, transfer them to the other Mac, and make sure they're in exactly the same folders — otherwise, iDVD can't find them.

To avoid this headache, iDVD provides the Archive Project command. This command gathers up all the files the project needs, so that you can move the project as a whole to another Mac.

Here's how to archive a project.

1. **Open the project.**

   If you're at the iDVD opening screen, click the Open an Existing Project button.

   If you're already in the iDVD interface, choose File ⇨ Open Recent or File ⇨ Open.

   If the project is already open, save any unsaved changes.

2. **Choose File ⇨ Archive Project.** iDVD displays the Archive Project dialog box (see figure 11.39).

3. **Select the Include themes check box if you want to include the project's themes.** If the Mac on which you'll open the project contains the themes already, you can deselect this check box. If you're using a custom theme, select this check box.

4. **Change the suggested name in the Save As box if you want.** iDVD suggests the project's name with "Archived" added to it.

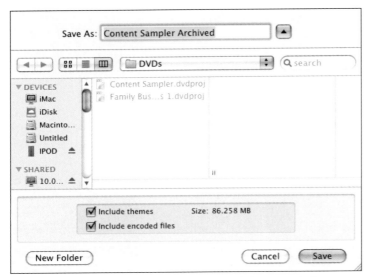

11.39 Archiving an iDVD project pulls together all the project's files.

5. **Choose the drive and folder on which to store the archive file.** For example, you can
   save the archive file to your Public folder or a network drive so that you can transfer it
   onto the other Mac across the network.

6. **Select the Include encoded files check box if you want to include all the files that
   iDVD has encoded already.** This is usually a good idea.

7. **Click Save.** iDVD creates the archive file.

Now transfer the archive file to the other Mac. You can then open it as you would any other
project.

Do You Have Any Troubleshooting Tips?

Normally iMovie runs well, and you can quickly build powerful, professional-quality movies using the techniques described earlier in this book. But all applications can suffer problems, so in this chapter I show you how to get around problems you may experience with iMovie. First, you'll learn several smart moves to make iMovie run as fast as possible. Next, you'll learn how to prevent iMovie from crashing or running unstably. After that, you'll see how to resolve problems when iMovie won't recognize your camcorder, import photos from iPhoto, or keep audio in sync. Lastly, you'll learn where to find information to troubleshoot other issues that arise.

Getting iMovie to Run as Well as Possible

To make iMovie run as fast and smoothly as possible, make sure you keep it up to date with the latest fixes and patches. You may also need to add RAM to your Mac or simply free up as much of its existing RAM as possible. And if your Mac's hard drive is nearly full, you may benefit from defragmenting it.

Installing the latest iMovie updates

To keep iMovie in good shape, you will want to install any updates that Apple releases — not only updates for iMovie itself, but also for the other iLife applications and for Mac OS X. Installing these updates ensures you have the latest features and fixes for problems.

The easiest way to get updates is to use Software Update. Choose Apple menu ➪ Software Update to check for updates to all your Mac's Apple software. If Software Update shows that new versions or fixes are available, follow through the procedure for downloading and installing them. Depending on the nature of the updates, you may need to restart your Mac.

Adding more RAM

Most Macs come with plenty of memory for everyday tasks such as Web browsing, e-mail, and creating documents. But iMovie is a demanding application that can use as much RAM as you can throw at it.

Note If you want to see how much RAM iMovie is grabbing, open Activity Monitor from your Utilities folder and click the System Memory tab near the bottom of the window. Click the RSIZE column heading once or twice (as needed) to get a descending sort by the RAM size. Chances are iMovie will be right up at the top of the list.

Given that adding RAM is usually the cheapest and easiest way to boost a Mac's performance, it's well worth looking into adding RAM to your Mac.

How difficult adding RAM is depends entirely on which Mac you have. For example:

- **Recent iMacs.** You need remove only a couple of screws from memory hatches.
- **Mac mini.** You need a delicate hand and a thin putty knife.
- **MacBook unibody.** You need to remove the hard drive and entire bottom panel.
- **MacBook Air.** You can't add RAM because the existing chip is soldered to the logic board.

You can buy RAM from the Apple Store (http://store.apple.com), but you will usually find better prices at sites such as these:

- Crucial.com (www.crucial.com) has a Mac System Scanner tool that shows your Mac's current memory configuration and your upgrade options.
- iFixit.com (www.ifixit.com) provides useful online guides that illustrate the upgrade process.
- Other World Computing (http://eshop.macsales.com/) makes it easy to find RAM for most Mac models.

Quitting other applications

If you can't add more RAM to your Mac, give iMovie as much of the existing RAM as possible, together with as many processor cycles as you can squeeze out. To do so, just close any other applications that you don't need while you're working in iMovie.

Defragmenting your Mac's hard drive

If your Mac's hard disk is running out of space, you may be able to improve iMovie's performance by defragmenting the disk. To defragment it, use an application such as TechTool Pro from Micromat (www.micromat.com).

Before you splash out on a defragmenter, though, make sure you need one. Normally, Mac OS X doesn't need defragmenting. This is for two reasons:

- **Built-in defragmentation.** Since Panther (10.3), Mac OS X automatically does some defragmentation in the background anyway. When Mac OS X finds a file that has been broken up over sectors spread around the disk, it automatically writes a new version of the file in a single location that has enough space.
- **Having enough disk space.** Most modern hard disks are so huge that there's plenty of space to store files. This means that the operating system can usually find an area of the disk that's big enough to contain each file it creates rather than having to split the file up and store it in sectors spread around the disk. This is an improvement over the olden days, when the operating system had to use every scrap of available space.

Under normal circumstances, the only times you'll need to defragment a Mac's hard drive are when you're working with large files and when the drive is running out of space. iMovie tends to create huge files (especially when capturing video from a camcorder) that eat up your Mac's hard disk space, so it's one of the applications most likely both to cause fragmentation problems and to benefit from your defragmenting the hard drive.

Caution If you've encrypted your home folder with FileVault, you'll get better performance by saving your movie project files outside your home folder. Otherwise, FileVault's encryption can slow iMovie down. Particular problems include imported video dropping frames or iMovie giving the message "The disk responded slowly" when you record a voiceover.

Dealing with iMovie Crashes and Instability

iMovie is usually pretty stable, but it sometimes crashes, either when you try to launch the application or when it has been running for a while.

Here's how to deal with the circumstances in which most crashes occur.

iMovie crashes on launch

If iMovie launches and then crashes — or if it launches and then displays the Spinning Beachball of Death, so that you need to force-quit it from the Dock icon — try as many of these troubleshooting fixes as are needed to get it running again:

- **Restart your Mac.** After the restart, try launching iMovie.
- **Disconnect any external hard drives you're using.** Open a Finder window, eject each drive by clicking its Eject button in the Sidebar, and then disconnect it physically. Restart your Mac, and then try launching iMovie.
- **Quit iMovie and repair disk permissions on your Mac's hard disk.**
    1. Quit iMovie. For example, press ⌘+Q or choose iMovie ➪ Quit iMovie.
    2. Click the Finder button on the toolbar to open a Finder window.
    3. Choose Go ➪ Utilities from the menu bar to open the Utilities folder.
    4. Double-click Disk Utility to open Disk Utility.
    5. In the Sidebar, click your Mac's hard drive. Figure 12.1 shows Disk Utility with a Mac's hard drive selected.
    6. Click the Repair Disk Permissions button. Disk Utility repairs the disk's permissions.
    7. Quit Disk Utility. For example, press ⌘+Q or choose Disk Utility ➪ Quit Disk Utility.
    8. Restart your Mac, and then launch iMovie.

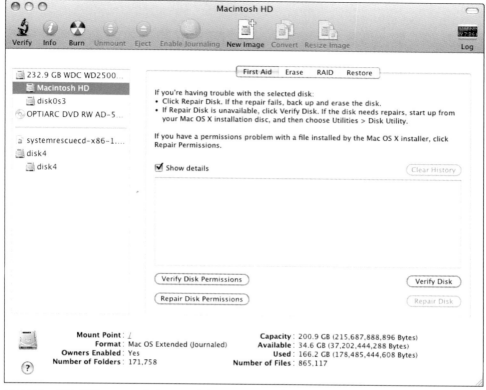

12.1 Using Disk Utility to repair the permissions on a Mac's hard drive.

● **Remove non-Apple QuickTime plug-ins.**

1. Quit iMovie. For example, press ⌘+Q or choose iMovie ➪ Quit iMovie.

2. Click the Finder button on the toolbar to open a Finder window.

3. Click your Mac's hard disk in the Devices category in the Sidebar.

4. Open the Library folder, and then open the QuickTime folder within it.

5. Select any non-Apple plug-ins, and then drag them to the Trash (or press ⌘+Backspace with them selected). You'll be able to recognize non-Apple plug-ins by their names. For example, AppleMPEG2Codec.component is an Apple plug-in, while Xvid_Codec 1.0 alpha.component is a third-party plug-in.

6. Restart your Mac, and then launch iMovie.

● **Reinstall iMovie from the iLife '09 DVD.** Launch iMovie after you reinstall it.

iMovie crashes after running for a while

If iMovie starts behaving unstably, you may need to trash your iMovie preferences and repair permissions on your Mac's hard disk. Follow these steps:

1. **Quit iMovie if it's running.** For example, press ⌘+Q or choose iMovie ⇨ Quit iMovie.

2. **Click the Finder button on the toolbar to open a Finder window.**

3. **Click your username in the Places list in the Sidebar to open your Home folder.**

4. **Open the Library folder, and then open the Preferences folder within it.**

5. **Click the file named com.apple.iMovie8.plist, and then press ⌘+Backspace to move it to the Trash.**

6. **Choose Go ⇨ Utilities from the menu bar to open the Utilities folder.**

7. **Double-click Disk Utility to open the utility.**

8. **In the Sidebar, click your Mac's hard drive.**

9. **Click the Repair Disk Permissions button.** Disk Utility repairs the disk's permissions.

10. **Quit Disk Utility.** For example, press ⌘+Q or choose Disk Utility ⇨ Quit Disk Utility.

11. **Restart your Mac.**

12. **Launch iMovie.** iMovie automatically creates a new preferences file.

13. **Press ⌘+, (comma) or choose iMovie ⇨ Preferences to open the Preferences window.**

14. **Set the permissions the way you prefer them.** Close the Preferences window.

Resolving Problems Recognizing Your Camcorder

iMovie is pretty good at recognizing camcorders you connect to your Mac, but sometimes you may find that iMovie simply doesn't notice your camcorder. This section shows you ways to solve this problem.

Check that iMovie can work with your camcorder

First, make sure that iMovie supports your camcorder. See the iMovie '09 Camcorder Support page on the Apple Web site (http://support.apple.com/kb/HT3290).

If iMovie Doesn't Support Your Camcorder

If iMovie doesn't support your camcorder, all is not lost: You'll just need to import your video footage in a different way. Try these workarounds:

- **Remove the memory card.** If the camcorder records onto removable memory (for example, an SDHC card or a MemoryStick), remove the memory card and insert it into a reader connected to your Mac.

- **Remove the DVD.** If the camcorder records onto a DVD, remove the DVD and insert it in your Mac's optical drive.

- **Import using a different camcorder.** For a tape camcorder, you may need to borrow a camcorder that iMovie does support, insert your tape, and import it.

- **Import using a different application or operating system.** If you can't borrow a suitable tape camcorder, you may need to import your video using a different application or operating system. For example, if you have a PC running Windows, see if the free Windows Movie Maker application can import video from your camcorder.

- **Use iPhoto.** If your camcorder is primarily a digital camera that also takes videos, you may need to import the videos into iPhoto and then transfer them to iMovie from there.

Check the connection

Next, check that the camcorder is connected correctly to your Mac:

- **Tape-based camcorder.** Use a FireWire connection. The connector on the camcorder may be marked IEEE 1394 (the Institute of Electrical and Electronics Engineers numeric designation for the FireWire standard) or i.LINK (Sony's term for its variant on FireWire).

- **Hard disk, DVD, or flash memory camcorder.** Use a USB connection.

Genius

If you can, connect the camcorder directly to your Mac rather than connecting it through a hub.

Caution You may need to disconnect an external FireWire drive before you can import video via FireWire from a camcorder. This is inconvenient at best, especially if you're planning to store the video on that FireWire drive. Connecting a camcorder via FireWire can also dismount an external FireWire drive without warning, so close any files open on such a drive before connecting a camcorder to your Mac.

If your camcorder offers only one type of connection, you'll have little choice. But if your camcorder has multiple outputs, as many camcorders do, check that you've chosen the right one. If the role of each output isn't clear, consult the camcorder's documentation. For example, many tape-based camcorders use FireWire for transferring video but use USB for transferring still images stored on internal memory or a memory card.

Check the output mode

With the camcorder properly connected, make sure it's turned on and that you've set it to the right output mode. Depending on the camcorder, the output mode may be called VTR mode (short for video tape recorder), VCR mode (short for video cassette recorder), DV mode, play mode, playback mode, or something else.

If your camcorder can handle HDV as well as regular DV, make sure the camcorder is switched to the mode you want to use.

Check that Mac OS X knows the camcorder is connected

Make sure Mac OS X knows the camcorder is connected:

1. **Choose Apple ➪ About This Mac.** The About This Mac window opens.
2. **Click the More Info button to open System Profiler.**
3. **In the Contents pane, expand the Hardware section by clicking its disclosure triangle**.
4. **Click the FireWire entry (for a FireWire-connected camcorder) or the USB entry (for a USB-connected camcorder).** Make sure that the FireWire Device Tree or USB Device Tree lists the camcorder. Figure 12.2 shows an example of a FireWire camcorder recognized by System Profiler.

Check that nobody else is using the camcorder

If the camcorder is correctly connected, but you still can't grab the video off it, make sure that nobody else is using the camcorder via Fast User Switching. Fast User Switching is a great feature for sharing a Mac among your family members, but it can give you headaches when you've connected a device that Fast User Switching isn't designed to share.

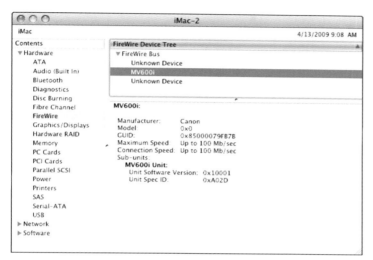

12.2 Use System Profiler to check that Mac OS X knows your camcorder is connected.

Genius

If your camcorder records in the AVCHD format, you can import it only if your Mac has an Intel processor. If the camcorder records in AVCHD on a DVD, you won't be able to import the video directly into iMovie. Use another application to import it, and then import the files into iMovie as described in Chapter 3.

Switch among import formats

Many high-definition camcorders can record in standard resolution as well. When you're importing from a tape, iMovie automatically stops importing when it detects a change in resolution. You may be able to start importing again right at the change, but iMovie may sometimes need you to fast-forward past the change before it will start importing.

Note

If iMovie still won't start importing, even after you fast-forward past a change of resolution, disconnect the camcorder and then reconnect it. If that doesn't solve the problem, remove the tape from the camcorder and then reinsert it.

273

Make sure the camcorder has plenty of power

It's a good idea to plug in the camcorder's AC power adapter while you're importing footage. This helps you avoid having the camcorder switch itself off automatically because its battery power has reached a low level. Most camcorders will export footage on battery power provided there's enough of it, but some camcorders actually require AC power for exporting.

Increase the camcorder's recording quality

Many tapeless camcorders can record video at several different qualities — for example, High, Normal (or Medium), and Low (or some better-sounding name such as "Economy" or "Space Saver"). These qualities typically use different compression settings or different codecs (*co*der/*dec*oders), with the higher qualities compressing the video less to give better results but a larger file size.

If iMovie refuses to recognize some of the movie clips on a tapeless camcorder, check the camcorder's settings and increase the quality to the next higher setting. Record some video and see if iMovie recognizes the new clips. If so, use that quality as your minimum; if not, raise the quality further and try again.

Troubleshoot an iSight or Web cam

If you're having trouble getting iMovie to recognize an iSight or Web cam you've connected to your Mac, work through this checklist.

1. **Make sure Mac OS X knows the iSight or Web cam is there:**

    1. Choose Apple ⇨ About This Mac. The About This Mac window opens.

    2. Click the More Info button to open System Profiler.

    3. In the Contents pane, expand the Hardware section by clicking its disclosure triangle.

    4. Click the FireWire entry (for a FireWire-connected Web cam) or the USB entry (for a USB-connected Web cam). Make sure that the FireWire Device Tree or USB Device Tree lists the Web cam.

Note   If Mac OS X doesn't recognize the iSight or Web cam, try unplugging it and then plugging it back in. Connect it directly to a port on your Mac rather than connecting it through a FireWire hub or USB hub. If you're still striking out, check whether the Web cam needs you to install a driver.

2. **Quit any other applications that are using the iSight or Web cam.** iChat and Photo Booth are the usual culprits here. If you're not running either of these applications yourself, make sure nobody else is logged on using Fast User Switching and running either application.

3. **Disconnect any other Web cam or camcorder you've connected.** Even if another camera is working fine in iMovie, disconnect it to give iMovie a better chance of identifying the camera that's not working.

4. **Disconnect the iSight or Web cam and restart your Mac.** Shut your Mac down, leave it off for a few minutes, and then restart it. When Mac OS X has finished loading, reconnect the iSight or Web cam.

Working Around Issues Dragging Photos into iMovie

As you saw in Chapter 9, iMovie makes it easy to use your still photos from iPhoto in your movies. But if you shoot your photos in the RAW format, you may get an error message saying that "The file could not be imported" because "QuickTime couldn't parse it" when you try to drag a photo into iMovie.

This error occurs because iMovie can't handle all the many RAW image formats that iPhoto supports. In particular, some Canon and Nikon RAW image files cause problems.

The workaround for this problem is to edit the photo in iPhoto. Editing the photo makes iPhoto create a JPEG file or TIFF file containing the edited version. You can then pull this JPEG file or TIFF file into iMovie without problems.

If the photo will benefit from a constructive edit, make that edit. If not, make a minimal edit such as cropping a pixel off one side of the photo or tweaking its color balance a tad.

When you click the Done button to accept the edit, iPhoto creates the new file. iPhoto creates a JPEG unless you've selected the Save edits as 16-bit TIFF files check box in the Advanced pane of the iPhoto Preferences window, which makes iPhoto create a TIFF file instead.

Curing Out-of-sync Audio

If you've ever watched a movie whose audio is out of sync, you'll know how an apparently minor timing problem can wreck a movie for the audience by making it look as though the actors are speaking in a foreign language.

There are two main causes of out-of-sync audio in iMovie: custom slow-motion percentages and import sync problems.

Avoiding custom slow-motion percentages

The usual cause for out-of-sync audio in iMovie is using custom slow-motion percentages.

Being able to slow down (or speed up) the action to precisely the degree you want is fantastic. But if you find that custom slo-mo percentages produce audio-sync problems, try using the preset stops on the slider instead. This limits your choices to 12.5%, 25%, 50%, 100%, 200%, 400%, and 800%, but it usually eliminates sync problems.

If you were using custom slo-mo to make a clip precisely the right length for its audio, you'll need to either edit the clip to allow for the new speed or edit the audio to match the new duration.

Dealing with import sync problems

The other main cause of out-of-sync audio is import problems from analog sources. The analog-to-digital converter (ADC) delivers the audio out of sync with the video, and iMovie records the audio and video that way. This shouldn't happen, but it does.

If the audio for a whole clip is out of sync by the same amount, you can extract the audio from the video and then insert the audio where you need it. See Chapter 7 for instructions on extracting the audio from video clips, trimming audio, and positioning audio

Genius

You can also use a video clip as its own audio track without extracting the audio. Use the Inspector window to mute the audio for the video clip in the Project window. Then drag another copy of the same clip from the Event browser to the Project window, drop it on the muted video clip, and choose Audio Only from the pop-up menu. iMovie positions a second copy of the clip; this instance will play audio only. Drag the audio copy to the appropriate starting position to play along with the video copy.

Using the Apple Support Pages to Resolve Other Issues

If iMovie starts acting up in ways other than those described in this chapter, consult the iMovie Support pages on the Apple Web site for advice. You can reach these pages easily one of two ways:

- **Go directly to Support.** Open Safari, type the URL (www.apple.com/support/imovie/), and press Return.

- **Open Support from iMovie.** Choose Help ➪ iMovie Help, and then click the "FAQ, discussions, and more" link in the More Information box on the iMovie Help screen. iMovie launches or activates Safari, which displays the iMovie Support page.

Index

The Genius is in.

Macs
PORTABLE GENIUS

978-0-470-29052-1

Mac OS X Leopard
PORTABLE GENIUS

978-0-470-29050-7

iPhone 3G S
PORTABLE GENIUS
Also covers iPhone 3G!

978-0-470-52422-0

Final Cut Pro
PORTABLE GENIUS

978-0-470-38760-3

iMac
PORTABLE GENIUS

978-0-470-29061-3

MacBook Air
PORTABLE GENIUS

978-0-470-38108-3

MacBook
PORTABLE GENIUS

978-0-470-29169-6

MacBook Pro
PORTABLE GENIUS

978-0-470-29170-2

Switching to a Mac
PORTABLE GENIUS

978-0-470-43677-6

iPod & iTunes
PORTABLE GENIUS

978-0-470-38259-2

iLife '09
PORTABLE GENIUS

978-0-470-41732-4

iPhoto '09
PORTABLE GENIUS

978-0-470-47569-0

The essentials for every forward-thinking Apple user are now available on the go. Designed for easy access to tools and shortcuts, the *Portable Genius* series has all the information you need to maximize your digital lifestyle. With a full-color interior and easy-to-navigate content, the *Portable Genius* series offers innovative tips and tricks as well as savvy advice that will save you time and increase your productivity.

WILEY
Now you know.

Available wherever books are sold.